How Will Capitalism End?

How Will Capitalism End?

Essays on a Failing System

Wolfgang Streeck

VERSO

London • New York

First published by Verso 2016
© Wolfgang Streeck 2016
Translation of Chapter 5 © Tessa Hauswedell 2016
Translation of Chapter 7 © Rodney Livingstone 2016

A version of Chapter 1 was delivered as the Anglo-German Foundation Lecture at the British Academy on 23 January 2014. Published in: *New Left Review* 87, May/June 2014, 35–64. Chapter 2 was first presented as the 2011 Max Weber Lecture at the European University Institute, Florence. I am grateful to Daniel Mertens for his research assistance. Published in: *New Left Review* 71, September/October 2011, 5–29. Chapter 3 was first published in *New Left Review* 76, July/August 2012, 27–47. Chapter 4 first published as MPIfG Discussion Paper 15/1, Cologne: Max-Planck-Institut für Gesellschaftsforschung, 2015. Chapter 5 first published in *New Left Review* 73, January/February 2012, 63–71. Chapter 6 first published in *European Law Journal* 21(3), 2015, 361–70. Chapter 7 originated as the Distinguished Lecture in the Social Sciences, Wissenschaftszentrum Berlin, 21 April 2015. Published in: *New Left Review* 95, September/October 2015, 5–26. Chapter 8 first published in *Zeitschrift für Vergleichende Politikwissenschaft* 9, 2015, H. 1–2, 49–60. Chapter 9 was first presented at a plenary session on 'Studying Contemporary Capitalism', 10th Conference of the European Sociological Association, 'Social Relations in Turbulent Times', Geneva, 7–10 September, 2011. Published in: *European Journal of Sociology* 53 (1), 2012, 1–28. Chapter 10 first published in Julian Go (ed.), *Political Power and Social Theory*, Bingley: Emerald Group Publishing Limited, Vol. 23, 2012, 311–21. Chapter 11 was first presented at a conference organized by the SSRC and the Wissenschaftszentrum Berlin, The Public Mission of the Social Sciences and Humanities: Transformation and Renewal, 16–17 September 2011.

3 5 7 9 10 8 6 4

Verso
UK: 6 Meard Street, London W1F 0EG
US: 20 Jay Street, Suite 1010, Brooklyn, NY 11201
versobooks.com

Verso is the imprint of New Left Books

ISBN-13: 978-1-78478-401-0 (HB)
ISBN-13: 978-1-78478-403-4 (US EBK)
ISBN-13: 978-1-78478-402-7 (UK EBK)

British Library Cataloguing in Publication Data
A catalogue record for this book is available from the British Library

Library of Congress Cataloging-in-Publication Data
Names: Streeck, Wolfgang, 1946- author.
Title: How will capitalism end? : essays on a failing system / Wolfgang
    Streeck.
Description: Brooklyn, New York : Verso, 2016.
Identifiers: LCCN 2016018054| ISBN 9781784784010 (hardback) | ISBN
    9781784784034 (ebook)
Subjects: LCSH: Capitalism–History. | Economic policy. | Oligarchy. |
    Poverty. | Political corruption. | Anarchism. | BISAC: POLITICAL SCIENCE /
    Economic Conditions. | POLITICAL SCIENCE / Political Ideologies /
    Democracy. | POLITICAL SCIENCE / Globalization.
Classification: LCC HB501 .S919515 2016 | DDC 330.12/2—dc23
LC record available at https://lccn.loc.gov/2016018054

Typeset in Minion Pro by Hewer Text UK Ltd, Edinburgh, Scotland
Printed and bound by CPI Group (UK) Ltd, Croydon, CR0 4YY

Contents

List of Figures

A Note on the Text

Apart from the Introduction, the chapters in this collection have all been previously published: five out of eleven in *New Left Review*, one as a discussion paper of the research institute of which I served as director for almost two decades, and the rest in various books and journals. Pieces first appeared in print between 2011 (Chapter 2, based on a Max Weber Lecture at the European University Institute in Florence) and 2015 (Chapters 4, 6, 7 and 8). Two were originally written in German and then translated, the rest I wrote in English. The help of outstandingly competent editors notwithstanding, I am painfully aware that this remains noticeable in all too many places.

The chapters included in this volume have in common that they have sprung from my continuing attempt to understand the implications of the financial crisis of 2008 for social science and sociological theory, in particular for political macrosociology and its relationship to political economy. This explains why certain themes return, resulting in occasional overlap between chapters. Eliminating that overlap would have destroyed the integrity of the chapters and would ultimately have required merging them into a systematic monograph. Not only would this have changed the purpose of the book – which is to make dispersed articles on different aspects of a common theme jointly available in one place – but it would also have by far exceeded both my current theoretical capacities and my available time.

The main subject of the collection is the enduring crisis of capitalism and capitalist society at the centre of the modern-capitalist global system. The thrust of the book is to inspire more concrete thinking on how that system might in a not-too-distant future come to an end, even without a successor regime in sight, as a consequence of its internal contradictions unfolding. The Introduction may be read as elaborating on and complementing Chapter 1, which gave the collection its title. Chapter 2 provides background to both, while Chapter 3 addresses some of the sources of the apparent stability of what might be an emerging neoliberal 'society lite'. Chapters 4 to 8 deal in diverse ways with the changing relationship between capitalism and democracy, as exemplified by the evolution of the institutions of the European Union in their intermediary position between global capitalism and European nation states. Finally, Chapters 9, 10 and 11 turn to what I believe is the homework that needs to be done by today's sociology to restore its ability to account for the dynamics of contemporary society and its ongoing critical transformation.

Wolfgang Streeck
Cologne, 6 April 2016

Introduction

Capitalism has always been an improbable social formation, full of conflicts and contradictions, therefore permanently unstable and in flux, and highly conditional on historically contingent and precarious supportive as well as constraining events and institutions. Capitalist society may be described in shorthand as a 'progressive' society in the sense of Adam Smith[1] and the enlightenment, a society that has coupled its 'progress' to the continuous and unlimited production and accumulation of productive capital, effected through a conversion, by means of the invisible hand of the market and the visible hand of the state, of the private vice of material greed into a public benefit.[2] Capitalism promises infinite growth of commodified material wealth in a finite world, by conjoining itself with modern science and technology, making capitalist society the first industrial society, and through unending expansion of free, in the sense of contestable, risky markets, on the coat-tails of a hegemonic carrier state and its market-opening policies both domestically and internationally.[3] As a version

---

1 Adam Smith, *An Inquiry into the Nature and Causes of the Wealth of Nations*, New York: Oxford University Press 1993 [1776].

2 Bernard de Mandeville, *The Fable of The Bees: or, Private Vices, Publick Benefits*, Indianapolis, IN: Liberty Fund 1988 [1714].

3 Definitions of capitalism abound and tend to be both elaborate and eclectic, in the sense of consisting of changing combinations of selected characteristics. There is no need to explore them in detail here. Different definitions emphasize different elements of the capitalist configuration, in line with writers' individual preoccupations or ideologies; they also reflect different stages in the evolution of the beast, pointing to its historical dynamism. For a sample see Sombart: 'Capitalism designates an economic system significantly characterized by the predominance of "capital" (. . .) [A]n economic system is a unitary mode of providing for material wants, animated by a definite spirit, regulated and organized according to a definite plan and applying a definite technical knowledge' (Werner Sombart, 'Capitalism'. In: Johnson, Alvin and Edwin Seligman, eds, *Encyclopedia of the Social Sciences*, Vol. 3, New York: Macmillan 1930, p. 196); Weber: 'Capitalism is present wherever the industrial provision for the needs of a human group is carried out by the method of enterprise, irrespective of what need is involved. More specifically, a rational capitalistic establishment is one with capital accounting, that is, an establishment which determines its income yielding power by calculation according to the methods of modern bookkeeping and the striking of a balance' (Max Weber, *General Economic History*, New Brunswick, NJ: Transaction Publishers 2003 [1927], p. 275); Schumpeter: 'Capitalism is that form of private property economy in which innovations are carried out by means of borrowed money, which in general, though not by logical necessity, implies credit creation' (Joseph A. Schumpeter, *Business Cycles*, Vol. 1, Philadelphia, PA: Porcupine Press 1982 [1939], p. 223); Keynes: '. . . the essential characteristic of capitalism [seems to me] the

of industrial society, capitalist society is distinguished by the fact that its collective productive capital is accumulated in the hands of a minority of its members
who enjoy the legal privilege, in the form of rights of private property, to dispose
of such capital in any way they see fit, including letting it sit idle or transferring
it abroad. One implication of this is that the vast majority of the members of a
capitalist society must work under the direction, however mediated, of the
private owners of the tools they need to provide for themselves, and on terms
set by those owners in line with their desire to maximize the rate of increase of
their capital. Motivating non-owners to do so – to work hard and diligently in
the interest of the owners – requires artful devices – sticks and carrots of the
most diverse sorts that are never certain to function – that have to be continuously reinvented as capitalist progress continuously renders them obsolescent.

The tensions and contradictions within the capitalist political-economic
configuration make for an ever-present possibility of structural breakdown
and social crisis. Economic and social stability under modern capitalism must
be secured on a background of systemic restlessness[4] produced by competition
and expansion, a difficult balancing act with a constantly uncertain outcome.
Its success is contingent on, among other things, the timely appearance of a
new technological paradigm or the development of social needs and values
complementing changing requirements of continued economic growth. For
example, for the vast majority of its members, a capitalist society must manage
to convert their ever-present fear of being cut out of the productive process,
because of economic or technological restructuring, into acceptance of the
highly unequal distribution of wealth and power generated by the capitalist
economy and a belief in the legitimacy of capitalism as a social order. For this,
highly complicated and inevitably fragile institutional and ideological
provisions are necessary. The same holds true for the conversion of *insecure*

---

dependence upon an intense appeal to the money-making and money-loving instincts of individuals
as the main motive force of the economic machine' (John Maynard Keynes, *The End of Laissez-Faire:
The Collected Writings of John Maynard Keynes*, Vol. 9, London: Macmillan Press Ltd 1972 [1931],
p. 293). As to Marx, Chiapello, in a penetrating article, claims that he never used the concept (Eve
Chiapello, 'Accounting and the Birth of the Notion of Capitalism', *Critical Perspectives on Accounting*,
vol. 18, no. 3, pp. 263–96; see also Ivan Tibor Berend, 'Capitalism'. In: Smelser, Neil and Paul Baltes,
eds, *International Encyclopedia of the Social and Behavioral Sciences*, Vol. 3, Amsterdam: Elsevier
2001, pp. 1454–9; Jürgen Kocka, *Geschichte des Kapitalismus*, München: Verlag C. H. Beck 2013)
although 'the capitalist system as described by [him] is more or less the same as capitalism according
to Sombart and Weber, at least when they produce a critical definition. The irony of history is that
Marx . . . never or hardly mentions accounting, unlike Sombart and Weber. And yet Marx certainly
knew more about the accounting practices of his time than the two German sociologists who were
to follow him' (Chiapello, 'Accounting and the Birth of the Notion of Capitalism', p. 293). Sombart,
in turn, claimed that Marx, 'who virtually discovered the *phenomenon*, defined only certain aspects
of capitalism as the occasion required' (Sombart, 'Capitalism', p. 195).

4   William H. Sewell Jr., 'The Temporalities of Capitalism', *Socio-Economic Review*, vol. 6, 2008.

workers – kept insecure to make them obedient workers – into *confident consumers* happily discharging their consumerist social obligations even in the face of the fundamental uncertainty of labour markets and employment.[5]

In light of the inherent instability of modern societies founded upon and dynamically shaped by a capitalist economy, it is small wonder that theories of capitalism, from the time the concept was first used in the early 1800s in Germany[6] and the mid-1800s in England,[7] were always also theories of crisis. This holds not just for Marx and Engels but also for writers like Ricardo, Mill, Sombart, Keynes, Hilferding, Polanyi and Schumpeter, all of whom expected one way or other to see the end of capitalism during their lifetime.[8] What kind of crisis was expected to finish capitalism off differed with time and authors' theoretical priors; structuralist theories of death by overproduction or under-consumption, or by a tendency of the rate of profit to fall (Marx), coexisted with predictions of saturation of needs and markets (Keynes), of rising resistance to further commodification of life and society (Polanyi), of exhaustion of new land and new labour available for colonization in a literal as well as figurative sense (Luxemburg), of technological stagnation (Kondratieff), financial-political organization of monopolistic corporations suspending liberal markets (Hilferding), bureaucratic suppression of entrepreneurialism aided by a worldwide *trahison des clercs* (Weber, Schumpeter, Hayek) etc., etc.[9]

---

5   Colin Crouch, 'Beyond the Flexibility/Security Trade-Off: Reconciling Confident Consumers with Insecure Workers', *British Journal of Industrial Relations*, vol. 50, no. 1, pp. 1–22.

6   Ingomar Bog, 'Kapitalismus'. In: Albers, Willi et al., eds, *Handwörterbuch der Wirtschaftswissenschaft (HdWW)*, Stuttgart: Gustav Fischer, 1988, pp. 418–32.

7   R. M. Hartwell and Stanley L. Engerman, 'Capitalism'. In: Mokyr, Joel, ed., *The Oxford Encyclopedia of Economic History*, Vol. 1, New York: Oxford University Press 2003, pp. 319–325.

8   This is reflected in the periodicizations of the history of capitalism typically offered by its theorists. Thus Sombart distinguishes between 'early' (merchant), 'high' (industrial) and 'late' capitalism, the latter referring to the 1920s and 1930s. For Hilferding, the transition he observed during his lifetime from liberal to organized and from industrial to financial capitalism was a transition out of capitalism into something else. Marx and Engels, just as after them Rosa Luxemburg, expected the socialist revolution to take place while they were still alive. Polanyi believed he had seen the end of capitalism, coincident with the end of the Second World War. The 'Frankfurt School' located 'late capitalism' (*Spätkapitalismus*) in the 1970s, having taken the place of liberal capitalism or free market capitalism after 1945. Schumpeter was certain already in 1918 that there would come a time when 'capitalism has done its work and an economy exists which is satiated with capital and thoroughly rationalized by entrepreneurial brains. Only then is it possible to look forward calmly to that inevitable slowing down of merely economic development which is the concomitant of socialism, for socialism means liberation of life from the economy and alienation from the economy. This hour has not yet struck. . . . Nevertheless the hour will come. By and by private enterprise will lose its social meaning through the development of the economy and the consequent expansion of the sphere of social sympathy. The signs of this are already with us . . .' (Joseph A. Schumpeter, 'The Crisis of the Tax State'. In: Swedberg, Richard, ed., *The Economics and Sociology of Capitalism*, Princeton, NJ: Princeton University Press 1991 [1918], p. 131.

9   For a good if somewhat tendentious summary of previous predictions of an 'end of capitalism' see Hartwell and Engerman, 'Capitalism'.

While none of these theories came true as imagined, most of them were not entirely false either. In fact, the history of modern capitalism can be written as a succession of crises that capitalism survived only at the price of deep transformations of its economic and social institutions, saving it from bankruptcy in unforeseeable and often unintended ways. Seen this way, that the capitalist order still exists may well appear less impressive than that it existed so often on the brink of collapse and had continuously to change, frequently depending on contingent exogenous supports that it was unable to mobilize endogenously. The fact that capitalism has, until now, managed to outlive all predictions of its impending death, need not mean that it will forever be able to do so; there is no inductive proof here, and we cannot rule out the possibility that, next time, whatever cavalry capitalism may require for its rescue may fail to show up.

A short recapitulation of the history of modern capitalism serves to illustrate this point.[10] Liberal capitalism in the nineteenth century was confronted by a revolutionary labour movement that needed to be politically tamed by a complex combination of repression and co-optation, including democratic power sharing and social reform. In the early twentieth century, capitalism was commandeered to serve national interests in international wars, thereby converting it into a public utility under the planning regimes of a new war economy, as private property and the invisible hand of the market seemed insufficient for the provision of the collective capacities countries needed to prevail in international hostilities. After the First World War, restoration of a liberal-capitalist economy failed to produce a viable social order and had to give way in large parts of the industrial world to either Communism or Fascism, while in the core countries of what was to become 'the West' liberal capitalism was gradually succeeded, in the aftermath of the Great Depression, by Keynesian, state-administered capitalism. Out of this grew the democratic welfare-state capitalism of the three post-war decades, with hindsight the only period in which economic growth and social and political stability, achieved through democracy, coexisted under capitalism, at least in the OECD world where capitalism came to be awarded the epithet, 'advanced'. In the 1970s, however, what had with hindsight been called the 'post-war settlement' of social-democratic capitalism began to disintegrate, gradually and imperceptibly at first but increasingly punctuated by successive, ever more severe crises of both the capitalist economy and the social and political

---

10   There is no need to get into the unending discussion about when capitalism came into the world. The best bet seems to be the 1600s, although *modern* capitalism, or *capitalism as a social system* or a *society,* may only have originated with its marriage with science and technology in early industrialization, i.e., at the end of the eighteenth century. See, among others, Kocka, *Geschichte des Kapitalismus.*

institutions embedding, that is, supporting as well as containing it. This was the period of both intensifying crisis and deep transformation when 'late capitalism', as impressively described by Werner Sombart in the 1920s,[11] gave way to neoliberalism.

Crisis Theory Redux

Today, after the watershed of the financial crisis of 2008, critical and indeed crisis-theoretical reflection on the prospects of capitalism and its society is again *en vogue. Does Capitalism Have a Future?* is the title of a book published in 2013 by five outstanding social scientists: Immanuel Wallerstein, Randall Collins, Michael Mann, Georgi Derluguian and Craig Calhoun. Apart from the introduction and the conclusion, which are collectively authored, the contributors present their views in separate chapters, and this could not be otherwise since they differ widely. Still, all five share the conviction that, as they state in the introduction, 'something big looms on the horizon: a structural crisis much bigger than the recent Great Recession, which might in retrospect seem only a prologue to a period of deeper troubles and transformations'.[12] On what is causing this crisis, however, and how it will end, there is substantial disagreement – which, with authors of this calibre, may be taken as a sign of the multiple uncertainties and possibilities inherent in the present condition of the capitalist political economy.

To give an impression of how leading theorists may differ when trying to imagine the future of capitalism today, I will at some length review the prospects and predictions put forward in the book. A comparatively conventional crisis theory is probably the one offered by Wallerstein (pp. 9–35), who locates

---

11 To get an idea of the magnitude of the about-face that took place, although only gradually and thus for a long time imperceptibly, see Sombart's model of the 'form of economic life' under 'late capitalism': 'Freedom from external constraint characteristic of the period of full capitalism is superseded in the period of late capitalism by an increase in the number of restrictions until the entire system becomes regulated rather than free. Some of these regulations are self-imposed – the bureaucratization of internal management, the submission to collective decisions of trade associations, exchange boards, cartels and similar organizations. Others are prescribed by the state – factory legislation, social insurance, price regulation. Still others are enforced by the workers – works councils, trade agreements. The relation between employer and employee becomes public and official. The status of the wage worker becomes more like that of a government employee: his activity is regulated by norms of a quasi-public character, the manner of his work approaches that of a civil servant (no overtime), his wage is determined by extra-economic, non-commercial factors. The sliding wage scale of earlier times is replaced by its antithesis, the living wage, expressing the same principle as that underlying the salary scale of civil servants; in case of unemployment the worker's pay continues, and in illness or old age he is pensioned like a government employee . . . By and large, flexibility is being replaced by rigidity . . .' ('Capitalism', p. 207). Reading Sombart one becomes convinced that the term, 'neoliberalism', for the present period of capitalist development, makes a lot of sense indeed.

12 Immanual Wallerstein, Randall Collins, Michael Mann, Georgi Drerluguian and Craig Calhoun, *Does Capitalism Have a Future?*, Oxford: Oxford University Press 2013, pp. 1–2.

contemporary capitalism at the bottom of a Kondratieff cycle (Kondratieff B) with no prospect of a new (Kondratieff A) upturn. This is said to be due to a 'structural crisis' that began in the 1970s, as a result of which 'capitalists may no longer find capitalism rewarding'. Two broad causes are given, one a set of long-term trends 'ending the endless accumulation of capital', the other the demise, after the 'world revolution of 1968', of the 'dominance of centrist liberals of the geoculture' (p. 21). Structural trends include the exhaustion of virgin lands and the resulting necessity of environmental repair work, growing resource shortages, and the increasing need for public infrastructure. All of this costs money, and so does the pacification of a proliferating mass of discontented workers and the unemployed. Concerning global hegemony, Wallerstein points to what he considers the final decline of the U.S.-centred world order, in military and economic as well as ideological terms. Rising costs of doing business combine with global disorder to make restoration of a stable capitalist world system impossible. Instead Wallerstein foresees 'an ever-tighter gridlock of the system. Gridlock will in turn result in ever-wilder fluctuations, and will consequently make short-term predictions – both economic and political – ever more unreliable. And this in turn will aggravate . . . popular fears and alienation. It is a negative cycle' (p. 32). For the near future Wallerstein expects a global political confrontation between defenders and opponents of the capitalist order, in his suggestive terms: between the forces of Davos and of Porto Alegre. Their final battle 'about the successor system' (p. 35) is currently fomenting. Its outcome, according to Wallerstein, is unpredictable, although 'we can feel sure that one side or the other will win out in the coming decades, and a new reasonably stable world-system (or set of world-systems) will be established'.

Much less pessimistic, or less optimistic from the perspective of those who would like to see capitalism close down, is Craig Calhoun, who finds prospects of reform and renewal in what he, too, considers a deep and potentially final crisis (pp. 131–61). Calhoun assumes that there is still time for political intervention to save capitalism, as there was in the past, perhaps with the help of a 'sufficiently enlightened faction of capitalists' (p. 2). But he also believes 'a centralized socialist economy' to be possible, and even more so 'Chinese-style state capitalism': 'Markets can exist in the future even while specifically capitalist modes of property and finance have declined' (p. 3). Far more than Wallerstein, Calhoun is reluctant when it comes to prediction (for a summary of his view see pp. 158–61). His chapter offers a list of internal contradictions and possible external disruptions threatening the stability of capitalism, and points out a wide range of alternative outcomes. Like Wallerstein, Calhoun attributes particular significance to the international system, where he anticipates the emergence of a plurality of more or less capitalist political-economic regimes, with the attendant problems and pitfalls of coordination and competition. While he does not rule out a 'large-scale, more or less simultaneous collapse of capitalist markets . . . not only bringing economic upheaval but also upending political and social institutions' (p. 161), Calhoun believes in the possibility of states, corporations and social movements re-establishing effective governance for a transformative renewal of capitalism. To quote,

> The capitalist order is a very large-scale, highly complex system. The events of the last forty years have deeply disrupted the institutions that kept capitalism relatively well organized through the postwar period. Efforts to repair or replace these will change the system, just as new technologies and new business and financial practices may. Even a successful renewal of capitalism will transform it . . . The question is whether change will be adequate to manage systemic risks and fend off external threats. And if not, will there be widespread devastation before a new order emerges? (p. 161)

Even more agnostic on the future of capitalism is Michael Mann ('The End May Be Nigh, But for Whom?', pp. 71–97). Mann begins by reminding his readers that in his 'general model of human society', he does 'not conceive of societies as systems but as multiple, overlapping networks of interaction, of which four networks – ideological, economic, military and political power relations – are the most important. Geopolitical relations can be added to the four . . .' Mann continues:

> Each of these four or five sources of power may have an internal logic or tendency of development, so that it might be possible, for example, to identify tendencies toward equilibrium, cycles, or contradictions within capitalism, just as one might identify comparable tendencies within the other sources of social power. (p. 72)

Interactions between the networks, Mann points out, are frequent but not systematic, meaning that 'once we admit the importance of such interactions we are into a more complex and uncertain world in which the development of capitalism, for example, is also influenced by ideologies, wars and states' (p. 73). Mann adds to this the possibility of uneven development across geographical space and the likelihood of irrational behaviour interfering with rational calculations of interest, even of the interest in survival. To demonstrate the importance of contingent events and of cycles other than those envisaged in the Wallerstein–Kondratieff model of history, Mann discusses the Great

Depression of the 1930s and the Great Recession of 2008. He then proceeds to demonstrate how his approach speaks to the future, first of U.S. hegemony and second of 'capitalist markets'.

As to the former, Mann (pp. 83–4) offers the standard list of American weaknesses, both domestic and international, from economic decline to political anomy to an increasingly less effective military – weaknesses that 'might bring America down' although 'we cannot know for sure'. Even if U.S. hegemony were to end, however, 'this need not cause a systemic crisis of capitalism'. What may instead happen is a shift of economic power 'from the old West to the successfully developing Rest of the world, including most of Asia'. This would result in a sharing of economic power between the United States, the European Union and (some of) the BRICS, as a consequence of which 'the capitalism of the medium term is likely to be more statist' (p. 86). Concerning 'capitalist markets' (pp. 86–7), Mann believes, *pace* Wallerstein, that there is still enough new land to conquer and enough demand to discover and invent, to allow for both extensive and intensive growth. Also, technological fixes may appear any time for all sorts of problems, and in any case it is the working class and revolutionary socialism, much more than capitalism, for which 'the end is nigh'. In fact, if growth rates were to fall as predicted by some, the outcome might be a stable low-growth capitalism, with considerable ecological benefits. In this scenario, 'the future of the left is likely to be at most reformist social democracy or liberalism. Employers and workers will continue to struggle over the mundane injustices of capitalist employment [. . .] and their likely outcome will be compromise and reform . . .'

Still, Mann ends on a considerably less sanguine note, naming two big crises that he considers possible, and one of them probable – crises in which capitalism would go under although they would not be crises of capitalism, or of capitalism alone, since capitalism would only perish as a result of the destruction of all human civilization. One such scenario would be nuclear war, started by collective human irrationality, the other an ecological catastrophe resulting from 'escalating climate change'. In the latter case (pp. 93ff.), capitalism figures – together with the nation state and with 'citizen rights', defined as entitlements to unlimited consumption – as one of three 'triumphs of the modern period' that happen to be ecologically unsustainable. 'All three triumphs would have to be challenged for the sake of a rather abstract future, which is a very tall order, perhaps not achievable' (p. 95). While related to capitalism, ecological disaster would spring from 'a causal chain bigger than capitalism' (p. 97). However, 'policy decisions matter considerably', and 'humanity is in principle free to choose between better or worse future scenarios – and so ultimately the future is unpredictable' (p. 97).

The most straightforward theory of capitalist crisis in the book is offered by Randall Collins (pp. 37–69) – a theory he correctly characterizes as a 'stripped-down version of [a] fundamental insight that Marx and Engels had formulated already in the 1840s' (p. 38). That insight, as adapted by Collins, is that capitalism is subject to 'a long-term structural weakness', namely 'the technological displacement of labor by machinery' (p. 37). Collins is entirely unapologetic for his strictly structuralist approach, even more structuralist than Wallerstein's, as well as his mono-factorial technological determinism. In fact, he is convinced that 'technological displacement of labor' will have finished capitalism, with or without revolutionary violence, by the middle of this century – earlier than it would be brought down by the, in principle, equally destructive and definitive ecological crisis, and more reliably than by comparatively difficult-to-predict financial bubbles. 'Stripped-down' Collins's late-Marxist structuralism is, among other things, because unlike Marx in his corresponding theorem of a secular decline of the rate of profit, Collins fails to hedge his prediction with a list of countervailing factors,[13] as he believes capitalism to have run out of whatever saving graces may in the past have retarded its demise. Collins does allow for Mann's and Calhoun's non-Marxist, 'Weberian' influences on the course of history, but only as secondary forces modifying the way the fundamental structural trend that drives the history of capitalism from below will work itself out. Global unevenness of development, dimensions of conflict that are not capitalism-related, war and ecological pressures may or may not accelerate the crisis of the capitalist labour market and employment system; they cannot, however, suspend or avert it.

What exactly does this crisis consist of? While labour has gradually been replaced by technology for the past two hundred years, with the rise of information technology and, in the very near future, artificial intelligence, that process is currently reaching its apogee, in at least two respects: first, it has vastly accelerated, and second, having in the second half of the twentieth century destroyed the manual working class, it is now attacking and about to destroy the middle class as well – in other words, the new petty bourgeoisie that is the very carrier of the neocapitalist and neoliberal lifestyle of 'hard work and hard play', of careerism-cum-consumerism, which, as will be discussed *infra*, may indeed be considered the indispensable cultural foundation of contemporary capitalism's society. What Collins sees coming is a rapid

---

13 What Marx calls *entgegenwirkende Ursachen* in *Capital*, Vol. 3, in the context of the 'law of the tendency of the profit rate to fall' (Chs. 13ff. in the German original, Karl Marx, *Das Kapital. Kritik der Politischen Ökonomie*, Dritter Band, Berlin: Dietz Verlag 1966 [1894]). In fact, Collins does deal with countervailing factors, which he calls 'escapes', but to show that they are not or no longer effective. See below.

appropriation of programming, managerial, clerical, administrative, and educational work by machinery intelligent enough even to design and create new, more advanced machinery. *Electronicization* will do to the middle class what mechanization has done to the working class, and it will do it much faster. The result will be unemployment in the order of 50 to 70 per cent by the middle of the century, hitting those who had hoped, by way of expensive education and disciplined job performance (in return for stagnant or declining wages), to escape the threat of redundancy attendant on the working classes. The benefits, meanwhile, will go to 'a tiny capitalist class of robot owners' who will become immeasurably rich. The drawback for them is, however, that they will increasingly find that their product 'cannot be sold because too few persons have enough income to buy it. Extrapolating this underlying tendency', Collins writes, 'Marx and Engels predicted the downfall of capitalism and its replacement with socialism' (p. 39), and this is what Collins also predicts.

Collins's theory is most original where he undertakes to explain why technological displacement is only now about to finish capitalism when it had not succeeded in doing so in the past. Following in Marx's footsteps, he lists five 'escapes' that have hitherto saved capitalism from self-destruction, and then proceeds to show why they won't save it any more. They include the growth of new jobs and entire sectors compensating for employment losses caused by technological progress (employment in artificial intelligence will be miniscule, especially once robots begin to design and build other robots); the expansion of markets (which this time will primarily be labour markets in middle-class occupations, globally unified by information technology, enabling global competition among educated job seekers); the growth of finance, both as a source of income ('speculation') and as an industry (which cannot possibly balance the loss of employment caused by new technology, and of income caused by unemployment, also because computerization will make workers in large segments of the financial industry redundant); government employment replacing employment in the private sector (improbable because of the fiscal crisis of the state, and in any case requiring ultimately 'a revolutionary overturn of the property system' [p. 51]); and the use of education as a buffer to keep labour out of employment, making it a form of 'hidden Keynesianism' while resulting in 'credential inflation' and 'grade inflation' (which for Collins is the path most probably taken, although ultimately it will prove equally futile as the others, as a result of demoralization within educational institutions and problems of financing, both public and private).

All five escapes closed, there is no way society can prevent capitalism from causing accelerated displacement of labour and the attendant stark economic and social inequalities. Some sort of socialism, so Collins concludes, will finally have to take capitalism's place. What precisely it will look like, and what will come after socialism or with it, Collins leaves open, and he is equally agnostic on the exact mode of the transition. Revolutionary the change will be – but whether it will be a *violent social revolution* that will end capitalism or a *peaceful institutional revolution* accomplished under political leadership cannot be known beforehand. Heavy taxation of the super-rich for extended public employment or a guaranteed basic income for everyone, with equal distribution and strict rationing of very limited working hours by more or less dictatorial means à la Keynes[14] – we are free to speculate on this as Collins's 'stripped-down Marxism' does not generate predictions as to what kind of society will emerge once capitalism will have run its course. Only one thing is certain: that capitalism will end, and much sooner than one may have thought.

Something of an outlier in the book's suite of chapters is the contribution by Georgi Derluguian, who gives a fascinating inside account of the decline and eventual demise of Communism, in particular Soviet Communism (pp. 99–129). The chapter is of interest because of its speculations on the differences from and the potential parallels with a potential end of capitalism. As to the differences, Derluguian makes much of the fact that Soviet Communism was from early on embedded in the 'hostile geopolitics' (p. 110) of a 'capitalist world-system' (111). This linked its fate inseparably to that of the Soviet Union as an economically and strategically overextended multinational state. That state turned out to be unsustainable in the longer term, especially after the end of Stalinist despotism. By then the peculiar class structure of Soviet Communism gave rise to a domestic social compromise that, much unlike American capitalism, included political inertia and economic stagnation. The result was pervasive discontent on the part of a new generation of cultural, technocratic and scientific elites socialized in the revolutionary era of the late 1960s. Also, over-centralization made the state-based political economy of Soviet Communism vulnerable to regional and ethnic separatism, while the global capitalism surrounding it provided resentful opponents as well as opportunistic apparatchiks with a template of a preferable order, one in which the latter could ultimately establish themselves as self-made capitalist oligarchs.

Contemporary capitalism, of course, is much less dependent on the geopolitical good fortunes of a single imperial state, although the role of the United States in this respect must not be underestimated. More importantly, capitalism is not exposed to pressure from an alternative political-economic

---

14   John Maynard Keynes, 'Economic Possibilities for our Grandchildren'. In: Keynes, John Maynard, *Essays in Persuasion*, New York: W. W. Norton & Co. 1963 [1930].

model, assuming that Islamic economic doctrine will for a foreseeable future remain less than attractive even and precisely to Islamic elites (who are deeply integrated in the capitalist global economy). Where the two systems may, however, come to resemble each other is in their internal political disorder engendered by institutional and economic decline. When the Soviet Union lost its 'state integrity', Derluguian writes, this 'undermined all modern institutions and therefore disabled collective action at practically any level above family and crony networks. This condition became self-perpetuating' (p. 122). One consequence was that the ruling bureaucracies reacted 'with more panic than outright violence' when confronted by 'mass civic mobilizations like the 1968 Prague Spring and the Soviet perestroika at its height in 1989', while at the same time 'the insurgent movements . . . failed to exploit the momentous disorganization in the ranks of dominant classes' (p. 129). For different reasons and under different circumstances, a similar weakness of collective agency, due to de-institutionalization and creating comparable uncertainty among both champions and challengers of the old order, might shape a future transition from capitalism to post-capitalism, pitting against each other fragmented social movements on the one hand and disoriented political-economic elites on the other.

My own view builds on all five contributors but differs from each of them. I take the diversity of theories on what all agree is a severe crisis of capitalism and capitalist society as an indication of contemporary capitalism having entered a period of deep *indeterminacy* – a period in which unexpected things *can* happen any time and knowledgeable observers can legitimately disagree on what *will* happen, due to long-valid causal relations having become historically obsolete. In other words, I interpret the coexistence of a shared sense of crisis with diverging concepts of the nature of that crisis as an indication that traditional economic and sociological theories have today lost much of their predictive power. As I will point out in more detail, below, I see this as a result, but also as a cause, of a destruction of collective agency in the course of capitalist development, equally affecting Wallerstein's Davos and Porto Alegre people and resulting in a social context beset with unintended and unanticipated consequences of purposive, but in its effects increasingly unpredictable, social action.[15]

---

15 For a different, more 'optimistic' view of indeterminacy see Wallerstein et al. (*Does Capitalism Have a Future?*, p. 4): 'We find hope . . . exactly in the degree to which our future is politically underdetermined. Systemic crisis loosens and shatters the structural constraints that are themselves the inheritance of past dilemmas . . . Deep capitalist crisis may be an opportunity to reorganize the planetary affairs of humanity in a way that promotes more social justice and a more livable planet.' While I agree on the softening of structural constraints, I do not see who the collective agent is that

Moreover, rather than picking one of the various scenarios of the crisis and privilege it over the others, I suggest that they all, or most of them, may be aggregated into a diagnosis of *multi-morbidity* in which different disorders coexist and, more often than not, reinforce each other. Capitalism, as pointed out at the beginning, was always a fragile and improbable order and for its survival depended on ongoing repair work. Today, however, too many frailties have become simultaneously acute while too many remedies have been exhausted or destroyed. The end of capitalism can then be imagined as a death from a thousand cuts, or from a multiplicity of infirmities each of which will be all the more untreatable as all will demand treatment at the same time. As will become apparent, I do not believe that any of the potentially stabilizing forces mentioned by Mann and Calhoun, be it regime pluralism, regional diversity and uneven development, political reform, or independent crisis cycles, will be strong enough to neutralize the syndrome of accumulated weaknesses that characterize contemporary capitalism. No effective opposition being left, and no practicable successor model waiting in the wings of history, capitalism's accumulation of defects, alongside its accumulation of capital, may be seen, with Collins,[16] as an entirely endogenous dynamic of self-destruction, following an evolutionary logic moulded in its expression but not suspended by contingent and coincidental events, along a historical trajectory from early liberal via state-administered to neoliberal capitalism, which culminated for the time being in the financial crisis of 2008 and its aftermath.

For the decline of capitalism to continue, that is to say, no revolutionary alternative is required, and certainly no masterplan of a better society displacing capitalism. Contemporary capitalism is vanishing on its own, collapsing from internal contradictions, and not least as a result of having vanquished its enemies – who, as noted, have often rescued capitalism from itself by forcing it to assume a new form. What comes after capitalism in its final crisis, now under way, is, I suggest, not socialism or some other defined social order, but a lasting *interregnum* – no new world system equilibrium à la Wallerstein, but a prolonged period of social entropy, or disorder (and precisely for this reason a period of uncertainty and indeterminacy). It is an interesting problem for sociological theory whether and how a society can turn for a significant length of time into *less than a society*, a *post-social society* as it were, or a *society lite*, until it may or may not recover and again become a society in the full meaning

---

would be able to take advantage of this. To me indeterminacy results from and reinforces the pulverization of collective agency in the course of the neoliberal revolution.

16 Although Collins suggests a monocausal explanation, whereas I expect capitalism to be wrecked by a bundle, or syndrome, of more or less related causes.

of the term.[17] I suggest that one can attain a conceptual fix on this by drawing liberally on a famous article by David Lockwood[18] to distinguish between *system integration* and *social integration*, or integration at the macro and micro levels of society. An interregnum would then be defined as a breakdown of system integration at the macro level, depriving individuals at the micro level of institutional structuring and collective support, and shifting the burden of ordering social life, of providing it with a modicum of security and stability, to individuals themselves and such social arrangements as they can create on their own. A society in interregnum, in other words, would be a *de-institution-alized* or *under-institutionalized* society, one in which expectations can be stabilized only for a short time by local improvisation, and which for this very reason is essentially ungovernable.

Contemporary capitalism, then, would appear to be a society whose system integration is critically and irremediably weakened, so that the continuation of capital accumulation – for an intermediate period of uncertain duration – becomes solely dependent on the opportunism of collectively incapacitated *individualized individuals*, as they struggle to protect themselves from looming accidents and structural pressures on their social and economic status. Undergoverned and undermanaged, the social world of the post-capitalist interregnum, in the wake of neoliberal capitalism having cleared away states, governments, borders, trade unions and other moderating forces, can at any time be hit by disaster; for example, bubbles imploding or violence penetrating from a collapsing periphery into the centre. With individuals deprived of collective defences and left to their own devices, what remains of a social order hinges on the motivation of individuals to cooperate with other individuals on an ad hoc basis, driven by fear and greed and by elementary interests in individual survival. Society having lost the ability to provide its members with effective protection and proven templates for social action and social existence, individuals have only themselves to rely on while social order depends on the weakest possible mode of social integration, *Zweckrationalität*.

---

17   Durkheimians would here resort to the concept of anomy, signifying a less-than-normal condition of deficient social integration (Emile Durkheim, *The Division of Labor in Society*, New York: The Free Press 1964 [1893]). Not buying into Durkheim's firm belief that such 'pathological' conditions can be rectified by theoretically informed government intervention, this would imply that there may be regression in history, not just progress but also loss, and for more than an insignificant intermediate moment – a move from civilization to a prolonged period of barbarism, such as, apparently, followed the end of the Western Roman Empire. Of course this goes fundamentally against the grain of modern thinking, which is obliged to be 'optimistic'.

18   David Lockwood, 'Social Integration and System Integration'. In: Zollschan, George K. and Walter Hirsch, eds, *Explorations in Social Change*, London: Houghton Mifflin 1964, pp. 244–257.

As pointed out in Chapter 1 of this book, and partly elaborated in the rest of this introduction, I anchor this condition in a variety of interrelated developments, such as declining growth intensifying distributional conflict; the rising inequality that results from this; vanishing macroeconomic manageability, as manifested in, among other things, steadily growing indebtedness, a pumped-up money supply, and the ever-present possibility of another economic breakdown;[19] the suspension of post-war capitalism's engine of social progress, democracy, and the associated rise of oligarchic rule; the dwindling capacity of governments and the systemic inability of governance to limit the commodification of labour, nature and money; the omnipresence of corruption of all sorts, in response to intensified competition in winner-take-all markets with unlimited opportunities for self-enrichment; the erosion of public infrastructures and collective benefits in the course of commodification and privatization; the failure after 1989 of capitalism's host nation, the United States, to build and maintain a stable global order; etc., etc. These and other developments, I suggest, have resulted in widespread cynicism governing economic life, for a long time if not forever ruling out a recovery of normative legitimacy for capitalism as a just society offering equal opportunities for individual progress – a legitimacy that capitalism would need to draw on in critical moments – and founding *social integration* on *collective resignation* as the last remaining pillar of the capitalist social order, or disorder.[20]

Moving Disequilibrium

In my own recent work, much of it assembled in this volume, I have argued that OECD capitalism has been on a crisis trajectory since the 1970s, the historical turning point being when the post-war settlement was abandoned

---

19   Which is a theme that is commonplace in today's quality press. See, for example, Binyamin Appelbaum, 'Policy Makers Skeptical on Preventing Financial Crisis', *New York Times*, 4 October 2015, nytimes.com, last accessed 21 January 2016; and Paul Mason, 'Apocalypse Now: Has the Next Giant Financial Crash Already Begun?', *Guardian*, 1 November 2015, theguardian.com, last accessed 21 January 2016. Consider also the report on 'global risks' presented to the Davos meeting in January 2016.

20   As will be discussed at the end of this introduction, systemic disintegration and social entropy can be presented as historical progress towards individual liberty and a free society. This is the core of neoliberal libertarianism, which expects nothing more of a society than that it allows its members to maximize their utility in the market, thereby making political democracy and collective goods redundant (emblematic Ayn Rand, 'What is Capitalism?' In: Rand, Ayn, ed., *Capitalism: The Unknown Ideal*, New York: The New American Library 1967 [1965], pp. 11–34; Ayn Rand, *Atlas Shrugged*, New York: Penguin 1992 [1957]). According to the economist Bernard Maris (*Houellebecq, Économiste*, Paris: Flammarion 2014), the reality of neoliberal social – or better: post-social – life according to the prescriptions of economic theory has nowhere been better depicted than in the work of the writer Michel Houellebecq, who in his novels explores the multifaceted individual and collective deformations that come with undersocialized individualism, including the liability of individuals living by its prescriptions to be drawn into regressive-identitarian collectivism (see, for example, Michel Houellebecq, *Soumission*, Paris: Flammarion 2015).

by capital in response to a global profit squeeze. To be precise, three crises followed one another: the global inflation of the 1970s, the explosion of public debt in the 1980s, and rapidly rising private indebtedness in the subsequent decade, resulting in the collapse of financial markets in 2008 (for more see Ch. 2). This sequence was by and large the same for all major capitalist countries, whose economies have never been in equilibrium since the end of post-war growth at the end of the 1960s. All three crises began and ended in the same way, following an identical political-economic logic: inflation, public debt and the deregulation of private debt started out as politically expedient solutions to distributional conflicts between capital and labour (and, in the 1970s, between the two and the producers of raw material, the cost of which had ceased to be negligible), until they became problems themselves: inflation begot unemployment as relative prices became distorted and owners of monetary assets abstained from invest-ment; mounting public debt made creditors nervous and produced pressures for consolidation in the 1990s; and the pyramid of private debt that had filled the gaps in aggregate demand caused by public spending cuts imploded when the bubbles produced by easy money and excessive credit blew up. Solutions turned into problems requiring new solutions which, however, after another decade or so, became problems themselves, calling for yet other solutions that soon turned out to be as short-lived and self-defeating as their predecessors. Government policies vacillated between two equilib-rium points, one political, the other economic, that had become impossible to attain simultaneously: by attending to the need for democratic political legitimacy and social peace, trying to live up to citizen expectations of steadily increasing economic prosperity and social stability, they found themselves at risk of damaging economic performance – while efforts to restore economic equilibrium tended to trigger political dissatisfaction and undermine support for the government of the day and the capitalist market economy in general.

In fact, the situation was even more critical than that, although it was not perceived as such for a long time, since it unfolded only gradually, over roughly two political generations. Intertwined with the crisis sequence of the post-1970s was an evolving fiscal crisis of the democratic-capitalist state, again basically in all countries undergoing the secular transition from 'late' to neolib-eral capitalism. While in the 1970s governments still had a choice, within limits, between inflation and public debt to bridge the gap between the combined distributional claims of capital and labour and what was available for distribution, after the end of inflation at the beginning of the 1980s the 'tax state' of modern capitalism began to change into a 'debt state'. In this it was helped by the growth of a dynamic, increasingly global financial industry headquartered in the rapidly de-industrializing hegemonic country of global capitalism, the United States. Concerned about the power of its new clients – who were after all sovereign states – to unilaterally cancel their debt, the rising financial sector soon began to seek reassurance from governments with respect to their economic and political ability to service and repay their loans. The result was another transformation of the democratic state, this time into a 'consolidation state', which began in the mid-1990s. To the extent that consolidation of public finances through spending cuts resulted in overall gaps in demand or in citizen discontent, the financial industry was happy to step in with loans to private households, provided credit markets were sufficiently deregulated. This began in the 1990s at the latest and ultimately caused the financial crisis of 2008.

Unfolding alongside the *crisis sequence* and the transformation of the tax state into a *consolidation state* were three long-term trends, all starting more or less at the end of the post-war era and running in parallel, again, through the entire family of rich capitalist democracies: declining growth, growing inequality, and rising debt – public, private and overall. Over the years the three seem to have become mutually reinforcing: low growth contributes to inequality by intensifying distributional conflict; inequality dampens growth by restricting effective demand; high levels of existing debt clog credit markets and raise the prospect of financial crises; an overgrown financial sector both results from and adds to economic inequality etc., etc. Already the last growth cycle before 2008 was more imagined than real,[21] and post-2008 recovery remains anaemic at best, also because Keynesian stimulus, monetary or fiscal, fails to work in the face of unprecedented amounts of accumulated debt. Note that we are talking about long-term trends, not just a momentary unfortunate coincidence, and indeed about global trends, affecting the capitalist system as a whole and as such. Nothing is in sight that seems only nearly powerful enough to break the three trends, deeply engrained and densely intertwined as they have become.

---

21   Lawrence 'Larry' Summers, chief mechanic of the American capital accumulation machine, at the IMF Economic Forum in November, 2013: 'If you go back and study the economy prior to the crisis, there is something a little bit odd. Many people believe that monetary policy was too easy. Everybody agrees that there was a vast amount of imprudent lending going on. Almost everybody agrees that wealth, as it was experienced by households, was in excess of its reality. Too easy money, too much borrowing, too much wealth. Was there a great boom? Capacity utilization wasn't under any great pressure; unemployment wasn't under any remarkably low level; inflation was entirely quiescent, so somehow even a great bubble wasn't enough to produce any excess in aggregate demand.' (James Decker, 'Larry Summers at IMF Economic Forum, Nov. 8', 8 November 2013, youtube.com.)

Phase IV

Since 2008, we have lived in a fourth stage of the post-1970s crisis sequence, and the by now familiar dialectic of problems treated with solutions that turn into problems themselves is again making itself felt.[22] The three apocalyptic horsemen of contemporary capitalism – stagnation, debt, inequality – are continuing to devastate the economic and political landscape. With ever lower growth, as recovery from the Great Recession is making little or no progress, deleveraging has been postponed *ad calendas graecas* and overall indebtedness is higher than ever.[23] Within a total debt burden of unprecedented magnitude, public debt has climbed again (see Figure 1.4, below, p. 54), not only annihilating all gains made in the first phase of consolidation, but also effectively blocking any fiscal effort to restart growth. Thus unemployment remains high throughout the OECD world, even in a country like Sweden where it has for some time now settled on a plateau of around 8 per cent. Where employment has to some extent been restored it tends to be at lower pay and inferior conditions, due to technological change, to 'reforms' in social security systems lowering workers' effective reservation wage, and to de-unionization, with the attendant increase in the power of employers. Indeed, often enough, 'recovery' amounts to replacement of unemployment with underemployment. Although interest rates are at a record low, investment and growth refuse to respond, giving rise to discussions among policymakers about lowering interest rates further, to below zero. While in the 1970s inflation was public enemy number one, now desperate efforts are being made throughout the OECD world to raise it to at least 2 per cent, hitherto without success. By comparison with the 1970s, when it was the coincidence of inflation and unemployment that left economists clueless, now it is very cheap money coexisting with deflationary pressures, raising the spectre of 'debt deflation' and of a collapse of a pyramid of accumulated debt by far exceeding in size that of 2008.

How much of a mystery the present phase of the long crisis of contemporary capitalism presents to its would-be management[24] is nowhere

---

22 The fourth stage is still open-ended, and was only insufficiently recognizable when the first two chapters of this book were written.

23 McKinsey Global Institute, *Debt and (Not Much) Deleveraging*, London: McKinsey & Company 2015.

24 An interesting case is that of Paul Krugman, the favourite ideologue of the 'Keynesian' centre-left. Responding in the *New York Times* (16 November 2013) to Summers' 'secular stagnation' *pronunciamiento* (see Footnote 21), he begins by paraphrasing Keynes as having said, 'spending is good, and while productive spending is best, unproductive spending is better than nothing' – from which he derives the claim that 'private spending that is wholly or partially wasteful' could be 'a good thing'. For illustration, Krugman continues, 'suppose that U.S. corporations, which are currently sitting on a huge hoard of cash, were somehow to become convinced that it would be a great idea to fit out all their employees as cyborgs, with Google Glass and smart wristwatches everywhere. And suppose that

more visible than in the practice of 'quantitative easing', adopted, under different names, by the leading central banks of the capitalist world. Since 2008,
central banks have been buying up financial assets of diverse kinds, handing
out new cash, produced out of thin air, to private financial firms. In return they
receive titles to future income streams from debtors of all sorts, turning private
debt into public assets, or better: into assets of public institutions with the
privilege unilaterally to determine an economy's money supply. Right now, the
balance sheets of the largest central banks have increased in the past seven
years from around eight to more than twenty trillion dollars (see Figure 4.3, p.
127), not yet counting the gigantic asset buying programme started by the
European Central Bank in 2014. In the process, central banks, in their dual
roles as public authorities and guardians of the health of private financial
firms, have become the most important, and indeed effectively the only, players in economic policy, with governments under strict austerity orders and
excluded from monetary policymaking. Although quantitative easing has
completely failed to counter the deflationary pressures in an economy like
Japan – where it has been relied upon for a decade or more on a huge scale – it
is steadfastly pursued for lack of alternatives, and nobody knows what would
happen if cash-production by debt-purchasing was ended. Meanwhile in
Europe, banks sell their no-longer-secure securities, including government
papers, to the European Central Bank, either letting the cash they get in return
sit with it on deposit, even if they have to pay negative interest on it, or they
lend it to cash-strapped governments in countries where central banks are not
allowed to finance governments directly, collecting interest from them at a rate
above what they could earn in the private credit market. To this extent, quantitative easing at least serves to rescue, if nothing else, the financial sector.[25]

three years later they realized that there wasn't really much payoff to all that spending. Nonetheless, the
resulting investment boom would have given us several years of much higher employment, with no
real waste, since the resources employed would otherwise have been idle.' Concerning bubbles, 'we
now know that the economic expansion of 2003-2007 was driven by a bubble. You can say the same
about the latter part of the 90s expansion; and you can in fact say the same about the later years of
the Reagan expansion, which was driven at that point by runaway thrift institutions and a large
bubble in commercial real estate . . .' This, according to Krugman, has 'some radical implications',
among them, following Summers, that 'most of what would be done under the aegis of preventing a
future crisis would be counterproductive' under the new circumstances. Another implication would
be that 'even improved financial regulation is not necessarily a good thing' as it 'may discourage
irresponsible lending and borrowing at a time when more spending of any kind is good for the
economy.' Moreover, it might be advisable 'to reconstruct our whole monetary system – say, eliminate
paper money and pay negative interest rates on deposits'. Paul Krugman, 'Secular Stagnation,
Coalmines, Bubbles, and Larry Summers', New York Times, 16 November 2013, krugman.blogs.
nytimes.com, last accessed 4 August 2015).
    25   If 'quantitative easing' continues to have no effect on the economy as a whole, or if central
banks have to write off too many of the assets that they have bought with fresh money, the last bullet of

Decoupling Democracy

As the crisis sequence took its course, the post-war shotgun marriage between capitalism and democracy came to an end.[26] Again this was a slow, gradual development. There was no putsch:[27] elections continue to take place, opposition leaders are not sent to prison, and opinions can still by and large be freely expressed in the media, both old and new. But as one crisis followed the next, and the fiscal crisis of the state unfolded alongside them, the arena of distributional conflict shifted, moving upwards and away from the world of collective action of citizens towards ever more remote decision sites where interests appear as 'problems' in the abstract jargon of technocratic specialists. In the age of inflation in the 1970s, labour relations were the main conflict arena, and strikes were frequent throughout the OECD world, offering ordinary people an opportunity to engage with others in direct action against a visible adversary. In this way, they could experience conflict and solidarity directly and personally, with often life-changing consequences. When inflation ended in the early 1980s, strikes came to an end as well, and the defence of redistributive interests against the logic of capitalist markets shifted to the electoral arena where the issue of contestation was the social welfare state and its future role and size. Then, when fiscal consolidation got under way, income gains began to depend on access to credit, as determined by – increasingly loose – legal regulations of financial markets and by the profit interests of the financial industry. This left little if any space for collective action, also because it was hard for most people in financial markets to understand their own interests and identify their exploiter. Today, in Phase IV, with monetary expansion and fiscal austerity coinciding, the prosperity, relative and absolute, of millions of citizens depends on decisions of central bank executives, international organizations, and councils of ministers of all sorts, acting in an arcane space remote from everyday experience and entirely impenetrable to outsiders, dealing with issues so complex that even insiders often cannot be sure what they are to do and are in fact doing.

The upward shift of conflict arenas during 'the decades of neoliberal progress was accompanied by a gradual erosion of the post-war *standard*

---

monetary policy, and perhaps of policy generally, would be dishing out 'helicopter money' to citizens, perhaps by sending each taxpayer a cheque of, say, $3,000, circumventing the banking system in the hope that this would, finally, result in a take-off of effective demand. But it would equally be possible that people will invest their free cash in asset markets, causing another bubble, or was it to deleverage, or stuff it into their mattress. That, one suspects, might be the final end of capitalist wisdom.

26   I have dealt with this subject in more detail in Wolfgang Streeck, *Buying Time: The Delayed Crisis of Democratic Capitalism*, London and New York: Verso Books 2014.

27   Apart, of course, from the replacement, by their united colleagues on the European Council in 2011, of the prime ministers of Italy and Greece with functionaries of international *haute finance*.

model of democracy, pushed forward by, as well as allowing for, the gradual emergence of a new, 'Hayekian' growth model for OECD capitalism. By the standard model of democracy, I mean the peculiar combination, as had come to be considered normal in OECD capitalism after 1945, of reasonably free elections, government by established mass parties, ideally one of the Right and one of the Left, and strong trade unions and employer associations under a firmly institutionalized collective bargaining regime, with legal rights to strike and, sometimes, lock-out. This model reached its peak in the 1970s, after which it began to disintegrate[28]. The advance of neoliberalism coincided with steadily declining electoral turnout in all countries, rare and short-lived exceptions notwithstanding. The shrinking of the electorate was, moreover, highly asymmetrical: those that dropped out of electoral politics came overwhelmingly from the lower end of the income scale – ironically where the need for egalitarian democracy is greatest. Party membership declined as well, in some countries dramatically; party systems fragmented; and voting became volatile and often erratic. In a rising number of countries, the gaps in the electorate have begun to be filled in part by so-called 'populist' parties, mostly of the Right but lately also from the Left, who mobilize marginalized groups for protest against 'the system' and its 'elites'. Also declining is trade-union membership – a trend reflected in an almost complete disappearance of strikes, which like elections have long served as a recognized channel of democratic participation.

The demise of standard post-war democracy was and is of the highest significance. Coupled to state-managed capitalism, democracy functioned as an engine of economic and social progress. By redistributing parts of the proceeds of the capitalist market economy downward, through both industrial relations and social policy, democracy provided for rising standards of living among ordinary people and thereby procured legitimacy for a capitalist market economy; at the same time it stimulated economic growth by securing a sufficient level of aggregate demand. This twofold role was essential for Keynesian politics-cum-policies, which turned the political and economic power of organized labour into a productive force and assigned democracy a positive economic function. The problem was that the viability of that model was contingent on labour mobilizing a sufficient amount of political and economic power, which it could do in the more or less closed national economies of the post-war era. Inside these, capital had to content itself with low profits and confinement in a strictly delimited economic sphere, a condition it accepted in exchange for economic stability and social peace as long as it saw no way out

---

28   Schäfer and Streeck, 'Introduction'., *Politics in the Age of Austerity*.

of the national containers within which its hunting licence had been conditionally renewed after 1945. With the end of post-war growth, however, as distributional margins shrunk, the profit-dependent classes began to look for an alternative to serving as an infrastructure of social democracy, and found it in de-nationalization, also known as 'globalization'. As capital and capitalist markets began to outgrow national borders, with the help of international trade agreements and assisted by new transportation and communication technologies, the power of labour, inevitably locally based, weakened, and capital was able to press for a shift to a new growth model, one that works by redistributing from the bottom to the top. This was when the march into neoliberalism began, as a rebellion of capital against Keynesianism, with the aim of enthroning the Hayekian model in its place.[29] Thus the threat of unemployment returned, together with its reality, gradually replacing political legitimacy with economic discipline. Lower growth rates were acceptable for the new powers as long as they were compensated by higher profit rates and an increasingly inegalitarian distribution.[30] Democracy ceased to be functional for economic growth and in fact became a threat to the performance of the new growth model; it therefore had to be decoupled from the political economy. This was when 'post-democracy' was born.[31]

In the 1990s at the latest, 'globalization' became the dominant political-economic formula for the legitimation of neoliberal capitalism, conceived as what is called in German a *Sachzwang*: a factual constraint residing in the nature of things that leaves you no choice. Soon even the Left began to internalize the idea of globalization as a natural evolutionary process unstoppable by political means – while for capital globalization it offered a long-desired way out of the social-democratic prison, or workhouse, in which it had been kept during the *trente glorieuse*. *Now states were located in markets, rather than markets in states.* While governments, including those of the Left, redefined social policy as public provision for private 'competitiveness' – for the re-commodification of labour by reinstatement of work incentives, and for replacing social citizenship with educational and occupational achievement – capital used its newly gained mobility to push for lower taxes, less regulation, and generally, in Sombart's terms (see above, Footnote 11), for rigidity being

---

29   The political opposition of business to Keynesianism and its consequences for political economy has nowhere been better explained than by Michal Kalecki, 'Political Aspects of Full Employment', *Political Quarterly*, vol. 14, no. 4, 1943, pp. 322–331.

30   Indeed, as growth rates fell, profit recovered while wage shares declined. There were years after 2008 in which the entire (small) increase of the American economy went to the top 0.01 per cent of the population.

31   Colin Crouch, *Post-Democracy*, Cambridge: Polity Press 2004.

replaced with flexibility. Over two decades, globalization as a discourse gave birth to a new *pensée unique*, a TINA (There Is No Alternative) logic of political economy for which adaptation to the 'demands' of 'international markets' is both good for everybody and the only possible policy anyway. Measured against those demands, democracy as in the standard model could not but appear outdated: too slow and sluggish, too collectivistic and conservative, and not innovative enough compared to agile individuals responding instantly to market signals and competition. What was urgently needed, therefore, was a new, more flexible regime, for which an attractive name was soon found: 'global governance', organized by sectors rather than classes, run by a voluntaristic 'civil society' rather than coercive states, and based on international organizations and 'epistemic communities' substituting modern cooperative problem-solving by experts for old-fashioned class conflict.[32]

The fastest sector to 'globalize' was finance, where more than anywhere else the process was identifiable as one of a worldwide expansion of the U.S. economy, more specifically its increasingly dominant sector, driven by American needs, interests and policies.[33] Within a little over a decade, the financial sector of the United States mutated into the financial sector of global capitalism, absorbing or eliminating its counterparts in other countries. Aggressive deregulation of the U.S. financial industry attracted capital from all over the world, with multilateral international organizations and bilateral agreements employed to open up for American financial firms the capital markets of other countries. Reconstituted at the global level, the financial industry effectively escaped democratic control everywhere except, perhaps, the United States. Then, however, it became the most important source of economic growth, tax revenue and campaign contributions. Left essentially to govern itself, apart from weak and in any case American-dominated institutions of 'global governance', finance became a government of its own, to the extent that cash-hungry *debt states*, having lost the capacity to tax their richest citizens and firms due to the new opportunities for capital mobility, required loans and expert advice from the private financial sector. National democracies in debt began to face a second constituency, the financial industry, which had its own and very peculiar ideas as to the role of the state in society, in particular how much taxing and spending governments

---

32   The leading German exponent of this view, in addition to the late Ulrich Beck and, in part, Jürgen Habermas, is Helmut Willke (*Demokratie in Zeiten der Konfusion*, Berlin: Suhrkamp 2014).

33   Turning the world into an extended playing field for the American economy, and in the process into an extension of the United States domestic political-economic order, has been the objective of U.S. foreign policy since the end of the Second World War, as lucidly pointed out by Perry Anderson 'Imperium', *New Left Review*, no. 83, September/October 2013, pp. 5–111.

should be allowed and how public revenues are to be raised and expenditures allocated.

Today, after global financialization, democracy may be conceived as a struggle between two constituencies, the national state people and the international market people (see Table 4.1, p. 124). Whereas the rights of the state people are grounded in national political status, or citizenship, the market people of international finance derive their claim on public policy from commercial contracts, which in an encompassing global market, where lenders have alternatives, tend to take precedence. By providing its customers with liquidity, the financial industry establishes control over them, *as is the very nature of credit.* Financialization turns the financial sector into an international *private government* disciplining national political communities and their public governments, without being in any way democratically accountable. The power of money, wielded by central banks both independent from states and dependent for the success of their monetary policies on the cooperation of the private financial sector, takes the place of the power of votes, adding importantly to the decoupling of democracy from political economy that is the central requirement of the Hayekian model, if not of growth, then of profit growth.

Commodification Unbound

Together with the decoupling of democracy from political economy, which made the democratic process run dry while setting capitalism free to shift to a new, market-driven, non-egalitarian growth model, globalization caused a deep erosion of social regimes which had in the past more or less effectively limited the commodification of what Karl Polanyi has called the three 'fictitious commodities', labour, land and money.[34] According to Polanyi, it is in the logic of capitalist development and its 'utopia' of a 'self-regulating market' that in order to continue its advance it must strive ultimately to commodify everything. Labour, land and money, however, can be commodified only within narrow bounds if they are to retain their use value: complete commodification destroys them and thereby obstructs rather than enhances capital accumulation. Capitalism, that is to say, can survive only as long as it accepts, voluntarily or not, being prevented by 'society' from forcing under its logic what it can fully commodify only at its own detriment. Keeping labour, land and money from complete commodification and thereby protecting them

---

34 Karl Polanyi, *The Great Transformation: The Political and Economic Origins of Our Time,* Boston, MA: Beacon Press 1957 [1944]. The present section elaborates selectively on a part of Chapter 1 that could only be sketched for reasons of space.

against abuse requires the authority of government. That resource, however, has been thoroughly diminished by globalization. 'Governance' is not enough to keep capitalism from going too far and undermining itself. Globalization eats away at political capacities that Marx, in his seminal analysis of the politics of the working day, identified as necessary for solving an otherwise unsolvable collective action problem arising from competitive markets:

> For protection against 'the serpent of their agonies', the labourers must put their heads together, and, as a class, compel the passing of a law, an all-powerful social barrier that shall prevent the very workers from selling, by voluntary contract with capital, themselves and their families into slavery and death.[35]

To illustrate the relevance of Marx's analysis for modern conditions, and in particular for the question of how capitalism might end, I will restrict myself to the field of labour.[36] Globalization has moved the sweatshops that Marx and Engels and the factory inspectors of the nineteenth century found in Manchester to the capitalist periphery, out of sight of today's labour aristocracy inhabiting the centres of the contemporary capitalist production system. So the sweated workers of today and the middle-class workers in the countries of 'advanced' capitalism, being so remote from each other spatially that they never meet, do not speak the same language and never experience together the community and solidarity deriving from joint collective action. Those exposed to the very exploitation that workers in 'the West' are told has been eradicated by capitalist progress are becoming objects of charity at best, while the consumerist lifestyle of the Western middle-class, and also of large parts of its working class, depends on the low wages and the barbaric working conditions in the 'developing' world. At the same time, by buying cheap T-shirts or smartphones, workers in the rich capitalist countries *as consumers* put pressure on themselves *as producers*, accelerating the move of production abroad and thereby undermining their own wages, working conditions and employment.

---

35 Marx was aware that one reason why British workers were able to get the Factory Act passed was that employers themselves were concerned about the ongoing destruction of labour in the 'satanic mills' of their factories. Exposed to competition, however, and only weakly organized, they could not act on what they knew should have been their rational interest (Karl Marx, *Capital: A Critique of Political Economy*, Vol. 1, New York: International Publishers 1967 [1867], p. 285).

36 Of course regime erosion is blatant also with respect to land, or nature, where the fragmented politics of global capitalism has proved unable to contain the accelerating consumption and destruction of the natural environment. Everything that needs to be said here, incidentally, is said in the papal encyclical, *Laudatio si*. Another source of uncertainty and a permanent threat to systemic stability is the competitive creation of money by governments, central banks and financial firms and the transformation of debt into a tradable commodity, which remains largely unregulated by 'global governance' even after the collapse of 2008.

Moreover, globalization relocates not only jobs but also workers. Neoliberal ideology supports migration and open borders in the name of personal liberty and human rights, knowing that it provides employers in the receiving countries with an unlimited labour supply, thereby destabilizing protective labour regimes. Ethnic diversity is welcomed, not only by the liberal middle class, but also by employers desiring docile workers that are grateful for being allowed to be where they are, and anxious to avoid deportation for becoming unemployed or engaging in militant activities. Immigration thus makes the collective organization of workers difficult, especially in low-income occupations. It can also be used propagandistically to enlist indigenous workers' sense of solidarity for neoliberal policies aimed at abolishing minimum wages and employment protections, by accusing trade unions of racist discrimination against 'outsiders' for the benefit of 'insiders'. If then the labour market interests of the indigenous working class are articulated by right-wing populist parties and movements, labour protection suffers further de-legitimation while the working class becomes even more divided.

As post-war national labour regimes, established after intense political struggles to protect workers and their families from market pressures, are being subverted by international competition, labour markets in leading capitalist countries are changing to precarious employment, zero hours jobs, freelancing and standby work, not just in small local but also and often in large global firms. An extreme case in point is Uber, a giant of the so-called 'sharing economy', which with the help of new communication technologies functions almost entirely without a workforce of its own. In the United States alone, more than 160,000 people depend on Uber for their livelihood, only 4,000 of whom are regular employees.[37] For the rest, employment risks are being privatized and individualized, and life and work become inseparably fused. At the same time, labour-aristocratic middle-class families, striving to meet ever more demanding career and consumption obligations, depend on an underpaid labour force of domestic servants, in particular childminders, who typically are immigrants, mostly female. With employers under global competitive pressures and workers fearing for their jobs, trade unions are losing power or never come into existence in new industries and firms. As a result, no political capacity is available to soften the impact of technological change, which proceeds

---

37   On Uber as an example of evolving employment patterns, see 'Rising Economic Insecurity Tied to Decades-Long Trend in Employment Practices', *New York Times*, 12 July 2015, nytimes.com, last accessed 29 November 2015.

faster than ever to reorganize work, as predicted, for example, by Randall Collins for the new, overeducated middle class.[38]

Why should the uprooting of regulations that have hitherto stood in the way of full commodification of labour be considered a symptom of crisis of *capitalism*, rather than just of its workers? One reason, emphasized by Richard Sennett, might be that ever-increasing 'flexibility' requirements are incompatible with the development of capacities for productive work as vested in stable professional identities.[39] Perhaps more importantly, at the macro-level the fragmentation of the working class and the debasement of work through excessive commodification and flexibilization preclude the formulation of a coherent oppositional project, like socialism, aspiring to separate what is progressive from what is reactionary in capitalism and preserve it. A collective political project like this, aimed at *Aufhebung* of capitalism in a more advanced social order – the utopia of a modern life beyond a dictatorship of the market – not just challenges existing society but at the same time legitimates it as a transitional stage in an imagined history of human progress. The global dispersion of the working class and its division by language and ethnicity, the dependence of consumption, production and reproduction in the centre on imported labour from and exported jobs to the periphery, and the deterioration of class solidarity into charity make for a social structure that confounds rather than supports class consciousness and collective action,

---

38 An entire book could and should be written summarizing the profound transformation of the world of work that has been under way for at least two decades, in particular since the crisis of 2008. Everywhere in the 'rich' capitalist countries low-wage and low-conditions employment have proliferated, and low wages have become even lower. See 'Low-Income Workers See Biggest Drop in Paychecks', *New York Times*, 2 September 2015, nytimes.com, last accessed 29 November 2015. Also, where employment has 'recovered' after the crisis, better jobs have more often than not been replaced with bad jobs, which workers had no choice but to accept. Moreover, privatization of employment risks has often meant that retraining had to be paid for by the workers themselves, financed out of (additional) debt. 'Seeking New Start, Finding Steep Cost', *New York Times*, 17 August 2014, nytimes.com, last accessed 29 November 2015. Worldwide, increasingly flexible work schedules undermine family life and require extensive subsidization of parents by intergenerational transfers of resources and time. See 'The Perils of Ever-Changing Work Schedules Extend to Children's Well-Being', *New York Times*, 12 August 2015, nytimes.com, last accessed 29 November 2015. Also, in trend-setting corporations like Amazon and Google, new human resource management strategies are intensifying work, squeezing maximum effort out of workers, including vast amounts of unpaid overtime; see 'Inside Amazon: Wrestling Big Ideas in a Bruising Workplace', *New York Times*, 15 August 2015, nytimes.com, last accessed 29 November 2015. The same applies to firms in the high-end service sector, the preferred site of employment for the new middle class, such as investment banks and law firms; 'Work Policies may be Kinder, but Brutal Competition Isn't', *New York Times*, 19 August 2015, nytimes.com, last accessed 29 November 2015.

39 Richard Sennett, *The Corrosion of Character: The Personal Consequences of Work in the New Capitalism*, New York: W. W. Norton & Company 1998; Richard Sennett, *The Culture of the New Capitalism*, New Haven, CT: Yale University Press 2006; Richard Sennett, *The Craftsman*, London: Allen Lane 2008. See also Zygmunt Baumann's *Liquid Modernity*, Cambridge: Polity 2000.

leaving capitalism, not just without an alternative, but also without a prospect for progress.

Systemic Disorders: Oligarchy, Corruption

At the end of the lecture that later became Chapter 1 of this volume, I identified five 'systemic disorders' that have befallen contemporary capitalism and are likely to condition its future, or non-future. I called them stagnation, oligarchic redistribution, the plundering of the public domain, corruption and global anarchy. Re-reading what I said then, I see no reason to make modifications; in fact, in the short time of two years that has since passed, all five conditions became even more palpable. In the present section I will limit myself to just a few elaborations on oligarchy and corruption – the two, of course, being closely connected. Like secular stagnation, the private appropriation of public infrastructures, and global anarchy, they have in common that they critically weaken the systemic integration and stability of neoliberal capitalist societies.[40]

Beginning with *oligarchic inequality* – one could also speak of *neo-feudalism* – what matters here for the future of capitalism, or the lack of one, is not primarily that a tiny minority in today's capitalist societies is becoming unimaginably rich. On this entire libraries have recently been produced, with little to no political effect. From the perspective of systemic stability what seems more important than inequality as such is that it may already have gone so far that the rich may rightly consider their fate and that of their families to have become independent from the fates of the societies from which they extract their wealth. As a result, they can afford no longer to care about them. This becomes a problem – one of 'moral hazard' – when differences in wealth become so extensive that they give rise to a fusion of economic and political power – that is, to *oligarchy*. To assess the extent to which growing inequality in America has produced an oligarchic power structure, Jeffrey Winters has calculated what he calls a *Material Power Index* for the contemporary United

---

40   One important aspect of the plundering of the public domain that I did not mention in the original paper is the growing role played by private firms in modern warfare. As it appears, in both Afghanistan and Iraq a majority of the American ground forces were mercenaries employed by firms such as Blackwater, attracted by new opportunities for safe and profitable investment in what used to be a public sector industry (on Blackwater see Sean McFate, *The Modern Mercenary: Private Armies and What They Mean for World Order*, Oxford: Oxford University Press 2015). Subcontracting warfare to private industry is likely to give rise to active lobbying of domestic firms for an interventionist foreign policy, resembling what had been envisaged by older theories of a 'military-industrial complex'. Of course being able to rely on private providers of lethal force relaxes whatever inhibitions the American or British governments may have on military intervention on the capitalist periphery, not least because commercialized violence is easier to hide from public view.

States.[41] One version of that index considers the relation between the average income of the top 400 taxpayers and of the bottom 90 per cent. Using data from 2007, Winters finds a ratio of a stunning 10,327 to 1 (p. 215). In another version of the index, based on 2004 household wealth excluding home equity, the top 100 households are compared to, again, the bottom 90 per cent; here the ratio is more than ten times as high, at 108,765 to 1 (p. 217). According to Winters, this corresponds roughly to the difference in material power between a senator and a slave at the height of the Roman Empire.[42]

American oligarchs, unlike their counterparts in other societies like Ukraine or Russia, are of a 'non-ruling' type, since they are content to live alongside a public bureaucracy, a state of law, and an elected government run by professional politicians. But this does not mean that they are not becoming involved in the domestic politics of their country, at the minimum in order to maintain optimal conditions for the further accumulation and future conservation of their wealth. Today the 'material power' of American oligarchs has reached a dimension that allows for the gross economic inequality that underlies it to reproduce itself in spite of political democracy. This is because it enables the super-rich to buy both political majorities and social legitimacy, the former through campaign contributions of all sorts[43] and the latter by acts of philanthropy partly filling the very gaps in public provision that result from oligarchic fortunes having become safe from taxation in the course of globalization and with the help of their owners' friends.[44] Oligarchic elites, Winters

41   Jeffrey A. Winters, *Oligarchy*, New York: Cambridge University Press 2011.

42   Jeffrey A. Winters, 'Oligarchy and Democracy', *The American Interest*, vol. 7, no. 2, 2011.

43   According to the *New York Times* of 1 August 2015, it was 'fewer than four hundred families' that were 'responsible for almost half the money raised in the 2016 presidential campaign, a concentration of political donors that is unprecedented in the modern era'. By late July of the pre-election year of 2015, total campaign contributions already amounted to $388 million. 'Small Pool of Rich Donors Dominates Election Giving', *New York Times*, 1 August 2015, nytimes.com, last accessed 12 August 2015. For a broader account see David Cole, 'The Supreme Court's Billion-Dollar Mistake', *New York Review of Books*, 19 January 2015: 'Over the five years since [the Court's *Citizens United* rule], super PACs have spent more than one billion dollars on federal election campaigns . . . About 60 percent of that billion dollars has come from just 195 people . . . The average donation over $200 of the ironically named Ending Spending, a conservative PAC, was $502,188 . . .' For the 2016 election campaign, the brothers Charles G. and David H. Koch, two billionaire industrialists who rank among the richest people in the world, put together a campaign contribution fund of $889, which was as high as the budgets of each of the two major political parties. 'Koch Brothers' Budget of $889 Million for 2016 Is on Par with both Parties' Spending', *New York Times*, 26 January 2015, nytimes.com, last accessed 30 November 2015.

44   On billionaires deciding *de facto* which parks and playgrounds in New York City are renovated see 'The Billionaires' Park', *New York Times*, 30 November 2014: 'Central Park is now a gleaming jewel thanks to $700 million in private investments, and two years ago a hedge fund manager – who lives in a mansion steps from the park – gave $100 million to shine it further . . . Meanwhile, many parks, starved of funds, have fallen into disrepair. This fall Mayor Bill de Blasio pledged to spend $130 million to upgrade 35 parks in poor neighborhoods – the same amount

shows, while they may disagree on just about everything else, are firmly united in their desire to defend their wealth. For this they can afford to employ a huge and highly sophisticated 'wealth defense industry' of lawyers, PR specialists, lobbyists, active and retired politicians, and think tanks and ideologues of all kinds, including entire economics departments.[45]

Oligarchs from outside the United States typically take their money out of their countries to resettle it in New York or London. American oligarchs, by comparison, are both more cosmopolitan and more patriotic: they extract their wealth globally and park it locally in the global financial firms of Manhattan. While their counterparts exit their societies to let them rot, moving preferably to the U.S., American oligarchs exercise voice at home to make sure that their country remains a safe haven for themselves as well as their non-American fellow oligarchs. As long as they succeed in this, there is no need for American-style oligarchic neo-feudalism to be replicated, for example, in Western Europe. Given the structure of the contemporary capitalist world system, what matters for global oligarchic wealth defence, both politically and ideologically, is control over American politics to ensure, for example, that the American Congress will never agree to a global wealth tax as proposed, among others, by Thomas Piketty.[46] As long as this is certain, it does not really matter who governs with what ambitions in France or Germany.

The second disorder of capitalism to be briefly touched upon here is *corruption*. I use this concept broadly, beyond its definition in criminal law, to mean the gross violation of legal rules and the systematic betrayal of trust and moral expectations in pursuit of competitive success and personal or institutional enrichment, as elicited by rapidly growing opportunities for huge material gain in and around today's political economy. As pointed out before, corruption is endemic in finance where the highest profits are to be made by circumventing or outright breaking legal rules on, for example, insider trading, mortgage lending, money laundering, rate fixing and the like. Indeed

---

Mr. Diller and his wife, Diane von Furstenberg, pledged for [a] new 2.7-acre park', nytimes.com, last accessed 30 November 2015. Steven A. Cohen, founder of 'the giant hedge fund SAC Capital Advisers' and the target of several investigations for insider trading, is reported to patronize what is called the 'Robin Hood Foundation'. Its 2013 'annual gala in Manhattan . . . which featured performances by Bono, Sting and Elton John, raised $72 Million to fight poverty'. 'SAC Starts to Balk over Insider Trading Inquiry', *New York Times*, 17 May 2013, dealbook.nytimes.com, last accessed 30 November 2015.

45 A fascinating example is the Koch brothers' nurturing, over several decades, of James Buchanan's Center for Study of Public Choice at George Mason University. See Nancy MacLean, *Forget Chicago, It's Coming from Virginia: The 1970s Genesis of Today's Attack on Democracy*, Unpublished Manuscript 2015.

46 Thomas Piketty, *Capital in the Twenty-First Century*, Cambridge, MA: Harvard University Press 2014.

cheating can be assumed to be normal in finance and consequently fails to excite moral outrage, certainly among insiders.[47] In the United States alone, the leading banks had by June 2014 agreed to pay about $100 billion in out-of-court settlement fees for legal infractions in connection with the 2008 financial crisis alone.[48] A little more than a year later, the *Frankfurter Allgemeine* reported on a study by Morgan Stanley, according to which American and West European banks had together paid roughly $260 billion in settlement fees, again since 2008.[49] Note that none of these cases ever went to trial, testifying to a deep empathy on the part of the legal system with the competitive pressure on financial institutions to break the law in order to make a profit. To get a sense of the penalties that would have been due after conviction in a regular trial, one must add the banks' legal expenses to the settlement fees. Of course a goodly share of both will be eligible to be declared as business expenses for tax purposes.

Financial corruption does not end here, however. Making fortunes in finance requires not just confidential early information on likely developments in 'the market', but also intimate knowledge of government policies, preferably in advance, and a capacity to influence such policies, both their conception and their implementation. Not surprisingly, then, no other industry, except perhaps armaments, has developed anything like Wall Street's rotating door relationship with the U.S. government. There is Robert Rubin, treasury secretary from 1995 to 1999 under Clinton, and Henry Paulsen, in the same position under Bush the Younger, from 2006 to 2009 – both former CEOs of Goldman Sachs, the one instrumental for financial deregulation, the other presiding over its results in 2008. The two are, however, only the tip of a truly titanic iceberg, as there were and are literally hundreds of former and later Goldman people occupying a wide variety of government positions.[50]

47   An exception is David A. Stockman, 'State-Wrecked: The Corruption of Capitalism in America', *New York Times*, 31 March 2013, who may be considered particularly knowledgeable on the subject.

48   'Vernunft durch Strafen in Milliardenhöhe', *Frankfurter Allgemeine Zeitung*, 29 June 2015, faz.net, last accessed 2 December 2015. The estimate seems far too low, given that another source names the same sum for Bank of America alone: John Maxfield, 'The Complete List', *The Motley Fool*, 1 October 2014, fool.com, last accessed 2 December 2015.

49   'Banken zahlen 260 Milliarden Dollar Strafe', *Frankfurter Allgemeine Zeitung*, 24 August 2015, www.faz.net, last accessed 2 December 2015. Major cases were still pending, like the corrupt fixing of the price of gold and of the London Interbank Overnight Rate, Libor. All major banks are involved, from the United States as well as from France (Paribas), Germany (Deutsche), Switzerland (UBS) and the UK (HSBC), each in multiple cases.

50   The literature on Goldman Sachs is endless. For an introduction see the article by Matt Taibbi, 'The Great American Bubble Machine, *Rolling Stone*, no. 9, July 2009. It is impossible to name the endless number of senators, governors, Cabinet members, central bankers and so on that came out of Goldman Sachs or landed there. To get the feeling see Taibbi: 'There's Joshua Bolten, Bush's chief of

One may also take a figure like Lawrence ('Larry') Summers, Rubin's deputy and successor at the U.S. Treasury, for decades now untiringly moving from academia to government to finance and back, and being richly rewarded for it.[51] And not to be forgotten is the Attorney General of the Obama administration, Eric Holder, in office from 2008 to 2014. While negotiating one out-of-court settlement with Wall Street financial firms after another, he was on leave from a Wall Street law firm specializing in, of all things, representing those very same financial firms. Under Holder, not a single banker had to go to court, not to speak of prison. Having made around $2.5 million a year before joining the Cabinet, Holder resigned in 2015 to reassume his partnership, moving back into his old office.[52] Of course, President Obama, who appointed Holder, drew more than one third of his campaign contributions from the financial industry.[53]

Demoralization caused by an overabundance of money-grabbing opportunities in a global economy does not end in the financial industry. As is now common knowledge, management salaries have since the 1980s exploded everywhere in the corporate world, not just in the United States, even when profits were low or non-existent, and also in years of general economic crisis when unemployment rose and wages declined. There are many explanations

------

staff during the bailout, and Mark Patterson, the current [2009; WS] Treasury chief of staff, who was a Goldman lobbyist just a year ago, and Ed Liddy, the former Goldman director whom Paulson put in charge of bailed-out insurance giant AIG, which forked over $13 billion to Goldman after Liddy came on board. The heads of the Canadian and Italian national banks are Goldman alumns, as is the head of the World Bank, the head of the New York Stock Exchange, the last two heads of the Federal Reserve Bank of New York – which, incidentally, is now in charge of overseeing Goldman.'

   51   Summers' relentless pursuit of real money, in between high government appointments, defies any attempt at summary. For an introduction, already slightly dated, see Matt Taibbi, 'Obama's Top Economic Advisor Is Greedy and Highly Compromised', Alternet, 9 April 2009, alternet.org, last accessed 2 December 2012. In 2006 Summers had to resign after five years as president of Harvard University, in part because of a scandal involving insider trading with Russian stocks. Immediately he landed a job as 'part-time managing director' of a hedge fund. In 2008, the year at the end of which he was widely expected to join the Obama administration as head of the National Economic Council, that fund paid him a respectable $5.2 million for his part-time efforts. During that same year, Summers also collected more than $2.7 million in 'speaking fees' from several Wall Street firms, among them $130,000 from Goldman Sachs for one afternoon appearance. When Obama was considering appointing him to succeed Ben Bernanke at the Federal Reserve, Summers removed himself from the list for fear of having to report on his sources of income at his confirmation hearing.

   52   See 'Eric Holder, Wall Street Double Agent, Comes in from the Cold', Rolling Stone, 8 July 2015, rollingstone.com, last accessed 12 August 2015.

   53   Goldman Sachs was Obama's second-biggest single supporter in 2008. See 'Barack Obama (D): Top Contributors, 2008 Cycle', at opensecrets.org/PRES08/contrib.php?cid=N00009638, last accessed 7 December 2015. Its CEO visited the Obama White House ten times in 2009 and 2010, almost every other month. Small donors, unlike the public impression created by the Obama machine, accounted for no more than 30 per cent of Obama's 2008 campaign expenses.

for this, but the most credible ones involve extended reciprocity among a tight network of corporate oligarchs conspiring to raise their own pay by helping raise that of their co-conspirators. Another example of corruption can be found among political leaders who upon leaving office sell their inside knowledge and public goodwill, and especially the connections they acquired while presumably serving the public interest, to private consulting, lobbying and, above all, financial firms.[54] Corruption is also rampant in professional athletics, which has in recent decades become a huge global industry, financed by mushrooming marketing activities for sports equipment and fashion goods. In major disciplines, including swimming and track and field, not to mention cycling, one can safely assume that top competitors routinely employ the services of expensive specialists providing them with illegal, performance-enhancing treatment. Doping among athletes competing for ever-increasing sums of prize money and even more lucrative advertising contracts in worldwide winner-take-all markets is accompanied by corruption among officials of international sports associations, some of whom are reported to have been paid huge sums by athletes and their management for suppressing the results of positive doping tests, and by corporations and governments for locating events in places they prefer. Officials also own firms that sell television rights in the events their associations organize.[55]

---

54 On Tony Blair, the deals he helped make after his resignation and his complex conglomerate of consulting firms see 'Tony Blair Has Used His Connections to Change the World, and to Get Rich', *New York Times*, 5 August 2014, nytimes.com, last accessed 7 December 2015. According to the report, Blair collects, in addition to whatever else he collects, 'a total of $5 million to $7 million a year from three firms: JP Morgan, Khosla Ventures and the Zurich Insurance Group'. One of his own firms, Windrush Ventures Limited, 'reported $3.4 million in profit' in 2013. On members of the Blair Cabinet see Tariq Ali, *The Extreme Centre: A Warning*, London: Verso 2015, pp. 45–53. There is no end to the list of other examples; the impression is that high public office has become an apprenticeship for richly rewarded private sector jobs. For Germany see Schröder and Fischer, who have sold their know-how and celebrity status to competing pipeline projects. Fischer works through a consulting firm, Fischer & Company, which in addition to the energy interests linked to the NABUCCO pipeline advises companies such as Siemens and BMW on 'ecological issues'. Fischer also serves as 'freshness expert' for the largest German grocery chain, REWE.

55 See the case of the former middle-distance runner Sebastian Coe, aka Lord Coe, who recently advanced to the presidency of the infamously corrupt International Association of Athletics Federations (IAFF). Coe owns several sports marketing firms and serves as the international representative of Nike. Of course, compared to corruption in finance, all of this is small fish. All the more interesting is the fact that the American government is currently aggressively prosecuting the Swiss-based International Soccer Association, FIFA (Coe, incidentally, has been a member of its 'ethics committee' since 2006), effectively demonstrating to a worldwide public the claim of the American justice system to global jurisdiction. In a highly publicized effort, Eric Holder's successor, one Loretta Lynch, appeared several times in Switzerland to have a number of FIFA officials, all of them from Latin America, arrested and expedited to the United States. To get a sense of proportion, FIFA's average yearly revenue in the eight years from 2007 to 2014 amounted to $1.2 billion. In December 2015, it still remained to be specified what part of this was used or collected in corrupt ways. While FIFA does seem

Finally, take a global corporation like Volkswagen (which, incidentally, around 2010 raised the salary of its CEO, Martin Winterkorn, to an, in German terms, hitherto unimaginable €15 million per annum). In 2015 it became apparent that Volkswagen had engaged in a massive pattern of fraud in relation to both customers and public authorities. The purpose was, essentially, to save on research and development to meet environmental standards, to be able to spend more on other features more likely to attract sales in a highly competitive global automobile market suffering from saturation and overcapacity.

Unlike in the Mandevillean *Fable*, under financialized capitalism the private vice of greed is no longer magically converted into a public virtue – depriving capitalism even of its last, consequentialist moral justification. Stylizing owners and managers of capital as trustees of society has lost any remaining credibility, their much-publicized exercises in philanthropy notwithstanding. A pervasive cynicism has become deeply engrained in the collective common sense, which has come as a matter of course to regard capitalism as nothing but an institutionalized opportunity for the well-connected super-rich to become even richer. Corruption, in the sense of the word used here, is considered a fact of life, and so is steadily growing inequality and the monopolization of political influence by a small self-serving oligarchy and its army of wealth defence specialists. Converting public trust into private cash has become routine and is seen as such, effectively rendering the social order morally defenceless in possible future moments of open contestation. Elite calls for trust and appeals to shared values can no longer be expected to resonate with a populace nursed on materialistic-utilitarian self-descriptions of a society in which everything is and ought to be for sale. Morally defenceless as they have rendered themselves, political and economic elites will require great creativity if things came to a head and they had to mobilize legitimacy for themselves and the social order they represent. One ominous symptom of growing instability of the democratic-capitalist system is the rise of so-called populist parties, of both the Left and the Right, feeding on and fortifying a deeply emotional rejection of existing social elites.[56]

---

like a prime example of the corruption that befell sports generally after the money avalanche that began to rain down on it in the 1980s, remember that the total out-of-court settlement fees paid by banks to pre-empt serious action by the American government after 2008 was roughly twenty-seven times FIFA's entire revenue during the same period.

56   As a loose definition, Left and Right populists share a profound hatred of indigenous social elites. Right populists in addition hate at least one other, 'foreign' group of people.

Interregnum

Is capitalism coming to an end? The problem is, while we see it disintegrating before our eyes, we see no successor approaching. As indicated, by disintegration I mean an already far advanced decline of the capacity of capitalism as an economic regime to underwrite a stable society. Capitalist society is disintegrating, but not under the impact of an organized opposition fighting it in the name of a better social order. Rather it disintegrates from within, from the success of capitalism and the internal contradictions intensified by that success, and from capitalism having overrun its opponents and in the process become more capitalist than is good for it. Low growth, grotesque inequality and mountains of debt; the neutralization of post-war capitalism's progress engine, democracy, and its replacement with oligarchic neo-feudalism; the clearing away by 'globalization' of social barriers against the commodification of labour, land and money; and systemic disorders such as infectious corruption in the competitive struggle for ever bigger rewards for individual success, with the attendant culture of demoralization, and rapidly spreading international anarchy – all these together have profoundly destabilized the post-war capitalist way of social life, without a hint as to how stability might ever be restored.

Why, if capitalism is going out, is there no new social order waiting to succeed it? A social order breaks down if and when its elites are no longer able to maintain it; but for it to be cleared away there have to be new elites able to design and eager to install a new order. Obviously the incumbent management of advanced and not-so-advanced capitalism is uniquely clueless: consider the senseless production of money to stimulate growth in the real economy; the desperate attempts to restore inflation with the help of negative interest rates; and the apparently inexorable coming apart of the modern state system on its periphery.[57] But there is also the absence of a vision of a practically possible

---

57 Here the source of systemic entropy is the weakening position of the United States as the political host of global capitalist expansion, as pointed out by Wallerstein among others. Historically, capitalism always advanced on the coat-tails of a strong, hegemonic state opening up and preparing new landscapes for growth, through military force or free trade or, typically, both. Political preparation for capitalist development included not just the breaking-up of pre- or anti-capitalist social orders, but also the creation of new, 'modern' societies supportive of economic progress through private capital accumulation. After 1945, this meant the establishment of a global system of secular states with a 'development' agenda, sovereign but integrated in an international free trade regime. Also on the agenda was the 'containment' and, if necessary and possible, suppression of alternative, oppositional systems, a programme that at first glance had come to its victorious completion in 1989. In fact, however, it turned out that the United States, while still able to destroy enemy regimes, had lost the capacity to replace them with stable pro-American and pro-capitalist regimes: *the hegemon losing its constructive powers while retaining its destructive ones*. The causes of this cannot be explored here; one can assume, however, that they include the demonstration effect of the defeats suffered by the United

progressive future, of a renewed industrial or new post-industrial society developing further and at the same time replacing the capitalist society of today. Not just capital and its running dogs but also their various oppositions lack a capacity to act collectively. Just as capitalism's movers and shakers do not know how to protect their society from decay, and in any case would lack the means to do so, their enemies, when it comes to the crunch, have to admit that they have no idea of how to replace neoliberal capitalism with something else – see the Greek SYRIZA government and its capitulation in 2015 when the 'Eurogroup' began to play hardball and SYRIZA, to mix metaphors, was forced to show its hand.

Before capitalism will go to hell, then, it will for the foreseeable future hang in limbo, dead or about to die from an overdose of itself but still very much around, as nobody will have the power to move its decaying body out of the way. *Pace* Wallerstein, the final Manichaean battle between Davos and Porto Alegre is not about to happen in the foreseeable future. Much more likely, we are facing a long period of systemic disintegration, in which social structures become unstable and unreliable, and therefore uninstructive for those living in them. A society of this kind that leaves its members alone is, as noted above, less than a society. The social order of capitalism would then issue, not in another order, but in disorder, or entropy – in a historical epoch of uncertain duration when, in the words of Antonio Gramsci, 'the old is dying but the new cannot yet be born', ushering in 'an interregnum in which pathological phenomena of the most diverse sort come into existence'[58] – in a society devoid of reasonably coherent and minimally stable institutions capable of normalizing the lives of its members and protecting them from accidents and monstrosities of all sorts. Life in a society of this kind demands constant improvisation, forcing individuals to substitute strategy for structure, and offers rich opportunities to oligarchs

---

States in successive wars, as well as declining domestic support for what is now considered foreign 'adventures' by a majority of U.S. citizens. 'Nation-building' having failed in large parts of the world, the global system of sovereign development-friendly free-trade states as originally envisaged shows growing holes and gaps, with *failed states* as a permanent source of unpredictable and unmanageable political and economic disorder. In many of them, fundamentalist religious movements have taken control, rejecting modernism and international law and seeking an alternative to consumerist capitalism, which they can no longer expect to replicate in their countries. Others, having given up hope in peaceful capitalist development at home, are trying to become part of advanced capitalism by migrating from the periphery to the centre. There they meet with second-generation immigrants who have given up on ever becoming part of the capitalist-consumerist mainstream of their societies. One result is another migration, this time of the violence that is destroying the stateless societies of the periphery into the metropolis, in the form of the 'terrorism' of a new class of 'primitive rebels'.

58   From the *Prison Notebooks*: 'La crisi consiste nel fatto che il vecchio muore e il nuovo non può nascere . . . in questo interregno si verificano i fenomeni morbosi più svariati'.

and warlords while imposing uncertainty and insecurity on all others, in some ways like the long interregnum that began in the fifth century CE and is now called the Dark Age.

Summing up so far, the historical period after the end, inflicted by capitalism, of capitalist society will be one lacking collective political capacities, making it a long and indecisive transition, a time of crisis as the new normal, a crisis that is neither transformative nor adaptive, and unable either to restore capitalism to equilibrium or to replace it with something better. Deep changes will occur, rapidly and continuously, but they will be unpredictable and in any case ungovernable. Western capitalism will decay, but non-Western capitalism will not take its place, certainly not on a global scale, and neither will Western non-capitalism. As to non-Western capitalism, China will for many reasons not be able to take over as capitalism's historical host and provide an orderly global environment for its further progress. Nor will there be a co-directorate of China and the United States amicably dividing between them the task of making the world safe for capitalism. And concerning non-capitalism, there is no such thing today as a global socialist movement, comparable to the socialisms that in the nineteenth and early twentieth centuries so successfully confronted capitalism in national power struggles. As long as the capitalist dynamism continues to outrun collective order-making and the building of non-market institutions, as it has for several decades now, it disempowers both capitalism's government and its opposition, with the result that capitalism can be neither reborn nor replaced.

An Age of Entropy

At the micro-level of society, systemic disintegration and the resulting structural indeterminacy translate into an under-institutionalized way of life, a life in the shadow of uncertainty, always at risk of being upset by surprise events and unpredictable disturbances and dependent on individuals' resourcefulness, skillful improvisation, and good luck. Ideologically, life in an under-governed society of this sort can be glorified as a life in liberty, unconstrained by rigid institutions and autonomously constructed through voluntary agreements among consenting individuals freely pursuing their idiosyncratic preferences. The problem with this neoliberal narrative is, of course, that it neglects the very unequal distribution of risks, opportunities, gains and losses that comes with de-socialized capitalism, including the 'Matthew effect'[59] of cumulative advantage. This raises the question why the neoliberal life

---

59   Robert K. Merton, 'The Matthew Effect in Science', *Science*, vol. 159, no. 3810, 1968, pp. 56–63.

associated with the post-capitalist interregnum is not more powerfully opposed, indeed how it can enjoy as much apparent support as it does – a question that is not satisfactorily answered with reference to the structural and regional fragmentation of anti-capitalist opposition under conditions of 'globalization'.

It is here that 'culture' comes in, which seems to grow the more important for social order the less instructive the institutions become that would other-wise normalize social intercourse. Without supportive institutions, the burden of organizing everyday life is moved from the macro- to the micro-level, meaning that the onus of securing a minimum of stability and certainty – of creating a modicum of social order – is shifting to the individual.[60] The behavioral programme of the *post-social society* during the *post-capitalist interregnum* is governed by a neoliberal ethos of competitive self-improvement, of untiring cultivation of one's marketable human capital, enthusiastic dedication to work, and cheerfully optimistic, playful acceptance of the risks inherent in a world that has outgrown government. That this programme is dutifully implemented is essential, as the reproduction of the *post-capitalist society lite* hangs on the thin thread of an accommodating repertoire of individual action filling the widening gaps in the society's systemic architecture. Structuralist critique of *false institutions* may therefore have to be complemented by a renewed culturalist critique of *false conscious-ness*. What may also become relevant here is the old topic of the relationship between *social structure and social character*, as treated, among others, by Hans Gerth and Charles Wright Mills.[61] Here, the question is how a given social structure both requires and, as long as it lasts, produces a correspond-ing character among its occupants. In this tradition, I will in the following take a first cut at an initial phenomenology of the social character that corre-sponds to the absence of institutional supports under the present interregnum, helping to extend the duration of the latter by providing for a semblance of social integration and legitimacy. I begin by drawing attention to two key terms that have recently become fashionable in political-economic discourse, *disruption* and *resilience*, and then turn to a brief outline of four central features of the behavioural pattern that, it would appear, is required for delay-ing the final breakdown of under-governed post-capitalism.

What disruption and resilience have in common, in addition to their steep ascent as catchwords characterizing basic features of life in an age of social

---

60   And social theory shifts, or drifts, from institutionalism to rational choice, to the extent that it desires to be affirmative, or to biological behaviourism.

61   Hans Gerth and C. Wright Mills, *Character and Social Structure: The Psychology of Social Institutions*, New York: Harcourt, Brace 1953.

entropy, is that they carry at the same time ominous and auspicious connotations. While *disruption* has traditionally been associated with unanticipated, destructive and even violent discontinuity – with *disaster* for those affected by it – it is now to stand for radical economic and social *innovation*, and indeed the only innovation left to make a difference, as it attacks and destroys in particular firms and markets that operate to everybody's satisfaction.[62] Innovation that is not in this sense disruptive is not innovative enough as it respects too much of the old and may even be concerned, or politically constrained, not to cause too many casualties. It is therefore doomed to be overtaken in the competitive struggles of the contemporary marketplace, where it is not enough for something to *work* if something else promises higher *profits*. Disruption may be considered the neoliberal version of 'creative destruction': more ruthless, more out-of-the-blue, and less willing to take prisoners or accept delay in order to be 'socially compatible'. While for those at the receiving end disruptive innovation can be catastrophic, regrettably they have to be sacrificed as collateral damage on the Darwinian battlefield of global capitalism.

Resilience is the other term on the rise, having recently been imported into social science and policy from bacteriology, engineering and psychology.[63] In the political economy literature the term is, confusingly at first glance,

---

62 The term was invented by Clayton Christensen (*The Innovator's Dilemma: When New Technologies Cause Great Firms to Fail*, Boston, MA: Harvard Business Review Press 1997) and subsequently became vastly popular among business school academics and managers. For a critical assessment see Jill Lepore, 'The Disruption Machine: What the gospel of innovation gets wrong', *New Yorker*, 23 June 2014. In management discourse, the concept is associated especially with platform firms like Uber, Alibaba, Airbnb and Amazon, which have in common that they have ceased to offer their workers regular employment. According to the *Frankfurter Allgemeine Sonntagszeitung*, disruption has in 2015, with the usual delay, arrived in Germany as the leading management buzzword: 'Nicht mehr zu zählen sind die Bücher, Reden, Studien zu dem Thema. Regelmäßig werden die, Disrupter des Jahres' ausgezeichnet. Marketing-Leute können sich besoffen reden über die 'digital disruption', gewöhnliche Beratungsfirmen gönnen sich den Zusatz 'The Disruption Consultancy . . . Nicht mal Praktikanten sind sonst noch anzulocken: Ready to disrupt? Dann komm zu uns', wirbt ein Arbeitgeber in der Hauptstadt'. (Georg Meck and Bettina Weigunt, 'Disrupton, Baby Disruption!', *Frankfurter Allgemeine Sonntagszeitung*, 27 December 2015, faz.net, last accessed 1 January 2016.)

63 To sample a flavour of the hype around the term, as well as of the real-world condition to which its ascent responds, here is an extract from the Wikipedia article, 'Resilience (organizational)', en.wikipedia.org/wiki/Resilience_(organizational), last accessed 1 January 2016: 'In recent years, a new consensus of the concept of resilience emerged as a practical response to the decreasing lifespan of organisations and the [sic] from key stakeholders, including boards, governments, regulators, shareholders, staff, suppliers and customers to effectively address the issues of security, preparedness, risk, and survivability.

1. Being resilient is a proactive and determined attitude to remain a thriving enterprise (country, region, organization or company) despite the anticipated and unanticipated challenges that will emerge;

used both for the capacities of individuals and groups to withstand the onslaught of neoliberalism,[64] and for the ability of neoliberalism as a social order, or disorder, to persist in spite of its theoretical poverty and practical failure to prevent or repair its own collapse in 2008.[65] While the two meanings may seem to be opposed to each other, this may not necessarily be so, as the practices that make it possible for individuals to survive under neoliberalism may also help neoliberalism itself to survive. Note that resilience is not resistance but, more or less voluntary, adaptive adjustment. The more resilience individuals manage to develop at the micro-level of everyday life, the less demand will there be for collective action at the macro-level to contain the uncertainties produced by market forces – a demand that neoliberalism could and would not fill.[66]

Social life in an age of entropy is by necessity individualistic.[67] As collective institutions are eroded by market forces, accidents are to be expected any time, while collective agency to prevent them is lost. Everybody is reduced to fending for themselves, with *sauve qui peut* as the foundational principle of social life. Individualization of risk breeds individualization of protection, by competitive effort ('hard work') and, if at all, private insurance – or,

---

2. Resilience moves beyond a defensive security and protection posture and applies the entity's inherent strength to withstand crisis and deflect attacks of any nature;

3. Resilience is the empowerment of being aware of your situation, your risks, vulnerabilities and current capabilities to deal with them, and being able to make informed tactical and strategic decisions; and,

4. Resilience is an objectively measurable competitive differentiator (i.e., more secure, increased stakeholder and shareholder value).

[. . .] Prominent members in the United States Congress are embracing resilience. The Chairman of the Homeland Security Committee of the U.S. House of Representatives, Bennie Thompson (D-MS) declared May 2008 "Resilience Month" as the committee and its subcommittees held a series of hearings to examine the issue. President Obama and the Department of Homeland Security have also made resilience an integral component of homeland security policy. The Quadrennial Homeland Security Review, released by the Department of Homeland Security in February 2010, made resilience a prominent theme and one of the core missions of the U.S. homeland security enterprise.'

64   Peter Hall and Michèle Lamont, eds, *Social Resilience in the Neoliberal Era*, Cambridge: Cambridge University Press 2013.

65   Vivien A. Schmidt and Mark Thatcher, eds, *Resilient Liberalism in Europe's Political Economy*, Cambridge: Cambridge University Press 2013; Aldo Madariaga, *The Political Economy of Neoliberal Resilience: Developmental Regimes in Latin America and Eastern Europe*, Doctoral Dissertation, Wirtschafts- und Sozialwissenschaftliche Fakultät, Universität zu Köln 2015.

66   Similar with infectious diseases: as resilience to malaria increases, there is no need any more to wipe out the carrier mosquitoes.

67   Its basic principles are cogently summarized in Margret Thatcher's dictum, stated as an empirical claim but more adequately understood as a neoliberal project: 'There is no such thing as society. There are individual men and women, and there are families.' Interview for *Woman's Own*, 23 September 1987, margaretthatcher.org/document/106689, last accessed 21 January 2016.

interestingly, by older, pre-modern social ties like family.[68] In the absence of collective institutions, social structures must be devised individually bottom-up, anticipating and accommodating top-down pressures from 'the markets'. Social life consists of individuals building networks of private connections around themselves, as best they can with the means they happen to have in hand. Person-centred relation-making creates lateral social structures that are voluntary and contract-like, which makes them flexible but perishable, requiring continuous 'networking' to keep them together and adjust them on a current basis to changing circumstances. An ideal tool for this are the 'new social media' that produce social structures for individuals, substituting voluntary for obligatory forms of social relations, and *networks of users* for *communities of citizens.*[69]

What keeps an entropic, disorderly, stalemated post-capitalist interregnum society going, in the absence of collective regulation containing economic crises, limiting inequality, securing confidence in currency and credit, protecting labour, land and money from overuse, and procuring legitimacy for free markets and private property through democratic control of greed and prevention of oligarchic conversion of economic into political power? In a world without system integration, social integration has to carry the entire burden of structuration, as long as no new order begins to settle in. The de-socialized capitalism of the interregnum hinges on the improvised performances of structurally self-centered, socially disorganized and politically disempowered individuals. Four broad types of behaviours are required of the 'users' of post-capitalist social networks for the precarious reproduction of their entropic social life, bestowing resilience both on themselves and on an otherwise unsustainable neoliberal capitalism, summarily and provisionally to be identified as *coping, hoping, doping* and *shopping.*[70] Briefly and in need of much elaboration,

---

68   Consider the indispensable unpaid contribution by grandmothers to the raising of small children in societies in which fulltime employment of mothers is socially and economically obligatory. Another case in point is unemployed young adults in Mediterranean countries who still live with their parents and, in the absence of effective unemployment insurance, on their parents' pensions.

69   Fittingly, the electronic infrastructures of individualized social life are privately owned by huge, overwhelmingly American corporations. While they are dressed up as collective goods freely available to all, they are in reality highly profitable tools of social control rented out to, among others, vendors of consumer goods and services.

70   What follows is a brief idiosyncratic summary of some features of social life under neoliberalism, especially of what is expected of individuals struggling to survive its disorders. There is a broad literature on this already that I cannot discuss here (for many others Wendy Brown, 'Neo-liberalism and the End of Liberal Democracy', *Theory and Event*, vol. 7, no. 1, 2003; Michel Foucault, *The Birth of Biopolitics: Lectures at the College de France, 1978–1979*, London: Palgrave Macmillan 2008; Johanna Bockman, *Markets in the Name of Socialism: The Left-Wing Origins of Neoliberalism*, Stanford, CA: Stanford University Press 2011; Colin Crouch, *The Strange Non-Death of Neoliberalism*, Cambridge: Polity Press 2011; Pierre Dardot and Christian Laval, *The New Way of the*

coping refers to the way individuals respond with ever-new improvisations and stopgaps to the successive emergencies inflicted on them by an under-governed social environment and its unpredictable and ungovernable fluctuations – emergencies which they have to expect as normal and to which they must learn to resign themselves as to facts of life.[71] While coping may involve sometimes extreme individual exertion, it does not include organization for collective redress, as this is perceived to be useless and, also and increasingly, for losers only.[72] Coping tends to come with a social construction of life as an ongoing test of one's stamina, inventiveness, patience, optimism and self-confidence – of one's cultivated ability to live up to what has become a social obligation to struggle with adversity on one's own and in eternally good spirits.

Successful coping is assisted by confident *hoping*. Hoping is defined here as an individual mental effort to imagine and believe in a better life waiting for oneself in a not-so-distant, possible future, whatever writing may be on the wall. One could also speak of 'dreaming', in the way the word is used in American political and cultural discourse, where to have a dream for oneself is a moral duty that comes with being a member of the community, perhaps the last remaining duty under liberal individualism, regardless of the circumstances in which one may currently be living. Dreams are allowed and even encouraged to be unrealistic, and trying to talk someone out of his or her dream is considered rude, crude and socially unacceptable, however hopelessly naïve that dream may ever be. In the United States, the sacrosanct nature of dreams, never to be critically assessed, may be the most powerful impediment to political radicalization and collective action.[73] Hoping and dreaming

---

World: On Neo-Liberal Society, London: Verso 2013; Steffen Mau, *Inequality, Marketization and the Majority Class: Why Did the European Middle Classes Accept Neo-Liberalism?* Basingstoke: Palgrave Macmillan 2015). My objective is only to draw attention to the crucial significance of action patterns at the micro-level compensating for institutional deficiencies during the end-of-capitalism interregnum.

71   These include precarious employment, to be celebrated as a positive incentive for competitive self-improvement and the building of an optimized entrepreneurial identity.

72   On this see, among many others, David Brooks on the so-called 'millennials', under the title of 'The Self-Reliant Generation', *New York Times*, 8 January 2016, nytimes.com last accessed 21 January 2016. Brooks summarizes the results of survey of eighteen- to twenty-nine-year-old Americans. To quote: 'You see an abstract celebration of creative transformation but a concrete hunger for order, security and stability . . . Another glaring feature of millennial culture is they have been forced to be self-reliant and to take a loosely networked individualism as the normal order of the universe. Millennials have extremely low social trust . . . They want systemic change but there is no compelling form of collective action available . . . But there will be some giant cultural explosion down the road. You can't be as detached from solid supporting structures as millennials now are and lead a happy middle-aged life. Something is going to change.'

73   'The most telling polling result from the 2000 election was from a *Time* magazine survey that asked people if they are in the top 1 percent of earners. Nineteen percent of Americans say they are in the richest 1 percent and a further 20 percent expect to be someday. So right away you have 39 percent

require an optimistic outlook, and life under social entropy elevates being optimistic to the status of a public virtue and civic responsibility. In fact, one can say that even more than capitalism in its heyday, the entropic society of disintegrated, de-structured and under-governed post-capitalism depends on its ability to hitch itself onto the natural desire of people not to feel desperate, while defining pessimism as a socially harmful personal deficiency.

This is, thirdly, where *doping* comes in. Doping helps with both coping and hoping, and it takes many forms. Where it involves substance use and abuse, one may distinguish two kinds, performance-enhancing and performance-replacing. Performance-enhancing drugs are taken whenever the rewards of success are high, obviously in the winner-take-all markets of today's showbusiness, including sports. But they are also used far down the income scale in middle-class professional and occupational life where competitive pressures have been intensifying for decades, as well as in educational institutions where test results may decide a person's future career and earnings prospects. Here as elsewhere, doping is closely connected to corruption. Most of the substances used to enhance performance one way or other are highly profitable legal products of the pharmaceutical industry. Performance-replacing drugs, on the other hand, as consumed by the losers, are mostly illegal, supplied by criminal operators linked to worldwide trading networks.[74] Lower-class users are often sent to prison and die in comparatively large numbers from overdose.[75] Middle-class users, and in particular top performers, have not only better medical assistance but can also expect more lenient treatment from law enforcement agencies. This is likely to be because using drugs, even illegal ones, to increase one's productivity – as

of Americans who thought that when Mr. Gore savaged a plan that favored the top 1 percent, he was taking a direct shot at them.' David Brooks, 'The Triumph of Hope Over Self-Interest', *New York Times*, 12 January 2003, nytimes.com, last accessed 31 December 2015.

74 Although underclass drug users are kept desirably apathetic and politically incapacitated by their habit, they are the target of harsh law enforcement measures, and so are their suppliers. The reason may be that performance-replacing drugs, although they effectively disorganize the underclass as a potential political force, could subvert the competitive achievement ethic on which capitalism vitally depends. In fact, the United States government is prepared to destroy entire states in Latin America in an effort, wholly futile, to stop the inflow of hard drugs into its inner cities. In a country like Afghanistan, of course, the production of heroin has multiplied under the eyes of the American occupation forces, due to the need for the latter to secure the cooperation of the local war-and-drug lords.

75 In 2013, 37,947 people died in the United States from drug abuse, of which a little less than 40 per cent had used illegal drugs. The number of drug-related deaths had steadily increased from 2001, when it was 12,678. In 2011 it for the first time exceeded the number of deaths from gun violence, which rose to 33,636 in 2013. Deaths from traffic accidents had declined in the same period, from 42,196 in 2001 to 32,719 in 2013. Data are from the Center for Disease Control and Prevention, the National Highway Traffic Safety Administration, CNN and the U.S. State Department.

distinguished from generating unearned happiness in underclass dropouts – is more easily forgiven in a world dependent for capital accumulation on ever-increasing individual exertion. Indeed, if pop musicians and actors were imprisoned for drug abuse at the same rate as street corner heroin consumers, many movies and music recordings would have to be produced behind bars; the same might apply to the trading of financial assets. Cross-cutting the distinction between performance-enhancing and performance-replacing drug use is, incidentally, the daily provision of *synthetic happiness* to an astonishingly large number of customers by means of ecstatic-euphoric feel-good pop music, individually delivered and consumed with the help of advanced information technology.

Finally, *shopping*. It doesn't need repeating that today's markets for consumer goods in the rich capitalist countries are by and large saturated, making it essential for capitalist profitability to get individuals whose *needs* are covered to develop *desires* that give rise to new desires the moment they are fulfilled.[76] Product design and advertisement are instrumental for this,[77] but also low prices as made possible by the sweatshops of today, out-of-sight of final consumers and out-of-reach for collective solidarity. Competitive consumerism under the dictates of continuously changing and rising standards of appropriate consumption also secures the motivation to work hard and harder,[78] for only a constant or even a declining income, and to submit to the strict discipline of the contemporary labour market and labour process. That pressure is reinforced when consumers use credit to acquire, for example, a new flat-screen TV or the latest model SUV. At this point banks join employers as enforcers of capitalist work discipline. Social relations are redefined as relations of consumption when shopping becomes the occasion of choice to socialize with friends and family and the status of an individual

---

76   The prototypical desire that is intensified rather than reduced by its satisfaction, according to Sigmund Freud, is sex. This may explain the increasingly unapologetic employment of sexualized images in contemporary advertising, escalating since the 'sexual revolution' of the 1970s, feminist protests notwithstanding. Indeed, women no less than men seem to cherish pictures of naked bodies and the seductive *flair* they can apparently attach to just about any commodity.

77   A classic Marxian treatment of current developments, unfortunately not available in English, is Wolfgang Fritz Haug, *Kritik der Warenästhetik. Gefolgt von Warenästhetik im High-Tech-Kapitalismus*, Frankfurt am Main: Suhrkamp 2009. See also Ch. 3, this volume, for an extended discussion of how today's consumerism turns citizens into clients and customers of private, capital-accumulating corporations.

78   Where the American version of conspicuous consumption (Veblen) – to 'keep up with the Jones's' – is topped by the more collective, 'groupist' neo-Asian one. There one has to have the expensive gimmick of the day, or if necessary has to undergo cosmetic surgery, in order not to disgrace one's friends and family members, who may not want to be associated with someone not meeting the latest, 'Western' standards of visible prosperity and beauty.

in society is defined by his or her status as consumer in the economy. Product differentiation in particular, made possible by new production technology as well as new methods of advertisement, especially in the new, allegedly 'social', media, produces a kind of social integration that allows for a combined sense of individual singularity and collective identity in a community of customers, united in the consumption of continuously upgraded individualized commodities.

Summing up, social life and capital accumulation in the post-capitalist interregnum depend on individuals-as-consumers adhering to a culture of *competitive hedonism*, one that makes a virtue out of the necessity of having to struggle with adversity and uncertainty on one's own. For capital accumulation to continue under post-capitalism, that culture must make hoping and dreaming obligatory, mobilizing hopes and dreams to sustain production and fuel consumption in spite of low growth, rising inequality and growing indebtedness. It must also provide technical assistance enabling people to keep themselves *unreasonably happy*, while at the same time producing a stream of incentives and satisfactions motivating them to constantly intensify their work effort regardless of stagnant or declining pay, unpaid overtime and precarious employment.[79] Capitalism without system integration requires a labour market and labour process capable of sustaining a *neo-Protestant work ethic* alongside socially obligatory hedonistic consumerism. Enthusiastic hard work must be culturally defined and recognized as test and proof of individual value, corresponding to a meritocratic worldview that explains inequality with differences in effort or ability. For hedonism not to undermine productive discipline, as none less than Daniel Bell[80] was confident would happen, the attractions of consumerism must be complemented with a fear of social descent, while non-consumerist gratifications available outside of the money economy must be discounted and discredited. All of this presupposes the presence of a broad middle class willing to seek social integration through the labour market, accepting as a matter of course expectations of employers for full identification with whatever jobs they may be assigned and taking for granted the need for social life to respect the primacy of dedicated work and the pursuit of, it is hoped, life-structuring careers.[81]

---

79   Sabine Donauer, *Faktor Freude: Wie die Wirtschaft Arbeitsgefühle erzeugt*, Hamburg: edition Körber-Stiftung 2015.

80   Daniel Bell, *The Cultural Contradictions of Capitalism*, New York: Basic Books 1976.

81   It is precisely this category of people – the disciplined investors in ever more advanced educational degrees – whose employment prospects would be radically curtailed by a rise of artificial intelligence as predicted by Randall Collins (pp. 37–69 in Wallerstein et al., *Does Capitalism Have a Future?*). They are the core constituency of the post-capitalist interregnum, and their destruction would go to the very heart of the disorganized capitalism of today.

Capital accumulation after the end of capitalist system integration hangs on a thin thread: on the effectiveness, as long as it lasts, of the social integration of individuals into a capitalist culture of consumption and production. Institutional supports having fallen into disarray, post-capitalist capital accumulation depends on culture lagging behind structure, or substituting for a structure that has long dissolved, and on the difficulties of an alternative culture developing under the combined pressures of fragmented competition and precarious, all-too-easily lost access to the means of production and consumption. Ideology, in particular the exaltation of a life in uncertainty as a life in liberty, is of central importance here. Neoliberal ideological narratives offer a euphemistic reinterpretation of the breakdown of structured order as the arrival of a free society built on individual autonomy, and of de-institutionalization as historical progress out of an *empire of necessity* into an *empire of freedom*. For the interregnum to continue, those living in it must be continuously exhorted to experience the debris of what was once a capitalist society as an adventure playground for them to demonstrate their personal resourcefulness and with good luck get rich. With collective institutions disabled, disorder must be made to appear as spontaneous order based on individual rational choice and individual rights, free from collective rules and obligations. It is only when the manufacturing of ideological enthusiasm for a neoliberal everybody-for-themselves existence will no longer work, perhaps in the course of a major crisis in middle-class employment, as predicted by Collins, or generally when the prevailing disorder will begin on a large scale and seriously to frustrate individual projects and ambitions, that the post-capitalist interregnum may come to an end and a new order may emerge.

CHAPTER ONE

How Will Capitalism End?

There is a widespread sense today that capitalism is in critical condition, more so than at any time since the end of the Second World War.[1] Looking back, the crash of 2008 was only the latest in a long sequence of political and economic disorders that began with the end of post-war prosperity in the mid-1970s. Successive crises have proved to be ever more severe, spreading more widely and rapidly through an increasingly interconnected global economy. Global inflation in the 1970s was followed by rising public debt in the 1980s, and fiscal consolidation in the 1990s was accompanied by a steep increase in private-sector indebtedness.[2] For four decades now, disequilibrium has more or less been the normal condition of the 'advanced' industrial world, at both the national and the global levels. In fact, with time, the crises of post-war OECD capitalism have become so pervasive that they have increasingly been perceived as more than just economic in nature, resulting in a rediscovery of the older notion of a capitalist society – of capitalism as a social order and way of life, vitally dependent on the uninterrupted progress of private capital accumulation.

Crisis symptoms are many, but prominent among them are three long-term trends in the trajectories of rich, highly industrialized – or better, increasingly deindustrialized – capitalist countries. The first is a persistent decline in the rate of economic growth, recently aggravated by the events of 2008 (Figure 1.1). The second, associated with the first, is an equally persistent rise in overall indebtedness in leading capitalist states, where governments, private households and non-financial as well as financial firms have, over forty years, continued to pile up financial obligations (for the U.S., see Figure 1.2). Third, economic inequality, of both income and wealth, has been on the ascent for several decades now (Figure 1.3), alongside rising debt and declining growth.

Steady growth, sound money and a modicum of social equity, spreading some of the benefits of capitalism to those without capital, were long considered prerequisites for a capitalist political economy to command the legitimacy it needs. What must be most alarming from this perspective is that the three

---

1 A version of this text was delivered as the Anglo-German Foundation Lecture at the British Academy on 23 January 2014. Published in: *New Left Review*, vol. 87, May/June 2014, pp. 35–64.

2 I have explored these arguments more fully in *Buying Time*.

Figure 1.1: Annual average growth rates of twenty OECD countries, 1972–2010*

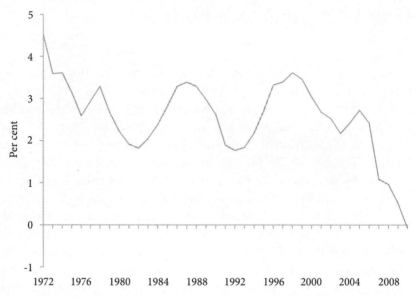

*Five-year moving average
Source: OECD Economic Outlook.

critical trends I have mentioned may be mutually reinforcing. There is mounting evidence that increasing inequality may be one of the causes of declining
growth, as inequality both impedes improvements in productivity and weakens demand. Low growth, in turn, reinforces inequality by intensifying
distributional conflict, making concessions to the poor more costly for the
rich, and making the rich insist more than before on strict observance of the
'Matthew principle' governing free markets: 'For unto every one that hath shall
be given, and he shall have abundance: but from him that hath not shall be
taken even that which he hath.'[3] Furthermore, rising debt, while failing to halt
the decline of economic growth, compounds inequality through the structural
changes associated with financialization – which in turn aimed to compensate
wage earners and consumers for the growing income inequality caused by
stagnant wages and cutbacks in public services.

   Can what appears to be a vicious circle of harmful trends continue forever?
Are there counterforces that might break it – and what will happen if they fail
to materialize, as they have for almost four decades now? Historians inform us
that crises are nothing new under capitalism, and may in fact be required for

---

   3   Matthew 25:29. This was first described as a social mechanism by Robert Merton in 'The
Matthew Effect in Science'. The technical term is cumulative advantage.

Figure 1.2: Liabilities as a percentage of U.S. GDP by sector, 1970–2011

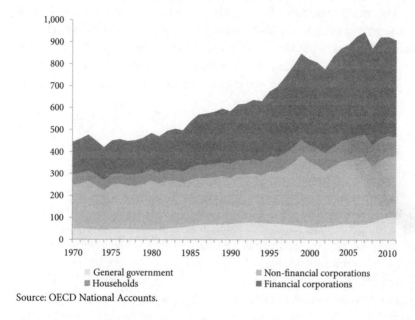

Source: OECD National Accounts.

Figure 1.3: Increase in GINI coefficient, OECD average

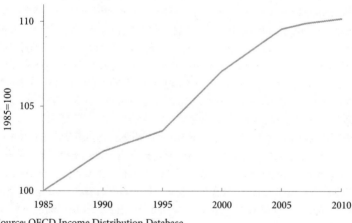

Source: OECD Income Distribution Database.

its longer-term health. But what they are talking about are cyclical movements or random shocks, after which capitalist economies can move into a new equilibrium, at least temporarily. What we are seeing today, however, appears in retrospect to be a continuous process of gradual decay, protracted but apparently all the more inexorable. Recovery from the occasional *Reinigungskrise* is one thing; interrupting a concatenation of intertwined, long-term trends quite another. Assuming that ever lower growth, ever higher inequality and ever rising debt are not indefinitely sustainable, and may together issue in a crisis that is systemic in nature – one whose character we have difficulty imagining – can we see signs of an impending reversal?

ANOTHER STOPGAP

Here the news is not good. Six years have passed since 2008, the culmination so far of the post-war crisis sequence. While memory of the abyss was still fresh, demands and blueprints for 'reform' to protect the world from a replay abounded. International conferences and summit meetings of all kinds followed hot on each other's heels, but half a decade later hardly anything has come from them. In the meantime, the financial industry, where the disaster originated, has staged a full recovery: profits, dividends, salaries and bonuses are back where they were, while re-regulation became mired in international negotiations and domestic lobbying. Governments, first and foremost that of the United States, have remained firmly in the grip of the money-making industries. These, in turn, are being generously provided with cheap cash, created out of thin air on their behalf by their friends in the central banks – prominent among them the former Goldman Sachs man Mario Draghi at the helm of the ECB – money which they then sit on or invest in government debt. Growth remains anaemic, as do labour markets; unprecedented liquidity has failed to jump-start the economy; and inequality is reaching ever more astonishing heights, as what little growth there is has been appropriated by the top 1 per cent of income earners – the lion's share by a small fraction of them.[4]

There would seem to be little reason indeed to be optimistic. For some time now, OECD capitalism has been kept going by liberal injections of fiat money, under a policy of monetary expansion whose architects know better than anyone else that it cannot continue forever. In fact, several attempts were made in 2013 to kick the habit, in Japan as well as in the U.S., but when stock prices plunged in response, 'tapering', as it came to be called, was postponed for the time being. In mid-June, the Bank for International Settlements (BIS)

---

4   See Emmanuel Saez, 'Striking It Richer: The Evolution of Top Incomes in the United States', 2 March 2012, available via Saez's personal web page at UC Berkeley; and Facundo Alvaredo, Anthony Atkinson, Thomas Piketty and Emmanuel Saez, 'The Top 1 per cent in International and Historical Perspective', *Journal of Economic Perspectives*, vol. 27, no. 3, 2013, pp. 3–20.

in Basel – the mother of all central banks – declared that 'quantitative easing' must come to an end. In its Annual Report, the Bank pointed out that central banks had, in reaction to the crisis and the slow recovery, expanded their balance sheets, 'which are now collectively at roughly three times their pre-crisis level – and rising'.[5] While this had been necessary to 'prevent financial collapse', now the goal had to be 'to return still-sluggish economies to strong and sustainable growth'. This, however, was beyond the capacities of central banks, which:

> cannot enact the structural economic and financial reforms needed to return economies to the real growth paths authorities and their publics both want and expect. What central-bank accommodation has done during the recovery is to borrow time . . . But the time has not been well used, as continued low interest rates and unconventional policies have made it easy for the private sector to postpone deleveraging, easy for the government to finance deficits, and easy for the authorities to delay needed reforms in the real economy and in the financial system. After all, cheap money makes it easier to borrow than to save, easier to spend than to tax, easier to remain the same than to change.

Apparently, this view was shared even by the Federal Reserve under Bernanke. By the late summer of 2013, it seemed once more to be signalling that the time of easy money was coming to an end. In September, however, the expected return to higher interest rates was again put off. The reason given was that 'the economy' looked less 'strong' than was hoped. Global stock prices immediately went up. The real reason why a return to more conventional monetary policies is so difficult, of course, is one that an international institution like BIS is freer to spell out than a – for the time being – more politically exposed national central bank. This is that as things stand, the only alternative to sustaining capitalism by means of an unlimited money supply is trying to revive it through neoliberal economic reform, as neatly encapsulated in the second subtitle of the BIS's 2012–13 Annual Report: 'Enhancing Flexibility: A Key to Growth'. In other words, bitter medicine for the many, combined with higher incentives for the few.[6]

---

5 Bank for International Settlements, *83rd Annual Report, 1 April 2012–31 March 2013*, Basel 2013, p. 5.
6 Even that may be less than promising in countries like the U.S. and U.K., where it is hard to see what neoliberal 'reforms' still remain to be implemented.

A PROBLEM WITH DEMOCRACY

It is here that discussion of the crisis and the future of modern capitalism must turn to democratic politics. Capitalism and democracy had long been considered adversaries, until the post-war settlement seemed to have accomplished their reconciliation. Well into the twentieth century, owners of capital had been afraid of democratic majorities abolishing private property, while workers and their organizations expected capitalists to finance a return to authoritarian rule in defence of their privileges. Only in the Cold War world did capitalism and democracy seem to become aligned with one another, as economic progress made it possible for working-class majorities to accept a free-market, private-property regime, in turn making it appear that democratic freedom was inseparable from, and indeed depended on, the freedom of markets and profit-making. Today, however, doubts about the compatibility of a capitalist economy with a democratic polity have powerfully returned. Among ordinary people, there is now a pervasive sense that politics can no longer make a difference in their lives, as reflected in common perceptions of deadlock, incompetence and corruption among what seems an increasingly self-contained and self-serving political class, united in their claim that 'there is no alternative' to them and their policies. One result is declining electoral turnout combined with high voter volatility, producing ever greater electoral fragmentation, due to the rise of 'populist' protest parties, and pervasive government instability.[7]

The legitimacy of post-war democracy was based on the premise that states had a capacity to intervene in markets and correct their outcomes in the interest of citizens. Decades of rising inequality have cast doubt on this, as has the impotence of governments before, during and after the crisis of 2008. In response to their growing irrelevance in a global market economy, governments and political parties in OECD democracies more or less happily looked on as the 'democratic class struggle' turned into post-democratic politainment.[8] In the meantime, the transformation of the capitalist political economy from post-war Keynesianism to neoliberal Hayekianism progressed smoothly: from a political formula for economic growth through redistribution from the top to the bottom, to one expecting growth through redistribution from the bottom to the top. Egalitarian democracy, regarded under Keynesianism as economically productive, is considered a drag on efficiency under

---

7   See Armin Schäfer and Wolfgang Streeck, eds, *Politics in the Age of Austerity*, Cambridge: Polity 2013.

8   Walter Korpi, *The Democratic Class Struggle*, London: Routledge and Kegan Paul 1983; and Crouch, *Post-Democracy*.

contemporary Hayekianism, where growth is to derive from insulation of markets – and of the cumulative advantage they entail – against redistributive political distortions.

A central topic of current anti-democratic rhetoric is the fiscal crisis of the contemporary state, as reflected in the astonishing increase in public debt since the 1970s (Figure 1.4). Growing public indebtedness is put down to electoral majorities living beyond their means by exploiting their societies' 'common pool', and to opportunistic politicians buying the support of myopic voters with money they do not have.[9] However, that the fiscal crisis was unlikely to have been caused by an excess of redistributive democracy can be seen from the fact that the build-up of government debt coincided with a decline in electoral participation, especially at the lower end of the income scale, and marched in lockstep with shrinking unionization, the disappearance of strikes, welfare-state cutbacks and exploding income inequality. What the deterioration of public finances *was* related to was declining overall levels of taxation (Figure 1.5) and the increasingly regressive character of tax systems, as a result of 'reforms' of top income and corporate tax rates (Figure 1.6). Moreover, by replacing tax revenue with debt, governments contributed further to inequality, in that they offered secure investment opportunities to those whose money they would or could no longer confiscate and had to borrow instead. Unlike taxpayers, buyers of government bonds continue to own what they pay to the state, and in fact collect interest on it, typically paid out of ever less progressive taxation; they can also pass it on to their children. Moreover, rising public debt can be and is being utilized politically to argue for cutbacks in state spending and for privatization of public services, further constraining redistributive democratic intervention in the capitalist economy.

Institutional protection of the market economy from democratic interference has advanced greatly in recent decades. Trade unions are on the decline everywhere and have in many countries been all but rooted out, especially in the U.S. Economic policy has widely been turned over to independent – i.e., democratically unaccountable – central banks concerned above all with the health and goodwill of financial markets.[10] In Europe, national economic

---

9 This is the Public Choice view of fiscal crisis, as powerfully put forward by James Buchanan and his school; see for example Buchanan and Gordon Tullock, *The Calculus of Consent: Logical Foundations of Constitutional Democracy*, Ann Arbor: University of Michigan Press 1962.

10 One often forgets that most central banks, including the BIS, have long been or still are partly under private ownership. For example, the Bank of England and the Bank of France were nationalized only after 1945. Central bank 'independence', as introduced by many countries in the 1990s, may be seen as a form of re-privatization.

Figure 1.4: Government debt as a percentage of GDP, 1970–2013

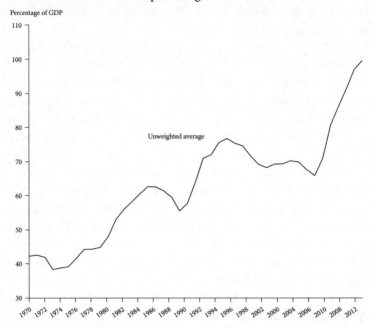

Countries included: Australia, Austria, Belgium, Canada, Denmark, Finland, France, Germany, Greece, Ireland, Italy, Japan, Netherlands, Norway, Portugal, Spain, Sweden, Switzerland, U.K., U.S. Source: OECD Economic Outlook No. 95.

Figure 1.5: Total tax revenue as a percentage of GDP, 1970–2011

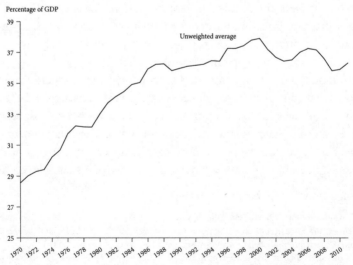

Countries included: Australia, Austria, Belgium, Canada, Denmark, Finland, France, Germany, Greece, Ireland, Italy, Japan, Netherlands, Norway, Portugal, Spain, Sweden, Switzerland, U.K., U.S. Source: OECD Revenue Statistics.

Figure 1.6: Top marginal income tax rates, 1900–2011

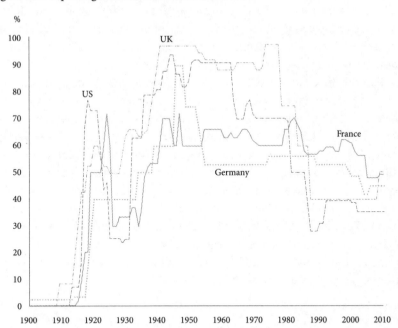

Source: Facundo Alvaredo, Anthony Atkinson, Thomas Piketty and Emmanuel Saez, 'The Top 1 per cent in International and Historical Perspective', *Journal of Economic Perspectives*, vol. 27, no. 3, 2013.

policies, including wage-setting and budget-making, are increasingly governed by supranational agencies like the European Commission and the European Central Bank that lie beyond the reach of popular democracy. This effectively de-democratizes European capitalism – without, of course, de-politicizing it.

Still, doubts remain among the profit-dependent classes as to whether democracy will, even in its emasculated contemporary version, allow for the neoliberal 'structural reforms' necessary for their regime to recover. Like ordinary citizens, although for the opposite reasons, elites are losing faith in democratic government and its suitability for reshaping societies in line with market imperatives. Public Choice's disparaging view of democratic politics as a corruption of market justice, in the service of opportunistic politicians and their clientele, has become common sense among elite publics – as has the belief that market capitalism cleansed of democratic politics will not only be more efficient but also virtuous and responsible.[11] Countries like China are complimented for their authoritarian political systems being so much better

---

11   Of course, as Colin Crouch has pointed out, neoliberalism in its actually existing form is a politically deeply entrenched oligarchy of giant multinational firms; see Crouch, *The Strange Non-Death of Neoliberalism*.

equipped than majoritarian democracy, with its egalitarian bent, to deal with what are claimed to be the challenges of 'globalization' – a rhetoric that is beginning conspicuously to resemble the celebration by capitalist elites during the interwar years of German and Italian Fascism (and even Stalinist Communism) for their apparently superior economic governance.[12]

For the time being, the neoliberal mainstream's political utopia is a 'market-conforming democracy', devoid of market-correcting powers and supportive of 'incentive-compatible' redistribution from the bottom to the top.[13] Although that project is already far advanced in both Western Europe and the United States, its promoters continue to worry that the political institutions inherited from the post-war compromise may at some point be repossessed by popular majorities, in a last-minute effort to block progress towards a neoliberal solution to the crisis. Elite pressures for economic neutralization of egalitarian democracy therefore continue unabated; in Europe this takes the form of a continuing relocation of political-economic decision-making to supranational institutions such as the European Central Bank and summit meetings of government leaders.

CAPITALISM ON THE BRINK?

Has capitalism seen its day? In the 1980s, the idea that 'modern capitalism' could be run as a 'mixed economy', both technocratically managed and democratically controlled, was abandoned. Later, in the neoliberal revolution, social and economic order was reconceived as benevolently emerging from the 'free play of market forces'. But with the crash of 2008, the promise of self-regulating markets attaining equilibrium on their own was discredited as well, without a plausible new formula for political-economic governance coming into view. This alone may be regarded as a symptom of a crisis that has become systemic, the more so the longer it lasts.

---

12   See Daniel A. Bell, *Beyond Liberal Democracy: Political Thinking for an East Asian Context*, Princeton, NJ: Princeton University Press 2006; and Nicolas Berggruen and Nathan Gardels, eds, *Intelligent Governance for the 21st Century: A Middle Way between West and East*, Cambridge: Polity 2012.

13   The expression 'market-conforming' is from Angela Merkel. The Chancellor's public rhetoric appears deliberately designed to obfuscate and mystify. Here is her September 2011 statement on the subject in original Merkelspeak: 'Wir leben ja in einer Demokratie und sind auch froh darüber. Das ist eine parlamentarische Demokratie. Deshalb ist das Budgetrecht ein Kernrecht des Parlaments. Insofern werden wir Wege finden, die parlamentarische Mitbestimmung so zu gestalten, dass sie trotzdem auch marktkonform ist, also dass sich auf den Märkten die entsprechenden Signale ergeben.' A rough translation might run: 'We certainly live in a democracy and are also glad about this. This is a parliamentary democracy. Therefore the budget right is a core right of parliament. To this extent we will find ways to shape parliamentary co-decision in such a way that it is nevertheless also market-conforming, so that the respective signals emerge on the market.'

In my view it is high time, in the light of decades of declining growth, rising inequality and increasing indebtedness – as well as of the successive agonies of inflation, public debt and financial implosion since the 1970s – to think again about capitalism as a historical phenomenon, one that has not just a beginning, but also an end. For this, we need to part company with mislead-ing models of social and institutional change. As long as we imagine the end of capitalism being decreed, Leninist-style, by some government or central committee, we cannot but consider capitalism eternal. (In fact it was Communism, centralized as it was in Moscow, that could be and was termi-nated by decree.) Matters are different if, instead of imagining it being replaced by collective decision with some providentially designed new order, we allow for capitalism to collapse by itself.

I suggest that we learn to think about capitalism coming to an end without assuming responsibility for answering the question of what one proposes to put in its place. It is a Marxist – or better: modernist – prejudice that capitalism as a historical epoch will end only when a new, better society is in sight, and a revolutionary subject ready to implement it for the advancement of mankind. This presupposes a degree of political control over our common fate of which we cannot even dream after the destruction of collective agency, and indeed the hope for it, in the neoliberal-globalist revolution. Neither a utopian vision of an alternative future nor superhuman foresight should be required to vali-date the claim that capitalism is facing its *Götterdämmerung*. I am willing to make exactly this claim, although I am aware of how many times capitalism has been declared dead in the past. In fact, all of the main theorists of capital-ism have predicted its impending expiry, ever since the concept came into use in the mid-1800s. This includes not just radical critics like Marx or Polanyi, but also bourgeois theorists such as Weber, Schumpeter, Sombart and Keynes.[14]

That something has failed to happen, in spite of reasonable predictions that it would, does not mean that it will never happen; here, too, there is no inductive proof. I believe that this time is different, one symptom being that even capitalism's master technicians have no clue today how to make the system whole again – see, for example, the recently published minutes of the deliberations of the Federal Reserve's board in 2008,[15] or the desperate search of central bankers, mentioned above, for the right moment to end 'quantitative easing'. This, however, is only the surface of the problem. Beneath it is the stark fact that capitalist progress has by now more or less destroyed any agency that

---

14 So, if history proves me wrong, I will at least be in good company.

15 As reported by Gretchen Morgenson, 'A New Light on Regulators in the Dark', *New York Times*, 23 April 2014. The article presents 'a disturbing picture of a central bank that was in the dark about each looming disaster throughout 2008'.

could stabilize it by limiting it; the point being that the stability of capitalism as a socio-economic system depends on its *Eigendynamik* being contained by countervailing forces – by collective interests and institutions subjecting capital accumulation to social checks and balances. The implication is that capitalism may undermine itself by being too successful. I will argue this point in more detail below.

The image I have of the end of capitalism – an end that I believe is already under way – is one of a social system in chronic disrepair, for reasons of its own and regardless of the absence of a viable alternative. While we cannot know when and how exactly capitalism will disappear and what will succeed it, what matters is that no force is on hand that could be expected to reverse the three downward trends in economic growth, social equality and financial stability and end their mutual reinforcement. In contrast to the 1930s, there is today no political-economic formula on the horizon, Left or Rright, that might provide capitalist societies with a coherent new regime of regulation, or *régulation*. Social integration as well as system integration seem irreversibly damaged and set to deteriorate further.[16] What is most likely to happen as time passes is a continuous accumulation of small and not-so-small dysfunctions; none necessarily deadly as such, but most beyond repair, all the more so as they become too many for individual address. In the process, the parts of the whole will fit together less and less; frictions of all kinds will multiply; unanticipated consequences will spread, along ever more obscure lines of causation. Uncertainty will proliferate; crises of every sort – of legitimacy, productivity or both – will follow each other in quick succession while predictability and governability will decline further (as they have for decades now). Eventually, the myriad provisional fixes devised for short-term crisis management will collapse under the weight of the daily disasters produced by a social order in profound, anomic disarray.

Conceiving of the end of capitalism as a process rather than an event raises the issue of how to define capitalism. Societies are complex entities that do not die in the way organisms do: with the rare exception of total extinction, discontinuity is always embedded in some continuity. If we say that a society has ended, we mean that certain features of its organization that we consider essential to it have disappeared; others may well have survived. I propose that to determine if capitalism is alive, dying or dead, we define it as a modern society[17] that secures its collective reproduction as an unintended side-effect

16   On these terms, see Lockwood, 'Social Integration and System Integration', pp. 244–257.

17   Or, as Adam Smith has it, a 'progressive' society – one aiming at growth of its productivity and prosperity that is in principle boundless, as measured by the size of its money economy.

of individually rational, competitive profit maximization in pursuit of capital accumulation, through a 'labour process' combining privately owned capital with commodified labour power, fulfilling the Mandevillean promise of private vices turning into public benefits.[18] It is this promise, I maintain, that contemporary capitalism can no longer keep – ending its historical existence as a self-reproducing, sustainable, predictable and legitimate social order.

The demise of capitalism so defined is unlikely to follow anyone's blueprint. As the decay progresses, it is bound to provoke political protests and manifold attempts at collective intervention. But for a long time, these are likely to remain of the Luddite sort: local, dispersed, uncoordinated, 'primitive' – adding to the disorder while unable to create a new order, at best unintentionally helping it to come about. One might think that a long-lasting crisis of this sort would open up more than a few windows of opportunity for reformist or revolutionary agency. It seems, however, that disorganized capitalism is disorganizing not only itself but its opposition as well, depriving it of the capacity either to defeat capitalism or to rescue it. For capitalism to end, then, it must provide for its own destruction – which, I would argue, is exactly what we are witnessing today.

A PYRRHIC VICTORY

But why should capitalism, whatever its deficiencies, be in crisis at all if it no longer has any opposition worthy of the name? When Communism imploded in 1989, this was widely viewed as capitalism's final triumph, as the 'end of history'. Even today, after 2008, the Old Left remains on the brink of extinction everywhere, while a new New Left has, until now, failed to appear. The masses, the poor and powerless as much as the relatively well-to-do, seem firmly in the grip of consumerism, with collective goods, collective action and collective organization thoroughly out of fashion. As the only game in town, why should capitalism not carry on, by default if for no other reason? At first glance, there is indeed much that speaks against pronouncing capitalism dead, regardless of

---

18   Other definitions of capitalism emphasize, for example, the peaceful nature of capitalist commercial market exchange: see Albert Hirschman, 'Rival Interpretations of Market Society: Civilizing, Destructive or Feeble?', *Journal of Economic Literature*, vol. 20, no. 4, 1982, pp. 1463–1484. This neglects the fact that non-violent 'free trade' is typically confined to the centre of the capitalist system, whereas on its historical and spatial periphery violence is rampant. For example, illegal markets (drugs, prostitution, arms, etc.) governed by private violence raise huge sums of money for legal investment – a version of primitive accumulation. Moreover, legitimate public and illegal private violence often blend into one another, not only on the capitalist frontier but also in the support provided by the centre to its collaborators on the periphery. One also needs to include public violence in the centre against dissenters and, when they still meaningfully existed, trade unions.

all the ominous writing on the historical wall. As far as inequality is concerned, people may get used to it, especially with the help of public entertainment and political repression. Furthermore, examples abound of governments being re-elected that cut social spending and privatize public services, in pursuit of sound money for the owners of money. Concerning environmental deterioration, it proceeds only slowly compared to the human lifespan, so one can deny it while learning to live with it. Technological advances with which to buy time, such as fracking, can never be ruled out, and if there are limits to the pacifying powers of consumerism, we clearly are nowhere near them. Moreover, adapting to more time-consuming and life-consuming work regimes can be taken as a competitive challenge, an opportunity for personal achievement. Cultural definitions of the good life have always been highly malleable and might well be stretched further to match the onward march of commodification, at least as long as radical or religious challenges to pro-capitalist re-education can be suppressed, ridiculed or otherwise marginalized. Finally, most of today's stagnation theories apply only to the West, or just to the U.S., not to China, Russia, India or Brazil – countries to which the frontier of economic growth may be about to migrate, with vast virgin lands waiting to be made available for capitalist progress.[19]

My answer is that having no opposition may actually be more of a liability for capitalism than an asset. Social systems thrive on internal heterogeneity, on a pluralism of organizing principles protecting them from dedicating themselves entirely to a single purpose, crowding out other goals that must also be attended to if the system is to be sustainable. Capitalism as we know it has benefited greatly from the rise of counter-movements against the rule of profit and of the market. Socialism and trade unionism, by putting a brake on commodification, prevented capitalism from destroying its non-capitalist foundations – trust, good faith, altruism, solidarity within families and communities, and the like. Under Keynesianism and Fordism, capitalism's more or less loyal opposition secured and helped stabilize aggregate demand, especially in recessions. Where circumstances were favourable, working-class organization even served as a 'productivity whip', by forcing capital to embark on more advanced production concepts.

---

19   Although recent assessments of their economic performance and prospects are much less enthusiastic than they were two or three years ago. Lately the euphoric 'BRIC' discourse has been succeeded by anxious questioning of the economic prospects of the 'Fragile Five' (Turkey, Brazil, India, South Africa and Indonesia; Landon Thomas Jr., *New York Times*, 28 January 2014). Reports on accumulating problems in Chinese capitalism have also become more frequent, pointing, among other things, to the extensive indebtedness of local and regional governments. Since the Crimean crisis, we have also been hearing about the structural weaknesses of the Russian economy.

It is in this sense that Geoffrey Hodgson has argued that capitalism can survive only as long as it is not completely capitalist – as it has not yet rid itself, or the society in which it resides, of 'necessary impurities'.[20] Seen this way, capitalism's defeat of its opposition may actually have been a Pyrrhic victory, freeing it from countervailing powers which, while sometimes inconvenient, had in fact supported it. Could it be that victorious capitalism has become its own worst enemy?

FRONTIERS OF COMMODIFICATION

In exploring this possibility, we might wish to turn to Karl Polanyi's idea of social limits to market expansion, as underlying his concept of the three 'fictitious commodities': labour, land (or nature) and money.[21] A fictitious commodity is defined as a resource to which the laws of supply and demand apply only partially and awkwardly, if at all; it can therefore only be treated as a commodity in a carefully circumscribed, regulated way, since complete commodification will destroy it or make it unusable. Markets, however, have an inherent tendency to expand beyond their original domain, the trading of material goods, to all other spheres of life, regardless of their suitability for commodification – or, in Marxian terms, for subsumption under the logic of capital accumulation. Unless held back by constraining institutions, market expansion is thus at permanent risk of undermining itself, and with it the viability of the capitalist economic and social system.

In fact, the indications are that market expansion has today reached a critical threshold with respect to all three of Polanyi's fictitious commodities, as institutional safeguards that served to protect them from full marketization have been eroded on a number of fronts. This is what seems to be behind the search currently under way in all advanced capitalist societies for a new time regime with respect to labour, in particular a new allocation of time between social and economic relations and pursuits; for a sustainable energy regime in relation to nature; and for a stable financial regime for the

---

20   'Every socio-economic system must rely on at least one structurally dissimilar subsystem to function. There must always be a coexistent plurality of modes of production, so that the social formation as a whole has the requisite structural variety to cope with change': Geoffrey Hodgson, 'The Evolution of Capitalism from the Perspective of Institutional and Evolutionary Economics'. In: Hodgson, Geoffrey et al., eds, *Capitalism in Evolution: Global Contentions, East and West*, Cheltenham: Edward Elgar 2001, 71ff. For a less functionalist formulation of the same idea see my concept of 'beneficial constraint': 'Beneficial Constraints: On the Economic Limits of Rational Voluntarism'. In: Hollingsworth, Rogers and Robert Boyer, eds, *Contemporary Capitalism: The Embeddedness of Institutions*, Cambridge: Cambridge University Press 1997, pp. 197–219.

21   Polanyi, *The Great Transformation*, pp. 68–76.

production and allocation of money. In all three areas, societies are today groping for more effective limitations on the logic of expansion,[22] institutionalized as one of private enrichment, that is fundamental to the capitalist social order. These limitations centre on the increasingly demanding claims made by the employment system on human labour, by capitalist production and consumption systems on finite natural resources, and by the financial and banking system on people's confidence in ever more complex pyramids of money, credit and debt.

Looking at each of the three Polanyian crisis zones in turn, we may note that it was an excessive commodification of money that brought down the global economy in 2008: the transformation of a limitless supply of cheap credit into ever more sophisticated financial 'products' gave rise to a real-estate bubble of a size unimaginable at the time. As of the 1980s, deregulation of U.S. financial markets had abolished the restrictions on the private production and marketization of money devised after the Great Depression. 'Financialization', as the process came to be known, seemed the last remaining way to restore growth and profitability to the economy of the overextended hegemon of global capitalism. Once let loose, however, the money-making industry invested a good part of its enormous resources in lobbying for a further removal of prudential regulation, not to mention in circumventing whatever rules were left. With hindsight, the enormous risks that came with the move from the old regime of M–C–M′ to a new one of M–M′ are easy to see, as is the trend towards ever-increasing inequality associated with the disproportionate growth of the banking sector.[23]

Concerning nature, there is growing unease over the tension, now widely perceived, between the capitalist principle of infinite expansion and the finite supply of natural resources. Neo-Malthusian discourses of various denominations became popular in the 1970s. Whatever one may think of them, and although some are now considered prematurely alarmist, no one seriously denies that the energy consumption patterns of rich capitalist societies cannot be extended to the rest of the world without destroying essential preconditions of human life. What seems to be taking shape is a race between the advancing exhaustion of nature on the one hand and technological innovation on the other – substituting artificial materials for natural ones, preventing or repairing environmental damage, devising shelters against unavoidable degradation of the biosphere. One question that no one seems able to answer

---

22   Or even 'transgression', if we go by the German: *Steigerungslogik*.

23   Donald Tomaskovic-Devey and Ken-Hou Lin, 'Income Dynamics, Economic Rents and the Financialization of the US Economy', *American Sociological Review*, vol. 76, no. 4, 2011, pp. 538–559.

is how the enormous collective resources potentially required for this may be mobilized in societies governed by what C. B. MacPherson termed 'possessive individualism'.[24] What actors and institutions are to secure the collective good of a liveable environment in a world of competitive production and consumption?

Thirdly, the commodification of human labour may have reached a critical point. Deregulation of labour markets under international competition has undone whatever prospects there might once have been for a general limitation of working hours.[25] It has also made employment more precarious for a growing share of the population.[26] With the rising labour-market participation of women, due in part to the disappearance of the 'family wage', hours per month sold by families to employers have increased while wages have lagged behind productivity, most dramatically in the capitalist heartland, the U.S. (see Figure 1.7). At the same time, deregulation and the destruction of trade unions notwithstanding, labour markets typically fail to clear, and residual unemployment on the order of 7 to 8 per cent has become the new normal, even in a country like Sweden. Sweatshops have expanded in many industries including services, but mostly on the global periphery, beyond the reach of the authorities and what remains of trade unions in the capitalist centre, and out of view of consumers. As sweated labour competes with workers in countries with historically strong labour protections, working conditions for the former deteriorate while unemployment becomes endemic for the latter. Meanwhile, complaints multiply about the penetration of work into family life, alongside pressures from labour markets to join an unending race to upgrade one's 'human capital'. Moreover, global mobility enables employers to replace unwilling local workers with willing immigrant ones. It also compensates for sub-replacement fertility, itself due in part to a changed balance between unpaid and paid work and between non-market and market consumption. The result is a secular weakening of social counter-movements, caused by a loss of class and social solidarity and accompanied by crippling political conflicts over ethnic diversity, even in traditionally liberal countries such as the Netherlands, Sweden or Norway.

---

24   C. B. MacPherson, *The Political Theory of Possessive Individualism: Hobbes to Locke*, Oxford: Clarendon Press 1962.

25   Consider the attack on the last remnants of the thirty-five-hour week in France, under the auspices of a Socialist president and his party.

26   From the capitalist frontier, it is reported that leading investment banks have begun suggesting to their lowest-level employees that they 'should try to spend four weekend days away from the office each month, part of a broader effort to improve working conditions': 'Wall St. Shock: Take a Day Off, Even a Sunday', *New York Times*, 10 January 2014.

Figure 1.7: The broken social contract, U.S., 1947 to present

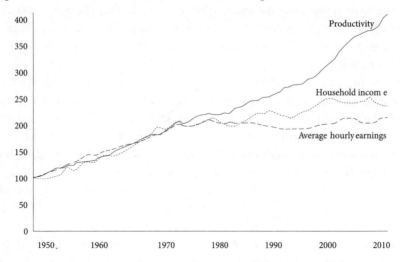

Source: Thomas Kochan, 'The American Jobs Crisis and the Implications for the Future of Employment Policy', *International Labor Relations Review*, vol. 66, no. 2, 2013.

The question of how and where capital accumulation must be restrained in order to protect the three fictitious commodities from total commodification has been contested throughout the history of capitalism. But the present worldwide disorder in all three border zones at the same time is something different: it results from a spectacularly successful onslaught of markets, expanding more rapidly than ever, on a wide range of institutions and actors that, whether inherited from the past or built up in long political struggles, had for a time kept capitalism's advance to some extent socially embedded. Labour, land and money have simultaneously become crisis zones after 'globalization' endowed market relations and production chains with an unprecedented capacity to cross the boundaries of national political and legal jurisdictions. The result is a fundamental disorganization of the agencies that have, in the modern era, more or less successfully domesticated capitalist 'animal spirits', for the sake of society as a whole as well as of capitalism itself.

It is not only with respect to fictitious commodities that capital accumulation may be hitting its limits. On the surface, consumption of goods and services continues to grow, and the implicit premise of modern economics – that the human desire and capacity to consume are unlimited – would seem to be easily vindicated by a visit to any large shopping mall. Still, fears that markets for consumer goods may at some point become saturated – perhaps in the course of a post-materialist decoupling of human aspirations from the purchase of commodities – are endemic among profit-dependent producers. This in itself reflects the fact that consumption in mature capitalist societies has long become dissociated from material need.[27] The lion's share of consumption expenditure today – and a rapidly growing one – is spent not on the use value of goods, but on their symbolic value, their aura or halo. This is why industry practitioners find themselves paying more than ever for marketing, including not just advertising but also product design and innovation. Nevertheless, in spite of the growing sophistication of sales promotion, the intangibles of culture make commercial success difficult to predict – certainly more so than in an era when growth could be achieved by gradually supplying all households in a country with a washing machine.[28]

FIVE DISORDERS

Capitalism without opposition is left to its own devices, which do not include self-restraint. The capitalist pursuit of profit is open-ended, and cannot be otherwise. The idea that less could be more is not a principle a capitalist society could honour; it must be imposed upon it, or else there will be no end to its progress, self-consuming as it may ultimately be. At present, I claim, we are already in a position to observe capitalism passing away as a result of having destroyed its opposition – dying, as it were, from an overdose of itself. For illustration I will point to five systemic disorders of today's advanced capitalism; all of them result in various ways from the weakening of traditional institutional and political restraints on capitalist advance. I call them stagnation, oligarchic redistribution, the plundering of the public domain, corruption and global anarchy.

Six years after Lehman, predictions of long-lasting economic stagnation are *en vogue*. A prominent example is a much-discussed paper by Robert Gordon, who argues that the main innovations that have driven productivity and economic growth since the 1800s could happen only once, like the increase

---

27   Think of the gigantic potlatch organized every year before Christmas by the consumer-goods and retail industries, or of the day after Thanksgiving, ominously referred to in the U.S. as 'Black Friday' because of the ubiquitous price reductions and the collective shopping hysteria it inaugurates. Imagine the desperation if nobody showed up!

28   The vital importance of a consumerist culture for the reproduction of contemporary capitalism cannot be underestimated. Consumers are the ultimate allies of capital in its distributional conflict with producers, even though producers and consumers tend to be the same people. By hunting for the best bargain, consumers defeat themselves as producers, driving their own jobs abroad; as they take up consumer credit to replenish their reduced purchasing power, they supplement consumerist incentives with legal obligations to work, entered into as debtors and enforced by lenders. See Lendol Calder, *Financing the American Dream: A Cultural History of Consumer Credit*, Princeton, NJ: Princeton University Press 1999.

in the speed of transportation or the installation of running water in cities.[29] Compared to them, the recent spread of information technology has produced only minor productivity effects, if any. While Gordon's argument may seem somewhat technologically deterministic, it appears plausible that capitalism can hope to attain the level of growth needed to compensate a non-capitalist working class for helping others accumulate capital only if technology opens up ever new opportunities for increasing productivity. In any case, in what looks like an afterthought, Gordon supports his prediction of low or no growth by listing six non-technological factors – he calls them 'headwinds' – which would make for long-term stagnation 'even if innovation were to continue . . . at the rate of the two decades before 2007'.[30] Among these factors he includes two that I argue have for some time been intertwined with low growth: inequality and 'the overhang of consumer and government debt'.[31]

What is astonishing is how close current stagnation theories come to the Marxist underconsumption theories of the 1970s and 1980s.[32] Recently, none other than Lawrence 'Larry' Summers – friend of Wall Street, chief architect of financial deregulation under Clinton, and Obama's first choice for president of the Federal Reserve, until he had to give way in face of congressional opposition[33] – has joined the stagnation theorists. At the IMF Economic Forum on 8 November last year, Summers confessed to having given up hope that close-to-zero interest rates would produce significant economic growth in the foreseeable future, in a world he felt was suffering from an excess of capital.[34]

---

29   Robert Gordon, *Is US Economic Growth Over? Faltering Innovation Confronts the Six Headwinds*, NBER Working Paper no. 18315, August 2012.

30   According to Gordon, that rate amounted to 1.8 per cent per annum. Under the impact of the six adverse forces, it would, in the future, fall to 0.2 per cent per annum for the bottom 99 per cent of the American population: Gordon, *Is US Economic Growth Over?*, pp. 18ff. (Growth for the top 1 per cent is of course a different matter.) Note that Gordon believes that, in fact, the basic growth rate will be lower than 1.8 per cent.

31   Gordon's exercise in forecasting was and is widely debated. Doubts have been raised in particular with respect to future technological progress in artificial intelligence and robotics. While progress on this front seems likely, however, it is unlikely that its fruits will be equitably shared. Without social protection, technological advances in these areas would be destructive of employment and would give rise to further social polarization. Whatever technological progress would add to growth would probably be cancelled out by what it would add to inequality.

32   See, among many others, Harry Magdoff and Paul Sweezy, *Stagnation and the Financial Explosion*, New York: Monthly Review Press 1987. For an interesting assessment of the applicability of underconsumption theory to post-2008 capitalism, see John Bellamy Foster and Fred Magdoff, *The Great Financial Crisis: Causes and Consequences*, New York: Monthly Review Press 2009.

33   Presumably also because he would have had to declare the substantial income he received from Wall Street firms after his resignation from the Obama administration at the end of 2010. See 'The Fed, Lawrence Summers, and Money', *New York Times*, 11 August 2013.

34   The same idea had been put forward in 2005 when Ben Bernanke, soon to follow Alan Greenspan at the Fed, invoked a 'savings glut' to account for the failure of the Fed's 'flooding the markets with liquidity' to stimulate investment. Today Summers casually subscribes to the view of Left

Summers' prediction of 'secular stagnation' as the 'new normal' met with surprisingly broad approval among his fellow economists, including Paul Krugman.[35] What Summers mentioned only in passing was that the conspicuous failure of even negative real interest rates to revive investment coincided with a long-term increase in inequality, in the United States and elsewhere. As Keynes would have known, concentration of income at the top must detract from effective demand and make capital owners look for speculative profit opportunities outside the 'real economy'. This may in fact have been one of the causes of the 'financialization' of capitalism that began in the 1980s.

The power elites of global capitalism would seem to be resigning themselves to low or no growth on aggregate for the foreseeable future. This does not preclude high profits in the financial sector, essentially from speculative trading with cheap money supplied by central banks. Few seem to fear that the money generated to prevent stagnation from turning into deflation will cause inflation, as the unions that could claim a share in it no longer exist.[36] In fact the concern now is with too little rather than too much inflation, the emerging received wisdom being that a healthy economy requires a yearly inflation rate of at least 2 per cent, if not more. The only inflation in sight, however, is that of asset-price bubbles, and Summers took pains to prepare his audience for a lot of them.

For capitalists and their retainers, the future looks like a decidedly bumpy ride. Low growth will refuse them additional resources with which to settle distributional conflicts and pacify discontent. Bubbles are waiting to burst, out of the blue, and it is not certain whether states will regain the capacity to take care of the victims in time. The stagnant economy that is shaping up will be far from a stationary or steady-state economy; as growth declines and risks increase, the struggle for survival will become more intense. Rather than restoring the protective limits to commodification that were rendered obsolete by globalization, ever new ways will be sought to exploit nature, extend and intensify working time, and encourage what the jargon calls creative finance, in a desperate effort to keep profits up and capital accumulation going. The scenario of 'stagnation with a chance of bubbles' may most plausibly be imagined as a battle of all against all, punctured by occasional panics and with the playing of endgames becoming a popular pastime.

---

stagnation theorists that the 'boom' of the 1990s and early 2000s was a chimera: 'Too easy money, too much borrowing, too much wealth. Was there a great boom? Capacity utilization wasn't under any great pressure, unemployment wasn't under any remarkably low level. Inflation was entirely quiescent. So somehow even a great bubble wasn't enough to produce any excess in aggregate demand.' A video of Summers' speech is available on the IMF website (see footnote 21 in the introduction).

35   Paul Krugman, 'A Permanent Slump?', *New York Times*, 18 November 2013.

36   Their absence, of course, was one of the reasons why excess profits could come about and depress demand in the first place.

PLUTOCRATS AND PLUNDER

Turning to the second disorder, there is no indication that the long-term trend towards greater economic inequality will be broken any time soon, or indeed ever. Inequality depresses growth, for Keynesian and other reasons. But the easy money currently provided by central banks to restore growth – easy for capital but not, of course, for labour – further adds to inequality, by blowing up the financial sector and inviting speculative rather than productive investment. Redistribution to the top thus becomes oligarchic: rather than serving a collective interest in economic progress, as promised by neoclassical economics, it turns into extraction of resources from increasingly impoverished, declining societies. Countries that come to mind here are Russia and Ukraine, but also Greece and Spain, and increasingly the United States. Under oligarchic redistribution, the Keynesian bond which tied the profits of the rich to the wages of the poor is severed, cutting the fate of economic elites loose from that of the masses.[37] This was anticipated in the infamous 'plutonomy' memorandums distributed by Citibank in 2005 and 2006 to a select circle of its richest clients, to assure them that their prosperity no longer depended on that of wage earners.[38]

Oligarchic redistribution and the trend toward plutonomy, even in countries that are still considered democracies, conjure up the nightmare of elites confident that they will outlive the social system that is making them rich. Plutonomic capitalists may no longer have to worry about national economic growth because their transnational fortunes grow without it; hence the exit of the super-rich from countries like Russia or Greece, who take their money – or that of their fellow citizens – and run, preferably to Switzerland, Britain or the United States. The possibility, as provided by a global capital market, of rescuing yourself and your family by exiting together with your possessions offers the strongest possible temptation for the rich to move into endgame mode – cash in, burn bridges, and leave nothing behind but scorched earth.

Closely related to this is the third disorder, the plundering of the public domain through underfunding and privatization. I have elsewhere traced its

---

37   In the United States and elsewhere, the rich mobilize against trade unions and minimum wage statutes, although low wages weaken aggregate demand. Apparently they can do so because the abundant supply of fresh money replaces mass purchasing power, by enabling those who have access to it to make their profit in the financial sector. Demand from below would make it attractive for the 'savings' of the rich to be invested in services and manufacturing. See, in this context, the call late last year by the director-general of the Confederation of British Industry, which represents manufacturing firms, for members to pay their workers better, as too many people are stuck in low-pay employment. See 'Companies urged to spread benefits widely', *Financial Times*, 30 December 2013.

38   Citigroup Research, 'Plutonomy: Buying Luxury, Explaining Global Imbalances', 16 October 2005; Citigroup Research, 'Revisiting Plutonomy: The Rich Getting Richer', 5 March 2006.

origin to the twofold transition since the 1970s from the tax state to the debt state to, finally, the consolidation or austerity state. Foremost among the causes of this shift were the new opportunities offered by global capital markets since the 1980s for tax flight, tax evasion, tax-regime shopping and the extortion of tax cuts from governments by corporations and earners of high incomes. Attempts to close public deficits relied almost exclusively on cuts in government spending – both to social security and to investment in physical infrastructures and human capital. As income gains accrued increasingly to the top 1 per cent, the public domain of capitalist economies shrank, often dramatically, starved in favour of internationally mobile oligarchic wealth. Part of the process was privatization, carried out regardless of the contribution public investment in productivity and social cohesion might have made to economic growth and social equity.

Even before 2008, it was generally taken for granted that the fiscal crisis of the post-war state had to be resolved by lowering spending instead of raising taxes, especially on the rich. Consolidation of public finances by way of austerity was and is being imposed on societies even though it is likely to depress growth. This would seem to be another indication that the economy of the oligarchs has been decoupled from that of ordinary people, as the rich no longer expect to pay a price for maximizing their income at the expense of the non-rich, or for pursuing their interests at the expense of the economy as a whole. What may be surfacing here is the fundamental tension described by Marx between, on the one hand, the increasingly social nature of production in an advanced economy and society, and private ownership of the means of production on the other. As productivity growth requires more public provision, it tends to become incompatible with private accumulation of profits, forcing capitalist elites to choose between the two. The result is what we are seeing already today: economic stagnation combined with oligarchic redistribution.[39]

CORROSIONS OF THE IRON CAGE

Along with declining economic growth, rising inequality and the transferral of the public domain to private ownership, corruption is the fourth disorder of contemporary capitalism. In his attempt to rehabilitate it by reclaiming its

---

39 *Nota bene* that capitalism is about profit, not about productivity. While the two may sometimes go together, they are likely to part company when economic growth begins to require a disproportionate expansion of the public domain, as envisaged early on in 'Wagner's law': Adolph Wagner, *Grundlegung der politischen Oekonomie*, 3rd edn, Leipzig: C. F. Winter 1892. Capitalist preferences for profit over productivity, and with them the regime of capitalist private property as a whole, may then get in the way of economic and social progress.

ethical foundations, Max Weber drew a sharp line between capitalism and greed, pointing to what he believed were its origins in the religious tradition of Protestantism. According to Weber, greed had existed everywhere and at all times; not only was it not distinctive of capitalism, it was even apt to subvert it. Capitalism was based not on a desire to get rich, but on self-discipline, method-ical effort, responsible stewardship, sober devotion to a calling and to a rational organization of life. Weber did expect the cultural values of capitalism to fade as it matured and turned into an 'iron cage', where bureaucratic regulation and the constraints of competition would take the place of the cultural ideas that had originally served to disconnect capital accumulation from both hedonistic-ma-terialistic consumption and primitive hoarding instincts. What he could not anticipate, however, was the neoliberal revolution in the last third of the twen-tieth century and the unprecedented opportunities it provided to get very rich.

Pace Weber, fraud and corruption have forever been companions of capi-talism. But there are good reasons to believe that with the rise of the financial sector to economic dominance, they have become so pervasive that Weber's ethical vindication of capitalism now seems to apply to an altogether different world. Finance is an 'industry' where innovation is hard to distinguish from rule-bending or rule-breaking; where the pay-offs from semi-legal and illegal activities are particularly high; where the gradient in expertise and pay between firms and regulatory authorities is extreme; where revolving doors between the two offer unending possibilities for subtle and not-so-subtle corruption;[40] where the largest firms are not just too big to fail, but also too big to jail, given their importance for national economic policy and tax revenue; and where the borderline between private companies and the state is more blurred than anywhere else, as indicated by the 2008 bailout or by the huge number of former and future employees of financial firms in the American government. After Enron and WorldCom, it was observed that fraud and corruption had reached all-time highs in the US economy. But what came to light after 2008 beat everything: rating agencies being paid by the producers of toxic securities to award them top grades; offshore shadow banking, money laundering and assistance in large-scale tax evasion as the normal business of the biggest banks with the best addresses; the sale to unsuspecting customers of securities constructed so that other customers could bet against them; the leading banks worldwide fraudulently fixing interest rates and the gold price, and so on. In recent years, several large banks have had to pay billions of dollars in fines for

40   Including at the highest level: both Blair and Sarkozy are now working for hedge funds, their time as elected national leaders apparently considered by them and their new employers as a sort of apprenticeship for a much better-paid position in the financial sector.

activities of this sort, and more developments of this kind seem to be in the offing. What at first glance may look like quite significant sanctions, however, appear minuscule when compared to the banks' balance sheets – not to mention the fact that all of these were out-of-court settlements of cases that governments didn't want or dare to prosecute.[41]

Capitalism's moral decline may have to do with its economic decline, the struggle for the last remaining profit opportunities becoming uglier by the day and turning into asset-stripping on a truly gigantic scale. However that may be, public perceptions of capitalism are now deeply cynical, the whole system commonly perceived as a world of dirty tricks for ensuring the further enrichment of the already rich. Nobody believes any more in a moral revival of capitalism. The Weberian attempt to prevent it from being confounded with greed has finally failed, as it has more than ever become synonymous with corruption.

A WORLD OUT OF JOINT

We come, finally, to the fifth disorder. Global capitalism needs a centre to secure its periphery and provide it with a credible monetary regime. Until the 1920s, this role was performed by Britain, and from 1945 until the 1970s by the United States; the years in between, when a centre was missing, and different powers aspired to take on the role, were a time of chaos, economically as well as politically. Stable relations between the currencies of the countries participating in the capitalist world economy are essential for trade and capital flows across national borders, which are in turn essential for capital accumulation; they need to be underwritten by a global banker of last resort. An effective centre is also required to support regimes on the periphery willing to condone the low-price extraction of raw materials. Moreover, local collaboration is needed to hold down traditionalist opposition to capitalist *Landnahme* outside the developed world.

Contemporary capitalism increasingly suffers from global anarchy, as the United States is no longer able to serve in its post-war role, and a multipolar world order is nowhere on the horizon. While there are (still?) no Great-Power clashes, the dollar's function as international reserve currency is contested – and cannot be otherwise, given the declining performance of the American economy, its rising levels of public and private debt and the recent experience of several highly destructive financial crises. The search for an international

---

41   Reports on banks having to pay fines for wrongdoings of various kinds can be found almost daily in quality newspapers. On 23 March 2014, the *Frankfurter Allgemeine Zeitung* reported that since the beginning of the financial crisis, American banks alone have been fined around one hundred billion dollars.

alternative, perhaps in the form of a currency basket, is getting nowhere since the United States cannot afford to give up the privilege of indebting itself in its own currency. Moreover, stabilizing measures taken by international organizations at Washington's behest have increasingly tended to have destabilizing effects on the periphery of the system, as in the case of the inflationary bubbles caused in countries like Brazil and Turkey by 'quantitative easing' in the centre.

Militarily, the United States has now been either defeated or deadlocked in three major land wars since the 1970s, and will in future probably be more reluctant to intervene in local conflicts with 'boots on the ground'. New, sophisticated means of violence are being deployed to reassure collaborating governments and inspire confidence in the United States as a global enforcer of oligarchic property rights, and as a safe haven for oligarchic families and their treasure. They include the use of highly secretive 'special forces' to seek out potential enemies for individualized destruction; unmanned aircraft capable of killing anybody at almost any place on the globe; confinement and torture of unknown numbers of people in a worldwide system of secret prison camps; and comprehensive surveillance of potential opposition everywhere with the help of 'big data' technology. Whether this will be enough to restore global order, especially in light of China's rise as an effective economic and, to a lesser extent, military rival to the United States may, however, be doubted.

In summary, capitalism, as a social order held together by a promise of boundless collective progress, is in critical condition. Growth is giving way to secular stagnation; what economic progress remains is less and less shared; and confidence in the capitalist money economy is leveraged on a rising mountain of promises that are ever less likely to be kept. Since the 1970s, the capitalist centre has undergone three successive crises, of inflation, public finances and private debt. Today, in an uneasy phase of transition, its survival depends on central banks providing it with unlimited synthetic liquidity. Step by step, capitalism's shotgun marriage with democracy since 1945 is breaking up. On the three frontiers of commodification – labour, nature and money – regulatory institutions restraining the advance of capitalism for its own good have collapsed, and after the final victory of capitalism over its enemies no political agency capable of rebuilding them is in sight. The capitalist system is at present stricken with at least five worsening disorders for which no cure is at hand: declining growth, oligarchy, starvation of the public sphere, corruption and international anarchy. What is to be expected, on the basis of capitalism's recent historical record, is a long and painful period of cumulative decay: of intensifying frictions, of fragility and uncertainty, and of a steady succession of 'normal accidents' – not necessarily but quite possibly on the scale of the global breakdown of the 1930s.

CHAPTER TWO

The Crises of Democratic Capitalism

The collapse of the American financial system that occurred in 2008 has since turned into an economic and political crisis of global dimensions.[1] How should this world-shaking event be conceptualized? Mainstream economics has tended to conceive society as governed by a general tendency towards equilibrium, where crises and change are no more than temporary deviations from the steady state of a normally well-integrated system. A sociologist, however, is under no such compunction. Rather than construe our present affliction as a one-off disturbance to a fundamental condition of stability, I will consider the 'Great Recession'[2] and the subsequent near-collapse of public finances as a manifestation of a basic underlying tension in the political-economic configuration of advanced-capitalist societies; a tension which makes disequilibrium and instability the rule rather than the exception, and which has found expression in a historical succession of disturbances within the socio-economic order. More specifically, I will argue that the present crisis can only be fully understood in terms of the ongoing, inherently conflictual transformation of the social formation we call 'democratic capitalism'.

Democratic capitalism was fully established only after the Second World War and then only in the 'Western' parts of the world, North America and Western Europe. There it functioned extraordinarily well for the next two decades – so well, in fact, that this period of uninterrupted economic growth still dominates our ideas and expectations of what modern capitalism is, or could and should be. This is in spite of the fact that, in the light of the turbulence that followed, the quarter century immediately after the war should be recognizable as truly exceptional. Indeed, I suggest that it is not the *trente glorieuses* but the series of crises which followed that represents the normal condition of democratic capitalism – a condition ruled by an endemic conflict between capitalist markets and democratic politics, which forcefully reasserted itself when high economic growth came to an end in the 1970s. In what follows I will first discuss the nature of that conflict and then turn to the

---

1 An earlier version of this chapter was given as the 2011 Max Weber Lecture at the European University Institute, Florence. I am grateful to Daniel Mertens for his research assistance. Published in: *New Left Review* 71, September/October 2011, pp. 5–29.

2 For the term 'Great Recession', see Carmen Reinhart and Kenneth Rogoff, *This Time Is Different: Eight Centuries of Financial Folly*, Princeton, NJ: Princeton University Press 2009.

sequence of political-economic disturbances that it produced, which both preceded and shaped the present global crisis.

MARKETS VERSUS VOTERS?

Suspicions that capitalism and democracy may not sit easily together are far from new. From the nineteenth century and well into the twentieth, the bourgeoisie and the political Right expressed fears that majority rule, inevitably implying the rule of the poor over the rich, would ultimately do away with private property and free markets. The rising working class and the political Left, for their part, warned that capitalists might ally themselves with the forces of reaction to abolish democracy, in order to protect themselves from being governed by a permanent majority dedicated to economic and social redistribution. I will not discuss the relative merits of the two positions, although history suggests that, at least in the industrialized world, the Left had more reason to fear the Right overthrowing democracy, in order to save capitalism, than the Right had to fear the Left abolishing capitalism for the sake of democracy. However that may be, in the years immediately after the Second World War there was a widely shared assumption that for capitalism to be compatible with democracy, it would have to be subjected to extensive political control – for example, nationalization of key firms and sectors, or workers' 'co-determination', as in Germany – in order to protect democracy itself from being restrained in the name of free markets. While Keynes and, to some extent, Kalecki and Polanyi carried the day, Hayek withdrew into temporary exile.

Since then, however, mainstream economics has become obsessed with the 'irresponsibility' of opportunistic politicians who cater to an economically uneducated electorate by interfering with otherwise efficient markets, in pursuit of objectives – such as full employment and social justice – that truly free markets would in the long run deliver anyway, but must fail to deliver when distorted by politics. Economic crises, according to standard theories of 'public choice', essentially stem from market-distorting political interventions for social objectives.[3] In this view, the right kind of intervention sets markets free from political interference; the wrong, market-distorting kind derives from an excess of democracy; more precisely, from democracy being carried over by irresponsible politicians into the economy, where it has no business. Not many today would go as far as Hayek, who in his later years advocated

---

3   The classic statement is Buchanan and Tullock, *The Calculus of Consent: Logical Foundations of Constitutional Democracy*.

abolishing democracy as we know it in defence of economic freedom and civil liberty. Still, the *cantus firmus* of current neo-institutionalist economic theory is thoroughly Hayekian. To work properly, capitalism requires a rule-bound economic policy, with protection of markets and property rights constitutionally enshrined against discretionary political interference; independent regulatory authorities; central banks, firmly protected from electoral pressures; and international institutions, such as the European Commission or the European Court of Justice, that do not have to worry about popular re-election. Such theories studiously avoid the crucial question of how to get there from here, however; very likely because they have no answer, or at least none that can be made public.

There are various ways to conceptualize the underlying causes of the friction between capitalism and democracy. For present purposes, I will characterize democratic capitalism as a political economy ruled by two conflicting principles, or regimes, of resource allocation: one operating according to marginal productivity, or what is revealed as merit by a 'free play of market forces', and the other based on social need or entitlement, as certified by the collective choices of democratic politics. Under democratic capitalism, governments are theoretically required to honour both principles simultaneously, although substantively the two almost never align. In practice they may for a time neglect one in favour of the other, until they are punished by the consequences: governments that fail to attend to democratic claims for protection and redistribution risk losing their majority, while those that disregard the claims for compensation from the owners of productive resources, as expressed in the language of marginal productivity, cause economic dysfunctions that will become increasingly unsustainable and thereby also undermine political support.

In the liberal utopia of standard economic theory, the tension in democratic capitalism between its two principles of allocation is overcome by turning the theory into what Marx would have called a material force. In this view, economics as 'scientific knowledge' teaches citizens and politicians that true justice is market justice, under which everybody is rewarded according to their contribution, rather than their needs redefined as rights. To the extent that economic theory became accepted as a social theory, it would 'come true' in the sense of being performative – thus revealing its essentially rhetorical nature as an instrument of social construction by persuasion. In the real world, however, it did not prove so easy to talk people out of their 'irrational' beliefs in social and political rights, as distinct from the law of the market and the right of property. To date, non-market notions of social justice have resisted efforts at economic rationalization, forceful as the latter may have become in the leaden age of advancing neoliberalism. People stubbornly refused to give up on the idea of a moral economy under which they have rights that take precedence over the outcomes of market exchanges.[4] In fact, where they have a chance – as they inevitably do in a working democracy – they tend in one way or another to insist on the primacy of the social over the economic; on social commitments and obligations being protected from market pressures for 'flexibility'; and on society honouring human expectations of a life outside the dictatorship of ever-fluctuating 'market signals'. This is arguably what Polanyi described as a 'counter-movement' against the commodification of labour in *The Great Transformation*.

For the economic mainstream, disorders like inflation, public deficits and excessive private or public debt result from insufficient knowledge of the laws governing the economy as a wealth-creation machine, or from disregard of such laws in selfish pursuit of political power. By contrast, theories of political economy – to the extent that they take the political seriously and are not just functionalist efficiency theories – recognize market allocation as just one type of political-economic regime, governed by the interests of those owning scarce productive resources and thus in a strong market position. An alternative regime, political allocation, is preferred by those with little economic weight but potentially extensive political power. From this perspective, standard economics is basically the theoretical exaltation of a political-economic social order serving those well-endowed with market power, in that it equates their interests with the general interest. It represents the distributional claims of the owners of productive capital as technical imperatives of good, in the sense of scientifically sound, economic management. For political economy, mainstream economics' account of dysfunctions in the economy as being the result of a cleavage between traditionalist principles of moral economy and rational-modern principles amounts to a tendentious misrepresentation, for it hides the fact that the 'economic' economy is *also* a moral economy, for those with commanding powers in the market.

In the language of mainstream economics, crises appear as punishment for governments failing to respect the natural laws that are the true governors of the economy. By contrast, a theory of political economy worth its name perceives crises as manifestations of the 'Kaleckian reactions' of the owners of productive resources to democratic politics penetrating into their exclusive domain, trying to prevent them from exploiting their market power to the

---

4   See Edward Thompson, 'The Moral Economy of the English Crowd in the Eighteenth Century', *Past & Present*, vol. 50, no. 1, 1971; and James Scott, *The Moral Economy of the Peasant: Rebellion and Subsistence in Southeast Asia*, New Haven, CT: Yale University Press 1976. The exact content of such rights obviously varies between different social and historical locations.

fullest and thereby violating their expectations of being justly rewarded for their astute risk-taking.[5] Standard economic theory treats social structure and the distribution of interests and power vested in it as exogenous, holding them constant and thereby making them both invisible and, for the purposes of economic 'science', naturally given. The only politics such a theory can envisage involves opportunistic or, at best, incompetent attempts to bend economic laws. Good economic policy is non-political by definition. The problem is that this view is not shared by the many for whom politics is a much-needed recourse against markets, whose unfettered operation interferes with what they happen to feel is right. Unless they are somehow persuaded to adopt neoclassical economics as a self-evident model of what social life is and should be, their political demands as democratically expressed will differ from the prescriptions of standard economic theory. The implication is that while an economy, if sufficiently conceptually disembedded, may be modelled as tending towards equilibrium, a political economy may not, unless it is devoid of democracy and run by a Platonic dictatorship of economist-kings. Capitalist politics, as will be seen, has done its best to lead us out of the desert of corrupt democratic opportunism into the promised land of self-regulating markets. Up to now, however, democratic resistance continues, and with it the dislocations in our market economies to which it continuously gives rise.

POST-WAR SETTLEMENTS

Post-war democratic capitalism underwent its first crisis in the decade following the late 1960s, when inflation began to rise rapidly throughout the Western world as declining economic growth made it difficult to sustain the political-economic peace formula between capital and labour that had ended domestic strife after the devastations of the Second World War. Essentially

---

5   In a seminal essay, Michał Kalecki identified the 'confidence' of investors as a crucial factor determining economic performance ('Political Aspects of Full Employment'). Investor confidence, according to Kalecki, depends on the extent to which current profit expectations of capital owners are reliably sanctioned by the distribution of political power and the policies to which it gives rise. Economic dysfunctions – unemployment in Kalecki's case – ensue when business sees its profit expectations threatened by political interference. 'Wrong' policies in this sense result in a loss of business confidence, which in turn may result in what would amount to an investment strike of capital owners. Kalecki's perspective makes it possible to model a capitalist economy as an interactive game, as distinguished from a natural or machine-like mechanism. In this perspective, the point at which capitalists react adversely to non-market allocation by withdrawing investment need not be seen as fixed and mathematically predictable but may be negotiable. For example, it may be set by a historically changeable level of aspiration or by strategic calculation. This is why predictions based on universalistic, i.e., historically and culturally indifferent, economic models so often fail: they assume fixed parameters where in reality these are socially determined.

that formula entailed the organized working classes accepting capitalist markets and property rights in exchange for political democracy, which enabled them to achieve social security and a steadily rising standard of living. More than two decades of uninterrupted growth resulted in deeply rooted popular perceptions of continuous economic progress as a right of democratic citizenship – perceptions that translated into political expectations, which governments felt constrained to honour but were less and less able to, as growth began to slow.

The structure of the post-war settlement between labour and capital was fundamentally the same across the otherwise widely different countries where democratic capitalism had come to be instituted. It included an expanding welfare state, the right of workers to free collective bargaining and a political guarantee of full employment, underwritten by governments making extensive use of the Keynesian economic toolkit. When growth began to falter in the late 1960s, however, this combination became difficult to maintain. While free collective bargaining enabled workers through their unions to act on what had become firmly ingrained expectations of regular yearly wage increases, governments' commitment to full employment, together with a growing welfare state, protected unions from potential employment losses caused by wage settlements in excess of productivity growth. Government policy thus leveraged the bargaining power of trade unions beyond what a free labour market would have sustained. In the late 1960s this found expression in a worldwide wave of labour militancy, fuelled by a strong sense of political entitlement to a rising standard of living and unchecked by fear of unemployment.

In subsequent years governments all over the Western world faced the question of how to make trade unions moderate their members' wage demands without having to rescind the Keynesian promise of full employment. In countries where the institutional structure of the collective-bargaining system was not conducive to the negotiation of tripartite 'social pacts', most governments remained convinced throughout the 1970s that allowing unemployment to rise in order to contain real wage increases was too risky for their own survival, if not for the stability of capitalist democracy as such. Their only way out was an accommodating monetary policy which, while allowing free collective bargaining and full employment to continue to coexist, did so at the expense of raising the rate of inflation to levels that accelerated over time.

In its early stages, inflation was not much of a problem for workers represented by strong trade unions and politically powerful enough to achieve *de facto* wage indexation. Inflation comes primarily at the expense of creditors and holders of financial assets, groups that do not as a rule include workers, or at least did not do so in the 1960s and 1970s. This is why inflation can be

described as a monetary reflection of distributional conflict between a working class, demanding both employment security and a higher share in their
country's income, and a capitalist class striving to maximize the return on its
capital. As the two sides act on mutually incompatible ideas of what is theirs by
right, one emphasizing the entitlements of citizenship and the other those of
property and market power, inflation may also be considered an expression of
anomie in a society which, for structural reasons, cannot agree on common
criteria of social justice. It was in this sense that the British sociologist, John
Goldthorpe, suggested in the late 1970s that high inflation was ineradicable in
a democratic-capitalist market economy that allowed workers and citizens to
correct market outcomes through collective political action.[6]

For governments facing conflicting demands from workers and capital in
a world of declining growth rates, an accommodating monetary policy was a
convenient ersatz method for avoiding zero-sum social conflict. In the immediate post-war years, economic growth had provided governments struggling
with incompatible concepts of economic justice with additional goods and
services by which to defuse class antagonisms. Now governments had to make
do with additional money, as yet uncovered by the real economy, as a way of
pulling forward future resources into present consumption and distribution.
This mode of conflict pacification, effective as it at first was, could not continue
indefinitely. As Hayek never tired of pointing out, accelerating inflation is
bound to give rise to ultimately unmanageable economic distortions in relative prices, in the relation between contingent and fixed incomes, and in what
economists refer to as 'economic incentives'. In the end, by calling forth
Kaleckian reactions from increasingly suspicious capital owners, inflation will
produce unemployment, punishing the very workers whose interests it may
initially have served. At this point at the latest, governments under democratic
capitalism will come under pressure to cease accommodating redistributive
wage settlements and restore monetary discipline.

LOW INFLATION, HIGHER UNEMPLOYMENT

Inflation was conquered after 1979 (Figure 2.1) when Paul Volcker, newly
appointed by President Carter as chairman of the Federal Reserve Bank, raised
interest rates to an unprecedented height, causing unemployment to jump to
levels not seen since the Great Depression. The Volcker 'putsch' was sealed
when President Reagan, said to have initially been afraid of the political fallout

---

6 John Goldthorpe, 'The Current Inflation: Towards a Sociological Account'. In: Hirsch, Fred and
John Goldthorpe, eds, *The Political Economy of Inflation*, Cambridge, MA: Harvard University Press 1978.

Figure 2.1: Inflation rates, 1970–2014

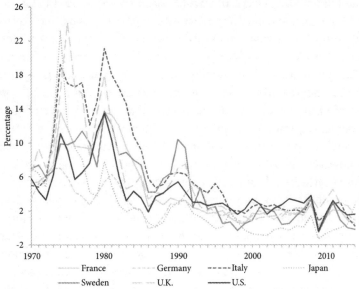

Source: OECD Main Economic Indicators.

Figure 2.2: Unemployment rates, 1970–2014

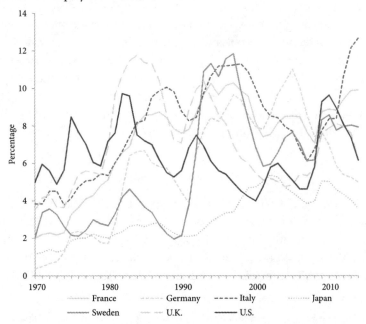

Source: OECD Economic Outlook Database Nos. 92 & 98.

of Volcker's aggressive disinflation policies, was re-elected in 1984. Thatcher, who had followed the American lead, had won a second term in 1983, also in spite of high unemployment and rapid de-industrialization caused, among other things, by a restrictive monetary policy. In both the United States and the United Kingdom, disinflation was accompanied by determined attacks on trade unions by governments and employers, epitomized by Reagan's victory over the air traffic controllers and Thatcher's breaking of the National Union of Mineworkers. In subsequent years, inflation rates throughout the capitalist world remained continuously low, while unemployment went more or less steadily up (Figure 2.2). In parallel, unionization declined almost everywhere, and strikes became so infrequent that some countries ceased to keep strike statistics (Figure 2.3).

The neoliberal era began with Anglo-American governments casting aside the received wisdom of post-war democratic capitalism, which held that unemployment would undermine political support, not just for the government of the day but also for democratic capitalism itself. The experiments conducted by Reagan and Thatcher on their electorates were observed with great attention by policymakers worldwide. Those who may have hoped that the end of inflation would mean an end to economic disorder were soon to be

Figure 2.3: Strike days per 1,000 employees, 1971–2007

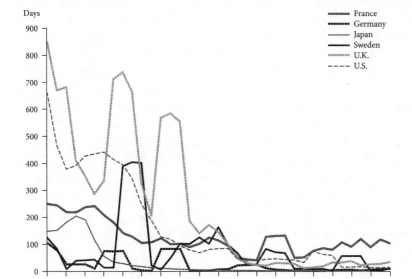

Source: Author's calculations of three-year moving averages based on ILO Labour Statistics Database and OECD Labour Force Statistics.

disappointed, however. As inflation receded, public debt began to increase, and not entirely unexpectedly.[7] Rising public debt in the 1980s had many causes. Stagnant growth had made taxpayers more averse than ever to taxation; and with the end of inflation, automatic tax increases through what was called 'bracket creep' also came to an end. The same held for the continuous devaluation of public debt through weakening national currencies, a process that had first complemented economic growth, and then increasingly substituted for it, reducing a country's accumulated debt relative to its nominal income. On the expenditure side, rising unemployment, caused by monetary stabilization, required rising expenditures on social assistance. Also the various social entitlements created in the 1970s in return for trade-union wage moderation – as it were, deferred wages from the neo-corporatist era – began to mature and become due, increasingly burdening public finances.

With inflation no longer available for closing the gap between the demands of citizens and those of 'the markets', the burden of securing social peace fell on the state. Public debt turned out, for a while, to be a convenient functional equivalent of inflation. As with inflation, public debt made it possible to introduce resources into the distributional conflicts of the time that had not yet in fact been produced, enabling governments to draw on future resources in addition to those already on hand. As the struggle between market and social distribution moved from the labour market to the political arena, electoral pressure replaced trade-union demands. Instead of inflating the currency, governments began to borrow on an increasing scale to accommodate demands for benefits and services as a citizen's right, together with competing claims for incomes to reflect the judgement of the market and thereby help maximize the profitable use of productive resources. Low inflation was helpful in this, since it assured creditors that government bonds would keep their value over the long haul; so were the low interest rates that followed when inflation had been stamped out.

Just like inflation, however, accumulation of public debt cannot go on forever. Economists had long warned of public deficit spending 'crowding out' private investment, causing high interest rates and low growth; but they were never able to specify where exactly the critical threshold was. In practice, it turned out to be possible, at least for a while, to keep interest rates low by deregulating financial markets while containing inflation through continued

7   Already in the 1950s Anthony Downs had noted that in a democracy the demands from citizens for public services tended to exceed the supply of resources available to government; see for example, 'Why the Government Budget Is Too Small in a Democracy', *World Politics*, vol. 12, no. 4, 1960. See also James O'Connor, 'The Fiscal Crisis of the State', *Socialist Revolution*, vol. 1, nos. 1 and 2, 1970.

union-busting.[8] Still, the US in particular, with its exceptionally low national savings rate, was soon selling its government bonds not just to citizens but also to foreign investors, including sovereign wealth funds of various sorts.[9] Moreover, as debt burdens rose, a growing share of public spending had to be devoted to debt service, even with interest rates remaining low. Above all, there had to be a point, although apparently unknowable beforehand, at which creditors, foreign and domestic alike, would begin to worry about getting their money back. By then at the latest, pressures would begin to mount from 'financial markets' for consolidation of public budgets and a return to fiscal discipline.

DEREGULATION AND PRIVATE DEBT

The 1992 presidential election in the United States was dominated by the question of the two deficits: that of the federal government and that of the country as a whole, in foreign trade. The victory of Bill Clinton, who had campaigned above all on the 'double deficit', set off worldwide attempts at fiscal consolidation, aggressively promoted under American leadership by international organizations such as the OECD and the IMF. Initially the Clinton administration seems to have envisaged closing the public deficit by accelerated economic growth brought about by social reform, such as increased public investment in education.[10] But once the Democrats lost their Congressional majority in the 1994 midterm elections, Clinton turned to a policy of austerity involving deep cuts in public spending and changes in social policy which, in the words of the president, were to put an end to 'welfare as we know it'. From 1998 to 2000, the U.S. federal government for the first time in decades was running a budget surplus.

This is not to say, however, that the Clinton administration had somehow found a way of pacifying a democratic-capitalist political economy without recourse to additional, yet-to-be-produced economic resources. The Clinton strategy of social-conflict management drew heavily on the deregulation of the financial sector that had already started under Reagan and was now driven further than ever before.[11] Rapidly rising income inequality, caused by

---

8   Greta Krippner, *Capitalizing on Crisis: The Political Origins of the Rise of Finance*, Cambridge, MA: Harvard University Press 2011.

9   David Spiro, *The Hidden Hand of American Hegemony: Petrodollar Recycling and International Markets*, Ithaca, NY: Cornell University Press 1999.

10   Robert Reich, *Locked in the Cabinet*, New York: Vintage 1997.

11   Joseph Stiglitz, *The Roaring Nineties: A New History of the World's Most Prosperous Decade*, New York: W. W. Norton 2003.

continuing de-unionization and sharp cuts in social spending, as well as the reduction in aggregate demand caused by fiscal consolidation, were counter-balanced by unprecedented new opportunities for citizens and firms to indebt themselves. The felicitous term, 'privatized Keynesianism', was coined to describe what was, in effect, the replacement of public with private debt.[12] Instead of the government borrowing money to fund equal access to decent housing, or the formation of marketable work skills, it was now individual citizens who, under a debt regime of extreme generosity, were allowed, and sometimes compelled, to take out loans at their own risk with which to pay for their education or their advancement to a less destitute urban neighbourhood.

The Clinton policy of fiscal consolidation and economic revitalization through financial deregulation had many beneficiaries. The rich were spared higher taxes, while those among them wise enough to move their interests into the financial sector made huge profits on the evermore complicated 'financial services' which they now had an almost unlimited licence to sell. But the poor also prospered, at least some of them and for a while. Subprime mortgages became a substitute, however illusory in the end, for the social policy that was simultaneously being scrapped, as well as for the wage increases that were no longer forthcoming at the lower end of a 'flexibilized' labour market. For African-Americans in particular, owning a home was not just the 'American dream' come true but also a much-needed substitute for the old-age pensions that many were unable to earn in the labour markets of the day and which they had no reason to expect from a government pledged to permanent austerity.

For a time, home ownership offered the middle class and even some of the poor an attractive opportunity to participate in the speculative craze that was making the rich so much richer in the 1990s and early 2000s – treacherous as that opportunity would later turn out to have been. As house prices escalated under rising demand from people who would, in normal circumstances, never have been able to buy a home, it became common practice to use the new financial instruments to extract part or all of one's home equity to finance the – rapidly rising – costs of the next generation's college education, or simply for personal consumption to offset stagnant or declining wages. Nor was it uncommon for home owners to use their new credit to buy a second or third dwelling, in the hope of cashing in on what was somehow expected to be an open-ended increase in the value of real estate. In this way, unlike the era of public debt when future resources were procured for present use by government borrowing, now such resources were made available by a myriad of individuals selling, in liberalized financial markets, commitments to pay a significant share of their expected future earnings to creditors, who in return provided them with the instant power to purchase whatever they liked.

Financial liberalization thus compensated for an era of fiscal consolidation and public austerity. Individual debt replaced public debt, and individual demand, constructed for high fees by a rapidly growing money-making industry, took the place of state-governed collective demand in supporting employment and profits in construction and other sectors (Figure 2.4). These dynamics accelerated after 2001, when the Federal Reserve switched to very low interest rates to prevent an economic slump and the return of high unemployment this implied. In addition to unprecedented profits in the financial sector, privatized Keynesianism sustained a booming economy that became the envy not least of European labour movements. In fact, Alan Greenspan's policy of easy money supporting the rapidly growing indebtedness of American society was held up as a model by European trade-union leaders, who noted with great excitement that, unlike the European Central Bank, the Federal Reserve was bound by law not just to provide monetary stability but also high levels of employment. All of this, of course, ended in 2008 when the international credit pyramid on which the prosperity of the late 1990s and early 2000s had rested suddenly collapsed.

SOVEREIGN INDEBTEDNESS

With the crash of privatized Keynesianism in 2008, the crisis of postwar democratic capitalism entered its fourth and latest stage, after the successive eras of inflation, public deficits and private indebtedness (Figure 2.5).[13] With the global financial system poised to disintegrate, nation states sought to restore economic confidence by socializing the bad loans licensed in compensation for fiscal consolidation. Together with the fiscal expansion necessary to prevent a breakdown of the 'real economy', this resulted in a dramatic new increase in public deficits and public debt – a development that, it may be noted, was not at all due to frivolous overspending by opportunistic politicians or

---

13   The diagram shows the development in the lead capitalist country, the United States, where the four stages unfold in ideal-typical fashion. For other countries it is necessary to make allowances reflecting their particular circumstances, including their position in the global political economy. In Germany, for example, public debt already began to rise sharply in the 1970s. This corresponds to the fact that German inflation was low long before Volcker, due to the independence of the Bundesbank and the monetarist policies it adopted as early as 1974; Fritz Scharpf, *Crisis and Choice in European Social Democracy*, Ithaca, NY: Cornell University Press 1991.

Figure 2.4: Fiscal consolidation and private debt, as a percentage of GDP, 1995–2008

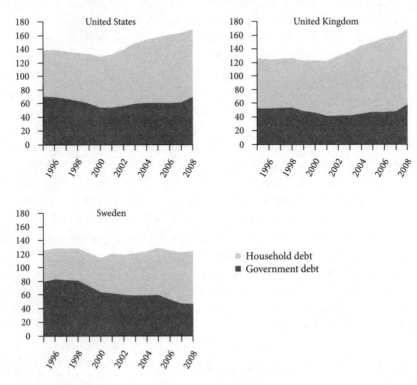

Source: OECD Economic Outlook Database No. 87, OECD National Accounts Database.

misconceived public institutions, as implied by theories of 'public choice' and the large institutional-economics literature produced in the 1990s under the auspices of, among others, the World Bank and the IMF.[14]

The quantum leap in public indebtedness after 2008, which completely undid whatever fiscal consolidation might have been achieved in the preceding decade, reflected the fact that no democratic state dared to impose on its society another economic crisis of the dimension of the Great Depression of the 1930s, as punishment for the excesses of a deregulated financial sector. Once again, political power was deployed to make future resources available for securing present social peace, in that states more or less voluntarily took

---

14   For a representative collection see Rolf R. Strauch and Jürgen von Hagen, eds, *Institutions, Politics and Fiscal Policy*, New York: Springer 2000.

Figure 2.5: Four crises of democratic capitalism in the U.S., 1970–2014

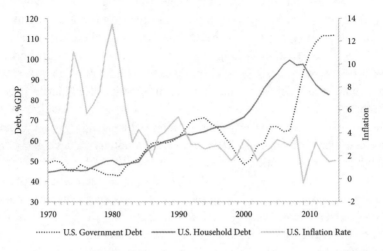

Source: OECD Economic Outlook Database No. 98, OECD National Accounts, OECD Main Economic Indicators Dataset.

upon themselves a significant share of the new debt originally created in the private sector, so as to reassure private-sector creditors. But while this effectively shored up the financial industry's money factories, quickly reinstating their extraordinary profits, salaries and bonuses, it could not prevent rising suspicions on the part of the same 'financial markets' that, in the process of rescuing them, national governments might have over-extended themselves. Even with the global economic crisis far from over, creditors began vociferously to demand a return to sound money through fiscal austerity, in search for reassurance that their vastly increased investment in government debt would not be lost.

In the three years since 2008, distributional conflict under democratic capitalism has turned into a complicated tug-of-war between global financial investors and sovereign nation states. Where in the past workers struggled with employers, citizens with finance ministers and private debtors with private banks, it is now financial institutions wrestling with the very states that they had only recently blackmailed into saving them. But the underlying configuration of power and interests is far more complex and still awaits systematic exploration. For example, since the crisis financial markets have returned to charging different states widely varying interest rates, thereby differentiating the pressure they apply on governments to make their citizens acquiesce in unprecedented spending cuts – in line, again, with a basically unmodified market logic of distribution. Given the amount of debt carried by most states today, even minor increases in the rate of interest on government bonds can cause fiscal disaster.[15] At the same time, markets must avoid pushing states into declaring sovereign bankruptcy, always an option for governments if market pressures become too strong. This is why other states have to be found that are willing to bail out those most at risk, in order to protect themselves from a general increase in interest rates on government bonds that the first default would cause. A similar type of 'solidarity' between states in the interest of investors is fostered where sovereign default would hit banks located outside the defaulting country, which might force the banks' home countries once again to nationalize huge amounts of bad debt in order to stabilize their economies.

There are still more ways in which the tension in democratic capitalism between demands for social rights and the workings of free markets expresses itself today. Some governments, including the Obama administration, have attempted to generate renewed economic growth through even more debt – in the hope that future consolidation policies will be assisted by a growth dividend. Others may be secretly hoping for a return to inflation, melting down accumulated debt by softly expropriating creditors – which would, like economic growth, mitigate the political tensions to be expected from austerity. At the same time, financial markets may be looking forward to a promising fight against political interference, once and for all reinstating market discipline and putting an end to all political attempts to subvert it.

Further complications arise from the fact that financial markets need government debt for safe investment; pressing too hard for balanced budgets may deprive them of highly desirable investment opportunities. The middle classes of the advanced-capitalist countries have put a good part of their savings into government bonds, while many workers are now heavily invested in supplementary pensions. Balanced budgets would likely involve states having to take from their middle classes, in the form of higher taxes, what these classes now save and invest, among other things in public debt. Not only would citizens no longer collect interest, but they would also cease to be able to pass their savings on to their children. However, while this should make them interested in states being, if not debt-free, then reliably able to fulfil their obligations to their creditors, it may also mean that they have to pay for their government's liquidity in the form of deep cuts in public benefits and services on which they also in part depend.

---

15   For a state with public debt equalling 100 per cent of GDP, an increase by 2 percentage points in the average rate of interest it has to pay to its creditors would raise its yearly deficit by the same amount. A current budget deficit of 4 per cent of GDP would as a result increase by half.

However complicated the cross-cutting cleavages in the emerging international politics of public debt, the price for financial stabilization is likely to be paid by those other than the owners of money, or at least of real money. For example, public pension reform will be accelerated by fiscal pressures; and to the extent that governments default anywhere in the world, private pensions will be hit as well. The average citizen will pay – for the consolidation of public finances, the bankruptcy of foreign states, the rising rates of interest on the public debt and, if necessary, for another rescue of national and international banks – with his or her private savings, cuts in public entitlements, reduced public services and higher taxation.

SEQUENTIAL DISPLACEMENTS

In the four decades since the end of post-war growth, the epicentre of the tectonic tension within democratic capitalism has migrated from one institutional location to the next, giving rise to a sequence of different but systematically related economic disturbances. In the 1970s the conflict between democratic claims for social justice and capitalist demands for distribution by marginal productivity, or 'economic justice', played itself out primarily in national labour markets, where trade-union wage pressure under politically guaranteed full employment caused accelerating inflation. When what was, in effect, redistribution by debasement of the currency became economically unsustainable, forcing governments to put an end to it at high political risk, the conflict re-emerged in the electoral arena. Here it gave rise to growing disparity between public spending and public revenues and, as a consequence, to rapidly rising public debt, in response to voter demands for benefits and services in excess of what a democratic-capitalist economy could be made to hand over to its 'tax state'.[16]

When efforts to rein in public debt became unavoidable, however, they had to be accompanied for the sake of social peace by financial deregulation, easing access to private credit, as an alternative route to accommodating normatively and politically powerful demands of citizens for security and prosperity. This, too, lasted not much longer than a decade until the global economy almost faltered under the burden of unrealistic promises of future payment for present consumption and investment, licensed by governments in compensation for fiscal austerity. Since then, the clash between popular ideas of social justice and economic insistence on market justice has once again changed sites, re-emerging this time in international capital markets and the complex contests currently

---

16   Schumpeter, 'The Crisis of the Tax State'.

taking place between financial institutions and electorates, governments, states and international organizations. Now the issue is how far states can go in imposing the property rights and profit expectations of the markets on their citizens, while avoiding having to declare bankruptcy and protecting what may still remain of their democratic legitimacy.

Toleration of inflation, acceptance of public debt and deregulation of private credit were no more than temporary stopgaps for governments confronted with an apparently irrepressible conflict between the two contradictory principles of allocation under democratic capitalism: social rights on the one hand and marginal productivity, as evaluated by the market, on the other. Each of the three worked for a while, but then began to cause more problems than they solved, indicating that a lasting reconciliation between social and economic stability in capitalist democracies is a utopian project. All that governments were able to achieve in dealing with the crises of their day was to move them to new arenas, where they reappeared in new forms. There is no reason to believe that this process – the successive manifestation of democratic capitalism's contradictions, in ever new varieties of economic disorder – should have ended.

POLITICAL DISORDER

At this point, it seems clear that the political manageability of democratic capitalism has sharply declined in recent years, more in some countries than in others, but also overall, in the emerging global political-economic system. As a result, the risks seem to be growing, both for democracy and for the economy. Since the Great Depression, policymakers have rarely, if ever, been faced with as much uncertainty as today. One example among many is that the markets expect not just fiscal consolidation but also, and at the same time, a reasonable prospect of future economic growth. How the two may be combined is not at all clear. Although the risk premium on Irish government debt fell when the country pledged itself to aggressive deficit reduction, a few weeks later it rose again, allegedly because the country's consolidation programme appeared so strict that it would make economic recovery impossible.[17] Moreover, there is a widely shared conviction that the next bubble is already building somewhere in a world that is more than ever flooded with cheap money. Subprime mortgages may no longer offer themselves for

---

17   In other words, not even 'the markets' are willing to put their money on the supply-side mantra according to which growth is stimulated by cuts in public spending. On the other hand, who can say how much new debt is enough, and how much too much, for a country to outgrow its old debt.

investment, at least not for the time being. But there are the markets for raw materials, or the new internet economy. Nothing prevents financial firms from using the surplus of money provided by the central banks to enter whatever appear to be the new growth sectors, on behalf of their favourite clients and, of course, themselves. After all, with regulatory reform in the financial sector having failed in almost all respects, capital requirements are little higher than they were, and the banks that were too big to fail in 2008 can count on being so also in 2012 or 2013. This leaves them with the same capacity for blackmailing the public that they were able to deploy so skilfully three years ago. But now the public bailout of private capitalism on the model of 2008 may be impossible to repeat, if only because public finances are already stretched to the limit.

Yet democracy is as much at risk as the economy in the current crisis, if not more. Not only has the 'system integration' of contemporary societies – that is, the efficient functioning of their capitalist economies – become precarious, but so has their 'social integration'.[18] With the arrival of a new age of austerity, the capacity of national states to mediate between the rights of citizens and the requirements of capital accumulation has been severely affected. Governments everywhere face stronger resistance to tax increases, particularly in highly indebted countries where fresh public money will have to be spent for many years to pay for goods that have long been consumed. Moreover, with ever-tighter global interdependence, it is no longer possible to pretend that the tensions between economy and society, between capitalism and democracy, can be handled inside national political communities. No government today can govern without paying close attention to international constraints and obligations, including those of the financial markets forcing the state to impose sacrifices on its population. The crises and contradictions of democratic capitalism have finally become internationalized, playing themselves out not just within states but also between them, in combinations and permutations as yet unexplored.

As we now read almost every day in the papers, 'the markets' have begun to dictate in unprecedented ways what presumably sovereign and democratic states may still do for their citizens and what they must refuse them. The same Manhattan-based ratings agencies that were instrumental in bringing about the disaster of the global money industry are now threatening to downgrade the bonds of states that accepted a previously unimaginable level of new debt to rescue that industry and the capitalist economy as a whole. Politics still contains and distorts markets, but only, it seems, at a level far remote from the

---

18   The concepts were laid out by David Lockwood in 'Social Integration and System Integration'.

daily experience and organizational capacities of normal people: the United States, armed to the teeth not just with aircraft carriers but also with an unlimited supply of credit cards, still gets China to buy its mounting debt. All others have to listen to what 'the markets' tell them. As a result, citizens increasingly perceive their governments, not as *their* agents, but as those of other states or of international organizations, such as the IMF or the European Union, immeasurably more insulated from electoral pressure than was the traditional nation state. In countries like Greece and Ireland, anything resembling democracy will be effectively suspended for many years; in order to behave 'responsibly', as defined by international markets and institutions, national governments will have to impose strict austerity, at the price of becoming increasingly unresponsive to their citizens.[19]

Democracy is not just being pre-empted in those countries that are currently under attack by 'the markets'. Germany, which is still doing relatively well economically, has committed itself to decades of public expenditure cuts. In addition, the German government will again have to get its citizens to provide liquidity to countries at risk of defaulting, not just to save German banks but also to stabilize the common European currency and prevent a general increase in the rate of interest on public debt, as is likely to occur in the case of the first country collapsing. The high political cost of this can be measured in the progressive decay of the Merkel government's electoral capital, resulting in a series of defeats in major regional elections over the past year. Populist rhetoric to the effect that perhaps creditors should also pay a share of the costs, as vented by the Chancellor in early 2010, was quickly abandoned when 'the markets' expressed shock by slightly raising the rate of interest on new public debt. Now the talk is about the need to shift, in the words of the German finance minister, from old-fashioned 'government', which is no longer up to the new challenges of globalization, to 'governance', meaning in particular a lasting curtailment of the budgetary authority of the Bundestag.[20]

The political expectations that democratic states are now facing from their new principals may be impossible to meet. International markets and institutions require that not just governments but also citizens credibly commit

---

19   Peter Mair, *Representative versus Responsible Government*, MPIfG Working Paper 09/8, Cologne: Max Planck Institute for the Sutdy of Societies 2009.

20   According to Wolfgang Schäuble: 'We need new forms of international governance, global governance and European governance.' *Financial Times*, 5 December 2010. Schäuble acknowledged that if the German parliament was asked to forfeit its jurisdiction over the budget immediately, 'you would not get a Yes vote' – '[but] if you would give us some months to work on this, and if you give us the hope that other member states will agree as well, I would see a chance.' Schäuble was, fittingly, speaking as winner of the FT competition for European finance minister of the year.

themselves to fiscal consolidation. Political parties that oppose austerity must be resoundingly defeated in national elections, and both government and opposition must be publicly pledged to 'sound finance', or else the cost of debt service will rise. Elections in which voters have no effective choice, however, may be perceived by them as inauthentic, which may cause all sorts of political disorder, from declining turnout to a rise of populist parties to riots in the streets.

One factor here is that the arenas of distributional conflict have become ever more remote from popular politics. The national labour markets of the 1970s, with the manifold opportunities they offered for corporatist political mobilization and inter-class coalitions, or the politics of public spending in the 1980s, were not necessarily beyond the grasp or the strategic reach of the 'man in the street'. Since then, the battlefields on which the contradictions of democratic capitalism are fought out have become ever more complex, making it exceedingly difficult for anyone outside the political and financial elites to recognize the underlying interests and identify their own.[21] While this may generate apathy at the mass level and thereby make life easier for the elites, there is no relying on it, in a world in which blind compliance with financial investors is propounded as the only rational and responsible behaviour. To those who refuse to be talked out of other social rationalities and responsibilities, such a world may appear simply absurd – at which point the only rational and responsible conduct would be to throw as many wrenches as possible into the works of *haute finance*. Where democracy as we know it is effectively suspended, as it already is in countries like Greece, Ireland and Portugal, street riots and popular insurrection may be the last remaining mode of political expression for those devoid of market power. Should we hope in the name of democracy that we will soon have the opportunity to observe a few more examples?

Social science can do little, if anything, to help resolve the structural tensions and contradictions underlying the economic and social disorders of

---

21   For example, political appeals for redistributive 'solidarity' are now directed at entire nations asked by international organizations to support other entire nations, such as Slovenia being urged to help Ireland, Greece and Portugal. This hides the fact that those being supported by this sort of 'international solidarity' are not the people in the streets but the banks, domestic and foreign, that would otherwise have to accept losses, or lower profits. It also neglects differences in national income. While Germans are on average richer than Greeks (although some Greeks are much richer than almost all Germans), Slovenians are on average much poorer than the Irish, who have statistically a higher per capita income than nearly all Euro countries, including Germany. Essentially, the new conflict alignment translates class conflicts into international conflicts, pitting against each other nations that are each subject to the same financial market pressures for public austerity. Ordinary people are told to demand 'sacrifices' from other ordinary people, who happen to be citizens of other states, rather than from those who have long since resumed collecting their 'bonuses'.

the day. What it can do, however, is bring them to light and identify the historical continuities in which present crises can be fully understood. It also can – and must – point out the drama of democratic states being turned into debt-collecting agencies on behalf of a global oligarchy of investors, compared to which C. Wright Mills's 'power elite' appears a shining example of liberal pluralism.[22] More than ever, economic power seems today to have become political power, while citizens appear to be almost entirely stripped of their democratic defences and their capacity to impress upon the political economy interests and demands that are incommensurable with those of capital owners. In fact, looking back at the democratic-capitalist crisis sequence since the 1970s, there seems a real possibility of a new, if temporary, settlement of social conflict in advanced capitalism, this time entirely in favour of the propertied classes now firmly entrenched in their politically unassailable stronghold, the international financial industry.

---

22   C. Wright Mills, *The Power Elite*, Oxford: Oxford University Press 1956.

CHAPTER THREE

Citizens as Customers: Considerations on the New Politics of Consumption

Four decades ago, in a landmark *Public Interest* article titled 'Public Goods and Private Status', Joseph Monsen and Anthony Downs took up the question of why American society was, in the phrase coined by John Kenneth Galbraith, 'privately rich but publicly poor'.[1,2] The authors were not convinced by what they took to be the received explanation at the time: the 'clever and nefarious advertising techniques' used by large corporations to manipulate consumers, so that they would 'buy private goods and services they do not relatively need or want'. Instead, Monsen and Downs suggested 'a more fundamental factor' was at work, accounting for the differential allocation of goods between the public and private sectors: a 'desire' on the part of consumers 'for emulation and differentiation', driving them 'to create visible distinctions between large groups and classes, and, within such groups, more subtle distinctions of individuality'. Drawing on Veblen's notion of conspicuous consumption in *The Theory of the Leisure Class*, as well as 1960s explanations of status-seeking consumer behaviour in American society, Monsen and Downs described this desire as 'an intrinsic part of man's character, evident to at least some degrees in all societies, past and present' – 'so fundamental that it can be considered a "law" of human nature.'

Why should this 'law of consumer differentiation', conceived as something close to an anthropological constant, affect the relative allocation of resources between the private and the public spheres of a modern political economy? The central point of Monsen and Downs's argument is that what they call 'government goods' – those produced or distributed by public authorities – are 'designed with an eye to uniformity'. The standardization of army rifles is the most evident case in point:

> Such goods are easier to produce and administer by the bureaucracy, and they accord with the ideal of equality which underlies the distribution of government goods. But by that very nature, such goods cannot be used easily for

---

1   This chapter first appeared in: *New Left Review* 76, July/August 2012, 27–47.

2   R. Joseph Monsen and Anthony Downs, 'Public Goods and Private Status', *National Affairs*, vol. 23, Spring 1971, pp. 64–77.

status differentiation which is a major function of most goods in advanced industrial societies.

In what follows, I shall make use of Monsen and Downs's productive distinction between these two modes of provision, with inherent capacities favouring different kinds of goods: one mode is public and collective, administered by state authorities; the other is private and individual, mediated by commercial markets. But rather than comparing the two modes synchronically, or examining them within the eternal property space of economic anthropology, I will take a longitudinal view on the development of their mutual relationship. Moreover, instead of anchoring product diversification in a timeless human disposition towards status-seeking, I will relate it to a particular mode of utility maximization favoured in the transition from a need-supplying to a want-supplying economy, from sellers' to buyers' markets, and from poor to saturated to affluent societies, which was getting under way around the time (1971) that Monsen and Downs's article appeared. In this sense, I will suggest a return to the 'institutionalist' explanation for the starvation of the public sphere, which Monsen and Downs rejected in favour of their human-nature theory.

CUSTOMIZED COMMODITIES

The late 1960s and early '70s were, we now know, a watershed in the history of post-war democratic capitalism. It has become customary to speak of the crisis and eventual collapse of a more-or-less coherent, international production and consumption regime which, having sustained unprecedented economic growth during the *trente glorieuses*, began to be referred to summarily as Fordism. Today what is most often remembered about its demise may be the worldwide wave of labour militancy at the end of the 1960s, and with it the refusal of growing sections of the working class to subject themselves to the discipline of Taylorist factories, together with claims for shorter hours, better pay and politically guaranteed rights of citizenship in employment.

It was not just labour markets, however, that turned into a bottleneck for the progress of capitalist accumulation. Quite similar developments took place in product markets, and in fact changes in the two were intricately related. Fordism had entailed the mass production of standardized goods for societies in a secular transition from rural to urban and industrial ways of life, in which people spent their rising incomes on consumer durables like cars and refrigerators, which they were able to acquire for the first time in their families' lives. Needs were still obvious, scarcity was a fact, and what people demanded and could afford were products that were both cheap and reliable, with robust and

mature technology offered at low prices, made possible by extensive economies of scale. Product markets, consequently, were governed by large
oligopolistic firms which benefited from steadily growing demand, often at a
rate that made it difficult for production to keep up. In fact, for Fordist mass
producers, selling was much less of a problem than producing; customers were
used to long delivery dates and waited patiently for firms to supply them once
their allotted time had come.

Interviewing German managers with first-hand experience of the
watershed years, I sometimes heard them speak nostalgically of the
Zuteilungswirtschaft, or 'allocation economy', of the 1950s and '60s: all you had
to do was produce one standard product and then allocate it among a deeply
deferential clientele, happy to be served whenever it fitted into the firm's
production schedule. (Another German term would be *Versorgungswirtschaft*,
which might be translated as 'provision economy'.) Given the structure of
competition and their desire for low prices, customers did not expect to have
much choice; Henry Ford's dictum about his T2 model, that 'you can have it
any colour you like as long as it's black', still applied *grosso modo* to the relationship between producers and consumers in the sellers' markets of post-war
Fordism. I even heard managers suggest that the differences between the
organized capitalism of the post-war years in the West and the state socialism
of the East were not as dramatic as one might have believed at the time: only
that delivery periods were even longer in the East. Nor was there much difference between the private and the state sector: applying to the Post Office for a
telephone was quite similar to applying to Volkswagen for a new car; in both
cases there was a waiting period of half a year or more. In Western Europe, the
first wave of motorization was in fact supplied by state-owned or heavily
state-supported companies: Volkswagen in Germany, Renault in France,
British Leyland in Britain, FIAT in Italy.

By 1971 there were clear signs that the – in hindsight, idyllic – world of
post-war Fordism was coming to an end. As workers began to rebel, demanding an increasing share of profits after two decades of uninterrupted growth
and full employment, customers were also becoming more difficult.
Throughout the West, markets for mass-produced, standardized consumer
durables were showing signs of saturation. Basic needs had by and large been
covered; if the washing machine was still washing, why buy a new one?
Replacement purchases, however, could not sustain comparable rates of
growth. The emerging crisis manifested itself most visibly among the prototypical mass producers of the Fordist age, the automobile industry, whose
manufacturing capacity had grown inordinately, but which now found itself
squeezed between increasing worker resistance to its Taylorist factory regime

and growing consumer indifference to its mass-market product regime. In the early 1970s sales of the Volkswagen Beetle suddenly plummeted and Volkswagen as a company entered into a crisis so deep that many took it as the beginning of its end.[3] 'Limits to growth' became a central topic of public discourse, with capitalist firms and democratic governments embarking on a desperate search for a new formula to overcome what threatened to be a fundamental crisis of capitalist political economy.

Today we can see how that crisis resulted in a wave of profound restructuring of both production processes and product lines. Worker militancy was vanquished, not least through a secular expansion of the available labour supply, first by the mass entry of women into paid employment, and then by the internationalization of production systems. More important for our context were the strategies that firms deployed in their attempt to overcome the crisis of the product markets. While some on the left were still hoping for an end to both 'alienated labour' and the 'tyranny of consumption', capitalist firms were busy re-engineering their products and processes, with the help of new micro-electronic technologies capable of dramatically shortening production cycles; making manufacturing machinery less dedicated, thereby lowering the break-even point for their products; and rendering much manual labour dispensable, or at least enabling firms to relocate to other parts of the world where it was cheaper and more deferential.

In short, capital's answer to the secular stagnation of markets for standardized goods at the end of the Fordist era included making goods less standardized. The re-engineering of product ranges now went far beyond the yearly changes in hubcaps and tail fins that American automakers had invented to accelerate product obsolescence (which in the late '60s provided Monsen and Downs with the evidence for their 'law of consumer differentiation'). By the 1980s, accelerated product design and more flexible production equipment and labour made it possible to customize the commodities of the Fordist world to an unprecedented extent, subdividing the large and uniform product runs of industrial mass production into ever-smaller series of differentiated sub-products, in an effort to get closer to the idiosyncratic preferences of ever-smaller groups of potential customers.[4] As mass production gave way to something

---

3   See Wolfgang Streeck, *Industrial Relations in West Germany: The Case of the Car Industry*, New York: St. Martin's Press 1984.

4   This was described at the time as a transition from mass production to 'flexible specialization' (see Michael Piore and Charles Sabel, *The Second Industrial Divide: Possibilities for Prosperity*, New York: Basic Books 1984) or 'diversified quality production': see Wolfgang Streeck, 'On the Institutional Conditions of Diversified Quality Production'. In: Matzner, Egon and Wolfgang Streeck, eds, *Beyond Keynesianism: The Socio-Economics of Production and Employment*, London: Edward Elgar 1991, pp. 21–61.

like large-scale boutique production, customers were increasingly spared the compromises they had had to make when purchasing the standardized goods of old – where there always remained a gap between what different buyers might ideally have liked and the one-size-must-fit-all product that producers were able to provide. Product differentiation matched manufactured goods – and, increasingly, services – more closely to individual consumers' particular utility functions. At the same time, it enabled and encouraged consumers to refine that function, by developing or paying more attention to their individual wants, on top of the common needs served by standardized products.

What made the customization of product ranges economically attractive, and eventually helped capitalist economies move on from the stagnation of the 1970s, was the degree to which it increased the value-added of industrial production: the closer products came to the specific preferences of consumers, the more consumers turned out to be willing to pay – and, indeed, the harder they were prepared to work and the more they were prepared to borrow for the purchasing power needed to participate in the new paradigm of economic growth, with the transition it involved from saturated to affluent markets. With the advance of the micro-electronic revolution, the range of available car models multiplied to such an extent that customers could be invited to design their new car themselves, by specifying their individual preferences. By the 1980s, no two cars built on the same day at the Volkswagen plant in Wolfsburg were completely identical. In the process, and not by accident, cars became both more complex and more expensive, with industry profits recovering where the new product strategy had been successfully implemented.

The customization of commodities that aimed to overcome the stagnation of capital accumulation at the end of the Fordist period was part and parcel of a powerful wave of commercialization of the capitalist societies of the time. Product diversification attends to the wants of consumers which, under mass production, had remained commercially untapped; now they could be activated and made profitable. I will not go into the important question of whether this process was consumer- or producer-driven – the issue over which Monsen and Downs, opting for the primacy of demand over supply, saw themselves at odds with critics of private business like John Kenneth Galbraith. An examination of modern marketing, a crucial development of the period, suggests that both may in part be true. Marketing discovers, but typically also *develops* consumer preferences; it asks consumers what they would like, but it also proposes to them things they might be prepared to like, including things they never imagined could have existed. Good marketing, in this sense, co-opts consumers as co-designers, in an effort to haul more of their as-yet commercially idle wants, or potential wants, into market relations. It is true that this turns the seller's markets of Fordism into buyers' markets, empowering consumers in ways inconceivable just a few years earlier, and making life much more difficult for producers. But it also amounts to a giant step forward in the secular invasion of social life by 'market forces' under capitalism, a process that Rosa Luxemburg metaphorically characterized as *Landnahme*, or land-grabbing, in *The Accumulation of Capital*. In any case, paying more attention to the customer strongly suggested itself to profit-dependent firms as a way out of stagnation when markets had become saturated and, it seemed to some, when material incentives among the working classes to exert themselves for economic growth appeared on the brink of being critically weakened.[5]

SOCIATION BY CONSUMPTION

It is important to bear in mind the sheer extent of the commercialization of social life that aimed to save capitalism from the spectre of saturated markets after the watershed years. In effect, what firms learned in the 1970s was to put the individualization of both customers and products at the service of commercial expansion. Diversified consumption entailed hitherto unknown opportunities for the individualized expression of social identities. The 1970s and 1980s were also a time when traditional families and communities were rapidly losing authority, offering markets the opportunity to fill a fast-growing social vacuum, which contemporary liberation theorists had mistaken for the beginning of a new age of autonomy and emancipation. The possibilities for diversified consumption and the rise of niche markets, with the accelerated obsolescence they inflicted on first-generation consumer durables, also helped to motivate renewed work discipline, among both traditional workers and the newcomers to paid employment, not least the women.

Commercialized diversification – the movement of markets and commercial relations from the satisfaction of needs to the servicing of wants – extended far beyond automobiles. Other growth industries after the end of Fordism included luxury goods, from perfumes to watches to fashion, all following the same pattern of increased product differentiation and accelerated product

---

5   So at least it appeared to many 'critical theorists' in the 1970s. An early formulation was Claus Offe's 1967 dissertation, published as *Leistungsprinzip und industrielle Arbeit*, Frankfurt am Main: Europäische Verlagsanst 1970, which envisaged a secular withering away of the motivation for waged labour, caused, however, not by saturated demand but by changes in the organization of production. Offe anticipated growing pressure for life chances to be allocated on the basis of social rights, rather than on grounds of 'competitively demonstrated individual performance' (p. 166). The irresistible attractions of a redesigned range of highly diversified commodities may well have helped to sustain, indeed extend, competitive-possessive individualism and the legitimacy of differential rewards for differential performance.

turnover, promoted by evermore highly targeted marketing. A prototypical example was the range of Swatch watches, a marketing creation *par excellence* which first appeared in 1983, as Asian manufacturers began replacing mechanical clockwork with quartz-based microprocessors. Mass production did not disappear but became much more sophisticated, characteristically developing a market niche of its own, and thus becoming another instance of niche production. Alongside McDonald's, which itself eventually moved towards something like product diversification, local and regional cuisines were rediscovered, and *haute cuisine* expanded as never before. Wine production followed automobile production almost step-by-step in the 1980s, as vintners gave up on generic blends of different grapes from various locations and returned to producing a range of diverse products, each with identifiably individual character and origin.

The scale of the general turn towards commercialization is perhaps best illustrated by the world of sport. Well into the 1970s, the Olympic Games were the protected domain of so-called 'amateurs', who were not supposed to make any money at all on what was officially considered to be no more than their personal obsession or, as the case may have been, their patriotic duty. In a very short time, however, what used to be 'the Olympic movement' turned into a giant money-making machine, both for the athletes and for numerous corporate sponsors, the advertising industry, the media and a vast complex of other firms producing a range of consumer goods related to physical exercise or the body in general. Moreover, looking at how sport was transformed in the transition to affluence, one cannot but be struck by the stark difference between the austere ethos of strict discipline and self-control, rewarded by nothing than the honour of being allowed to participate, and the atmosphere of hedonistic entertainment with a strong smell of money that surrounds today's sporting events. The quasi-battlefields of the past became sites for professionally staged open-air parties, offering fans and athletes ample opportunity for celebratory self-presentation and for demonstrating their unlimited capacity to have fun. Fashion has come to play an essential part in this, for athletes as well as spectators. The transformation of sport as a social institution – from an ethos of asceticism to one of consumerist narcissism, in less than three decades – can be symbolized by the simultaneous rise of the two German firms, Adidas and Puma, from local producers of no more than two or three styles of football and running shoes, to multi-billion-dollar global companies that essentially make their money from fashion products, ranging from hundreds of permanently changing models of running shoes to, of all things, perfumes, both masculine and feminine.[6]

---

6   Critical writing on sport has long emphasized its function as a model for the world of work,

I would suggest that commercialization has created opportunities, and apparently quite attractive ones, for a new type of what Simmel called *Vergesellschaftung*, or sociation – that is, a way for individuals to link up to others and thereby define their place in the world. The vast variety of alternative possibilities of consumption in affluent post-Fordist markets provides a mechanism that allows people to conceive of an act of purchase – concluding, as it often does, a lengthy period of introspective exploration of one's very personal preferences – as an act of self-identification and self-presentation, one that sets the individual apart from some social groups while uniting him or her with others. Compared to more traditional modes of social integration, *Vergesellschaftung* by consumer choice appears more voluntary, resulting in social bonds and identities that are less restrictive – indeed, entirely free from obligations, apart from what Marx and Engels called *bare Zahlung*, or naked cash. This is because in a mature affluent market, buying something involves no more than picking what you like best (and can afford) from what is in principle an infinite menu of alternatives awaiting your decision, with no need to negotiate or compromise as one had to in traditional social relations. In fact the only other actors that one encounters operating in a social structure of advanced consumption are firms whose marketing departments specialize in guessing your every want and striving to satisfy them, regardless of how idiosyncratic they may be. Such firms never argue with customers; they listen and comply, and indeed make every effort to know what their customers desire long before they themselves know.

Sociation by consumption, then, is monological rather than dialogical in nature, voluntary rather than obligatory, individual rather than collective. It is from this perspective that it seems productive to speak of a particular *politics* of consumption, associated with the affluent societies of today. In mature post-Fordist markets, where alternatives are in almost infinite supply, it is easy to exit from collective identities that have been established by purchase, without a need for certification by 'significant others'. Obviously this condition is widely experienced as one of liberation, compared not just to having to buy standardized mass products but also to the constraining nature of traditional communities, like families, neighbourhoods or nations, and the collective identities they furnish. In fact even fashion is today far less binding – one might also say less oppressive – than it used to be under the uniform-production regime. There are now numerous co-existing sub-fashions, as it were, in

---

characterized by competition, differential rewards and measured time. The changes of the past decades have included much wider participation by women and untiring efforts by event designers to convince spectators that strenuous exertion need not prevent one from looking sexy and having fun.

music just as in clothes, most of them lasting only a few months before they pass away, in rapid rotation.

Since communities of consumption are much easier to abandon than traditional 'real' communities, social identities become structured by weaker and looser ties, allowing individuals to surf from one identity to the next, free from any pressure to explain themselves. Diversified markets offer something for everybody, while internationalization increases the variety of available commodities and sharpens the contrast between the local communities of the past and the borderless societies of temporary co-consumers, chosen by a purchase – or just by clicking a 'Like' button – and deserted at pleasure. Sociation by social media – Twitter, Facebook and the like – represents an extension of this trend, not least in that it offers these companies a further set of tools for highly individualized marketing. Firms, politicians and celebrities of every sort have quickly learned to use social media to customize imagined communities of 'followers', ready to receive pseudo-personal messages at any time of the day. In politics, the hope is to deploy the new technology to compensate for the increasing atrophy of traditional party organizations. At the same time, it represents a further personalization of politics; the time is coming when Angela Merkel will instantly inform her 'followers' how much she enjoyed the opera performance she has just attended.

MARKETIZED PUBLIC SPHERE

The unprecedented commercialization of social life that aimed to rescue capitalism from its late-Fordist stagnation profoundly affected the relations between collective state and individual market provision in what used to be the 'mixed economies' of the post-war era. Even more consequentially, it transformed the relationship between citizens and states in what remains of the public sphere – and thereby, I will argue, the nature of politics as such. One result of states existing alongside the new, dynamic markets for advanced consumption goods was to aid pressures from investment capital for the privatization of several hitherto publicly provided services, among them telecommunications, radio broadcasting and television, which increasingly came to be perceived in their traditional format as old-fashioned, utilitarian, boring, and unresponsive to users-turned-consumers. When technological progress made possible the same multiplication and diversification of products as in the manufacturing industry, governments worldwide accepted and promoted the claim that only private firms would be able to satisfy the rising expectations of more exacting consumers for increased attention to their emerging wants, in particular for more customized products.

In subsequent years it was in the newly privatized sectors of telecommunications and television that commercialization progressed more than anywhere else. Not by chance, it was here that some of the largest fortunes of the late twentieth century were made, in particular by mass-entertainment entrepreneurs like Murdoch and Berlusconi. In Germany there had been no more than two national television channels well into the 1970s, both public, with extensive public-interest reporting and a legally enshrined educational mission, resulting in frequent broadcasts of plays by Goethe, Shakespeare and Brecht, as well as live transmissions of Bundestag debates. Today, by comparison, there are cities in Germany where one can receive over a hundred TV channels, many from abroad, with the two public channels now confined to an ageing minority audience – regardless of the fact that they have radically changed their programme structure to emulate the more entertaining, and more successful, private channels. In varying form, the same development took place in all other European countries, with commercialization also resulting in the shift of high-ratings programmes to pay-TV, as in Britain. Something similar may even be observed in the United States, where the national networks are now relegated to a small niche in a highly fragmented media market, almost entirely geared towards entertainment.

Telecommunications changed in much the same way. In the German case, the national telephone system was run by the Post Office until the late 1980s and its profits were actually used to subsidize the postal service. The spirit in which the system operated may be illustrated by the fact that public phone booths used to carry a sign saying, *Fasse Dich kurz*, or 'Keep It Short', urging citizens not to misuse their privileged access to the state's precious telephone lines for idle chatter. By comparison, a few years ago one of the many booming private phone companies, with their innumerable service plans customized to suit every conceivable group of consumers, ran advertisements showing young people talking on their mobile phones under the slogan, perhaps a conscious allusion to its precursor from the commercial stone age, *Quatsch Dich leer* – 'gabble yourself out' would be an approximate translation.

A third example of the ways in which new patterns of consumption in the private sector encouraged the privatization of existing public services is that of swimming pools. In the post-war period, almost every local community had a public pool. They were simple, even austere, but nevertheless well-used, due to a general belief that they were good for people's health, and that children had a duty to learn how to swim, both to build character and to be able to rescue others from drowning. In the 1970s, however, attendance declined and *Stadtbäder* underwent a financial crisis. At the same time, private pools, often called *Spaßbäder*, 'fun baths', began to flourish. They had hot whirlpools, saunas, restaurants, artificial beaches, even shopping malls. Entrance fees were much higher than in the declining *Stadtbäder*, but then there was much more fun to be had. With time, more and more communities closed their public pools, or sold them to private businesses that promised to rebuild them and run them as *Spaßbäder*. Where pools remained public, and communities had enough money to pay for the investment, they were redesigned in the spirit of the private competition, and subsequently often recovered. Generally, however, here as elsewhere the view began to prevail, not least among political leaders, that only the private sector was capable of properly attending to the changing needs of a richer and more demanding clientele, and that the best thing the state could do under the circumstances was to step out of the way, shut down its primitive-utilitarian facilities and invite private business in to provide colour, fun and, above all, freedom of choice.

In many ways, then, it became received political wisdom during the 1980s and '90s that the difference between public and private provision was that the state dictates to people what they are supposed to need – which will always in effect be the same for everybody – whereas private markets cater to what people really want, as individuals. While this was a strong motivation for privatization, it also radiated into core areas of government activity which, for whatever reason, could not be outsourced to the market. At a certain point, governments began to acknowledge the supposedly inherent superiority of the private over the public sector by encouraging citizens to perceive themselves, in their relations with state bureaucracies, as *customers*. Correspondingly, state officials in contact with the public were taught to act, no longer as representatives of the law, of legitimate public authority or of the general will, but on the pretence that they were providers of services in a competitive marketplace, driven simultaneously by the desires of their customers and the pressures of competition. It was in this spirit that in Germany, in the course of the Schröder reforms, the *Arbeitsamt* of old – the Labour Office – was renamed the *Arbeitsagentur*, an 'agency' that had to learn to speak of the unemployed as its customers. The model for this, of course, was New Labour's 'Third Way', which had much to say about alleged or actual inefficiencies of state-provided services, manifest among other things in their alleged lack of attention to clients' 'real needs'. The keystone of this development was the introduction of the 'new public management' paradigm, whereby barrages of minutely specified quantitative performance indicators are supposed to substitute for the corrective feedback from an unfortunately not-yet-existent commercial market.

COLLECTIVE MINIMA

The lateral effects, so to speak, of the new 'politics of consumption' on what one might call the old 'politics of the political' have been even more consequential than the privatization of state functions. As formerly public functions were moved to the private sector and the public sphere came to be simultaneously narrowed and discredited, with the support of reformist governments, the balance between private and public channels of provision shifted in favour of the former. Inevitably the material base for the legitimacy of states as states began to shrink. The decline of political legitimacy did not, however, stop in the area of service provision. Gradually it extended into the very core of citizenship, where the traditional relationship between citizens and the state became increasingly subject to unfavourable comparison with the relationship between customers and producers in the refurbished post-Fordist markets for consumer goods.

To be more explicit: I would argue that the restructuring of consumption aimed at restoring the dynamics of capitalist accumulation after the crisis of the 1970s made possible – indeed, invited and cultivated – attitudes and expectations on the part of customers-cum-citizens that inexorably began to radiate into what remained of the public sphere. Compared to the new consumption regime, states and the goods of which they still were in charge looked increasingly shabby and dull, very much like the uniform-product markets of the Fordist age as they were becoming saturated. It had been exactly this contrast that Monsen and Downs had invoked in their clairvoyant 1971 paper to explain the disparity between public poverty and private riches. We may note in passing that Monsen and Downs were far from happy with this condition and, rather than contenting themselves with celebrating the superiority of markets over states, offered a series of suggestions as to how the balance between public and private wealth in a capitalist political economy might be improved. The strategy they proposed to governments was not to fight 'the inherent striving for differential social status among consumers' but to accommodate it, and even to 'use the desire for consumer differentiation to further other public objectives'. In fact some of the remedies they suggested look conspicuously similar to what would become the public-sector reforms of the 1990s: less uniformity and more differentiation of 'government goods'; privatization of the provision of 'goods which need not be distributed by the government'; the use of 'private producers of goods and services' as 'purveyors of government goods'; a more diversified mix of government activities, 'such as less defence and more education and subsidized housing'; and more decentralization of government activities to local communities.[7]

If these proposals to restore the legitimacy of politics in competition with the attractions of private markets seem quite remarkable – not least because

7   Monsen and Downs, 'Public Goods and Private Status', pp. 73–75.

they are so far from the neoliberal anti-statism that reigned during the 1990s and early 2000s – they can nevertheless serve their purpose only for a limited range of government activities, while their application beyond that would in fact be counterproductive. For while the satisfaction of expectations of diversity, individuality and choice may increase the legitimacy of the delivery of certain goods and services by governments rather than by commercial firms, it may be quite subversive when it comes to the *production* of such goods, in particular where it involves duties of citizenship, including the collective deliberation of how entitlements and duties are to be weighed. Monsen and Downs identify 'public goods' with 'government goods'; their use of the terms implies that the former are not just divisible but can in principle be produced by specialized agencies separate from the individuals that consume them. Yet there are collective goods which are indivisible and must be produced, or at least decided upon, by those who benefit from them, and indeed by their collectivity: social solidarity, distributive justice and the general rights and duties that constitute citizenship. I call these *political* goods, and would maintain that not only do they need to be made attractive by other means than product diversification, but that allowing them to be judged by the same standards as modern commodities must ultimately result in a situation in which they are critically undersupplied.

More specifically, I am arguing that citizenship is by its very essence less comfortable than customership, and if measured by the same criteria must inevitably lose out. If seen in terms of customers' rights, citizenship is bound to look structurally similar to customership in the mass markets of old, as individuals must live with only some of their idiosyncratic preferences being attended to and others being compromised. Moreover, rather than just consuming political decisions, citizens in a functioning democracy are invited and indeed obliged to participate in their production. In the process, they must subject their specific, collectively unexamined 'raw' wants to critical scrutiny in some sort of public dialogue. Getting their way may demand collective rather than individual action, requiring in turn considerable investment, making for high transaction costs without guarantee that the result will be to one's personal liking. In fact the role of citizen requires a disciplined readiness to accept decisions that one had originally opposed, or that are contrary to one's interests. Results are thus only rarely optimal from an individual's perspective, so that lack of fit with what one would have preferred must be compensated by civic satisfaction about their having been achieved through a legitimate democratic procedure. Political participation in a democracy demands, in particular, a preparedness to justify and recalibrate one's choices in the light of general principles, developing preferences not in the sense of diversifying, but rather of aggregating and unifying them. Moreover, unlike customership, citizenship demands that one provide generalized support to the community as a whole, in particular by paying taxes, which may be put to as yet undecided uses by a lawfully constituted government, as distinguished from purchases of specific goods or services paid for one at a time, at market prices.

Political communities are republics that cannot by their very nature be turned into markets, or not without depriving them of some of their central qualities. Unlike the highly flexible communities of choice that emerge in societies governed by advanced patterns of consumption, political communities are basically communities of fate. At their core, they ask their members not to insist on their separate individuality but to accept a collectively shared identity, integrating the former into the latter. Compared to market relations, political relations are therefore by necessity rigid and persistent; they emphasize, and must emphasize, strong ties of duty rather than weak ties of choice. They are obligatory rather than voluntary, dialogical rather than monological, demanding sacrifices in utility and effort; and they insist on loyalty – providing, in the terms of Albert Hirschman, opportunities for 'voice', while frowning upon 'exit'.[8]

Politics, therefore, cannot undergo the same re-engineering that capitalist firms and product ranges underwent after the Fordist era. Rather than simply serving the idiosyncratic wants of individuals, it must subject them to public examination with the objective of aggregating them into a general will, which bundles and supersedes the many individual wills. There is a strong sense in which politics will always at its core remain structurally akin to mass production, and as a consequence compare unfavourably to the ease and freedom of choice in modern consumer markets. Political product diversification and innovation will never be able to keep pace with diversification and innovation in consumer markets. As politics is centrally about the creation and regulation of social order, its results cannot be decomposed into different individual products catering to individual tastes, just as their consumption and the participation of consumers in their production cannot ultimately be voluntary. This implies that, to the extent that modern markets for consumer goods become a general model for the optimal satisfaction of social needs, and citizens begin to expect the same kind of individuated response from public authorities that they have become used to receiving from private firms, they will inevitably be disappointed, even and precisely where political leaders try to endear themselves by keeping silent about the difference between public

---

8   Albert Hirschman, *Exit, Voice and Loyalty: Responses to Decline in Firms, Organizations and States*, Cambridge, MA: Harvard University Press 1970.

and private goods. The result will be that motivation to contribute to the joint production of civic goods will dry up, which in turn will undermine the capacity of states to produce the civic goods on which the legitimacy of politics as politics depends. As the new market mode leaches laterally into the public sphere, through the generalization of expectations cultivated in the consumerism of post-Fordist affluence, the capacity of states to impose public order on what is an increasingly de-politicized market society must evaporate.[9]

POLITICS AS CONSUMPTION?

What are the consequences of the superior attractiveness of markets to political provision in affluent societies? For one thing, it appears that the middle classes, who command enough purchasing power to rely on commercial rather than political means to get what they want, will lose interest in the complexities of collective preference-setting and decision-making, and find the sacrifices of individual utility required by participation in traditional politics no longer worthwhile. While one might call this political apathy, it need not imply that individuals will cease to keep informed about what is going on and, for example, give up following the news. Of course quite a few have done so in recent years, and in fact large sections of the generation that has come of age in the commercialized world of the 1980s and '90s have never adopted the habit. In Germany, hardly anyone below fifty ever watches either of the two public television channels that are still known for their relatively conventional public-interest reporting. While their ageing audiences still vote in disproportionately high numbers, for them, too, politics may be gradually turning into some form of entertainment, a spectator sport whose performers are almost habitually viewed with contempt: never since the War, it appears, have political parties and politicians been so despised by citizens as today.

Large-scale migration from politics into markets does not mean that people fail to make themselves heard through what has come to be called non-traditional or unconventional modes of political participation. In fact both the young and the affluent middle classes have grown pretty good at this, whenever they feel affected or concerned. It seems, however, that the majority of such initiatives are not for but against something – typically something

9   Much of my argument on politics and markets parallels Colin Crouch's seminal analysis in *Post-Democracy*. While Crouch emphasizes the 'push' out of the public into the commercial sphere, I call attention to the 'pull' exercised by a reinvigorated post-Fordist consumption model on an emaciated democratic polity. In both cases, the reorganization of political participation as consumption, and re-styling of citizens as consumers, reflects the decline of nationally constituted communities of fate in a marketized world.

started by government in the alleged collective interest of the community as a whole, and passionately rejected by parts of that community who, however, will not and cannot be held responsible for the broader consequences of their potential success. Of course, suspicions on the part of citizens that government projects are ill-conceived or even corrupt are often quite justified; but this does not change the fact that political participation of this sort is typically as de-contextualized as individual decisions on consumption or non-consumption. What is at stake for the participants is not whether a specific policy fits into an overarching collective project, but whether or not they have to 'buy' a public good, produced by political leaders and imposed on the citizenry by public authority. Participation of this kind is overwhelmingly negative, suggesting that citizens generally expect little from collective-political provision, and that governments have very few if any projects to offer, for whose sake people might be willing to subject themselves to majority decisions that do not entirely match their preferences.

As individual market choice trumps collective political choice, politics must become de-contextualized. Rather than related to a potentially coherent vision of how society as a whole is or wants to be organized, individual political decisions are bought or rejected by citizens, one at a time. In some ways this looks like what used to be called, decades ago, the 'end of ideology'. In the 1960s, however, in a much more organized and deferential society, 'pragmatic' elites were able to deal with 'the issues' 'on their merits'. In the fragmented societies of today, by comparison, the absence of a coherent and enforceable 'ideological' context for policy decisions makes for an omnipresence of sectional resistance to whatever decisions are under consideration. There is an obvious connection here with the widespread loss of status of political parties, which used to be the privileged intermediary organizations that took charge of aggregating the diverse demands of different sectors of society into more or less coherent platforms. In many countries, such programmes have lost their significance for parties and voters alike – or, as in the United States, have become opportunistically compiled lists of themes and promises, controlled by pollsters rather than party members and put together shortly before an election, only to be dispensed with immediately after.

The disjointedness of contemporary politics, with its striking similarity to the randomness and collective irresponsibility of private consumption, fits well with the fact that young people in particular seem more disinclined than ever to join a political party, and thereby identify with an entire political programme, including sections that they individually do not like but would have to accept for the sake of programmatic coherence and party unity. Again, this is not to say that parties cannot win young people at all. Experience in a country like Germany, however, with a reasonably strong tradition of party membership, suggests that this is most successful where participation is only on an issue-by-issue basis and in particular does not require formal acceptance of general duties, not to mention party discipline. (This, of course, disregards those who join a party in pursuit of a political career.) The door with the EXIT sign must always be visible and open.

The limited and easy-to-terminate individual commitments characteristic of single-issue politics are structurally not too different from the purchase of a specific automobile or mobile phone; if they cease to excite you, you can abandon them with no bad feelings and switch to a different model, or to something else altogether. Acts of political participation thus become like acts of consumption, or of hedonistic individual utility maximization. Generalized loyalty is not asked for; if it were, nobody might show up. Political participation as the duty of a citizen gives way, in affluent consumer cultures, to political participation as fun: one personal preference like any other, rather than a collective obligation. Not that political systems have not tried to emulate markets. Expenditure on market research and advertisements seems to have exploded as voter volatility has risen in parallel with the volatility of customers. Product innovation, however, is still rare in politics, and product differentiation is difficult. Note, however, the growing number of niche parties in many countries, like the 'Piraten', and the associated general decline of the old *Volksparteien*, the 'Fordist' catch-all mass producers of political consent, which seems to be quite analogous to the secular fragmentation of commercial markets.

Another consequence of the penetration of modern habits of consumption into the public sphere is that what is publicly perceived of politics is increasingly reduced to self-centred power games, scandals and the egotistic antics of its remaining personnel. Of course, being experienced as hopelessly inferior to commercial markets when it comes to attending to people's interests, politics may be bound to look increasingly self-referential in the eyes of citizens. It may be forced to mutate in this direction, given the fixation of its audience on what is left when serious matters have been relegated to market forces: that is, political personalities, their style and appearance. After a certain amount of time, it may no longer be possible to stop the rot: expectations of what politics can do may have eroded too far, and the civic skills and organizational structures needed to develop effective public demand may have atrophied beyond redemption, while the political personnel themselves may have adapted entirely to specializing in the management of appearances rather than the representation of some version, however biased, of the public interest.

As the middle classes and the post-Fordist generations shift their expectations for the good life away from public towards private consumption, those who, for lack of purchasing power, remain dependent on public provision are also affected. The attrition of the public sphere deprives them of their only effective means for making themselves heard, devaluing the political currency by which they might otherwise compensate for their lack of commercial currency. While those at the bottom of society have no place in commercial markets and their regime of resource allocation, they might extract benefits from potential allies more powerful than themselves in political coalitions in need of their support. Moreover, improving their lives might figure importantly in collective political visions of a good society, whereas markets can always do without them. In fact the poor suffer in several ways from the de-politicization of want satisfaction in affluent societies. Not only do the potentially reform-minded middle classes cease to take much interest or to place much confidence in collective projects: as they provide for themselves individually in the market, they become more resistant to paying taxes. Indeed with the declining social relevance of, and respect for, politics, tax resistance has increased almost everywhere, even in Scandinavia, and levels of taxation have fallen in almost all rich democracies.

Left to themselves, faced with a political system starved of both legitimacy and material resources, and as a result reduced to what has come to be called 'politainment', the lower classes follow the lead of the younger generation and refrain in growing numbers from voting, refusing even symbolically to participate in what might in principle be their last recourse in pursuit of a better life. Increasingly the picture in Western Europe is beginning to resemble that in the United States. The transformation of democracy under neoliberalism may also remind one of Albert Hirschman's observation about the Nigerian state railways: as the affluent lose interest in collective provision and instead turn to more expensive but, for them, affordable private alternatives, their exit from public in favour of private services accelerates the deterioration of the former and discourages their use even among those who depend upon them because they cannot afford the private alternatives.[10]

---

10   Hirschman, *Exit, Voice and Loyalty*, pp. 44ff.

CHAPTER FOUR

The Rise of the European Consolidation State

The rise of the *consolidation state* follows the displacement of the classical *tax state*, or *Steuerstaat*,[1] by what I have called the *debt state*,[2] a process that began in the 1980s in all rich capitalist democracies. Consolidation is the contemporary response to the 'fiscal crisis of the state' envisaged as early as the late 1960s when post-war growth had come to an end.[3] Both the long-term increase in public debt and the current global attempts to bring it under control were intertwined with the 'financialization' of advanced capitalism and its complex functions and dysfunctions.[4] As I will show, the ongoing shift towards a consolidation state involves a deep rebuilding of the political institutions of post-war democratic capitalism and its international order, in particular in Europe where consolidation coincides with an unprecedented increase in the scale of political rule under European Monetary Union (EMU) and the transformation of the latter into an asymmetric fiscal stabilization regime.

In this chapter I begin by briefly recounting the development that led to current consolidation efforts, with the financial crisis of 2008 as something like a critical juncture. Next I sketch out the domestic and international politics of fiscal consolidation at a time of low growth (or even secular stagnation), a long-term increase in economic inequality, and record-setting overall indebtedness. Following this I will discuss the specifically European dimension of consolidation, in particular the emergence, during the crisis, of an integrated *European consolidation state* as a unique configuration of national states, international relations and supranational agencies, with fundamental implications for both domestic democracy and the international order. Finally, I look at some of the political-economic consequences of consolidation, especially for the relationship between states, societies and markets, and for what citizens will be entitled to expect from democratic government and democratic participation in the future.

---

1   Schumpeter, 'The Crisis of the Tax State'.
2   Streeck, *Buying Time*.
3   James O'Connor, *The Fiscal Crisis of the State*, New York: St. Martin's Press 1973.
4   Magdoff and Sweezy, *Stagnation and the Financial Explosion*; Susan Strange, *Mad Money: When Markets Outgrow Government*, Ann Arbor: University of Michigan Press 1998; Greta R. Krippner, 'The Financialization of the American Economy', *Socio-Economic Review*, vol. 3, no. 2, 2005, pp. 173–208; Natascha van der Zwaan, 'Making Sense of Financialization', *Socio-Economic Review*, vol. 12, no. 1, 2014, pp. 99–129.

FROM THE FISCAL CRISIS OF THE STATE TO THE GREAT RECESSION

By the mid-1970s, the accumulated debt of states in the OECD world began to increase steeply and steadily (see above, Figure 1.4, p. 54). Indebtedness rose by and large simultaneously, regardless of country, national economic performance, or the political complexion of the government of the day. North Sea oil made a difference for Britain, unification for Germany, the rise and fall of defence spending for the United States, but always only temporarily. Indebtedness increased for two decades until the mid-1990s, when debt levels seemed to stabilize. After 2008, however, they rapidly returned to the long-term trend.

A growing level of public debt is the result of cumulative, non-Keynesian[5] deficits in public budgets: of an enduring inadequacy of government revenue compared to government spending. A popular explanation for this is offered by the 'public choice' school of institutional economics, which conceives public finance as a poorly managed 'common pool' from which democratic-electoral majorities and office-seeking politicians may satisfy ever more extravagant collective demands without having to assume responsibility for the costs.[6] As I have shown, however,[7] the secular rise of public debt in OECD countries coincided with a general, equally secular decline in the political power of organized labour and social-democratic politics, as indicated by long-term sinking rates of unionization, falling participation in national elections, an almost complete disappearance of strikes, high and steady rates of unemployment, stagnant wages and rising economic inequality.[8]

If redistributive democracy didn't do it, what did? As mentioned above, the Marxist theorist James O'Connor, writing in the tradition of authors such as Schumpeter and Goldscheid,[9] predicted already in the late 1960s a

---

5   Non-Keynesian, because Keynesian debt is supposed to be paid off as the economy returns to an adequate level of growth and public budgets generate a surplus of revenues over expenditure. Anti-Keynesian economists, in particular in the United States, tried early on to blur this difference by accusing Keynes of having provided spendthrift governments with a good conscience when they overdrew the public accounts (James M. Buchanan and Richard E. Wagner, *Democracy in Deficit: The Political Legacy of Lord Keynes,* New York: Academic Press 1977; James M. Buchanan and Richard E. Wagner, 'The Political Biases of Keynesian Economics'. In: Buchanan, James M. and Richard E. Wagner, eds, *Fiscal Responsibility in Constitutional Democracy,* Leiden: Martinus Nijhoff Social Sciences Division 1978, pp. 79–100.

6   Buchanan and Tullock, *The Calculus of Consent.*

7   Wolfgang Streeck, 'The Politics of Public Debt: Neoliberalism, Capitalist Development, and the Restructuring of the State', *German Economic Review,* vol. 15, no. 1, 2014, pp. 143–165.

8   Schäfer and Streeck, 'Introduction'. *Politics in the Age of Austerity,* pp. 1–25.

9   Rudolf Goldscheid, 'Staat, öffentlicher Haushalt und Gesellschaft'. In: Gerloff, Wilhelm and Fritz Neumark, eds, *Handbuch der Finanzwissenschaft,* Tübingen: Mohr 1926; Rudolf

widening gap between the fiscal means governments could mobilize under capitalist relations of production and ownership, and the demands on state support made by an advancing capitalist economy. States under capitalism, according to O'Connor, had to provide both the legitimacy and the efficiency of capital accumulation – the former through all sorts of social consumption, the latter through investment in a public infrastructure. O'Connor also expected mounting pressure on state finances by public-sector trade unions claiming the same wages and benefits as workers in private industry and thereby exposing the state to the 'cost disease' of the service sector.[10] It is interesting that Daniel Bell, almost at the opposite end of the political spectrum, found much to endorse in O'Connor's analysis, although he seems to have placed the emphasis, somewhat like the public choice school, less on functional needs and structural contradictions than on cultural change away from protestant values towards materialistic consumerism, or 'bourgeois hedonism'.[11]

In hindsight, the route from the tax state to the debt state looks less straightforward than one might have expected at its beginning. Empirically, deficits became endemic and debt started to accumulate after the end of inflation in the early 1980s. Before then, high inflation had substituted for real growth by wiping out parts of the public debt, thus slowing down its accumulation. For a while it had also kept up employment.[12] With monetary stabilization, unemployment became high and chronic, causing social spending to increase until, with a delay of a decade or so, it was again brought under control by neoliberal 'reforms'. Up to this point, public debt was basically a matter of the inertia of social security systems functioning as 'automatic stabilizers'.[13] In addition, however, the end of inflation ended what is called 'bracket creep' in the United States: the movement of taxpayers into higher income tax rates with rising nominal incomes. Moreover, it reinforced tax resistance in particular among the middle class and lent

Goldscheid, 'Finanzwissenschaft und Soziologie'. In: Hickel, Rudolf, ed., *Die Finanzkrise des Steuerstaats: Beiträge zur politischen Ökonomie der Staatsfinanzen*, Frankfurt am Main: Campus 1976 [1917], pp. 317–328.

10   William J. Baumol, 'Macroeconomics of Unbalanced Growth: The Anatomy of Urban Crisis', *American Economic Review*, vol. 57, no. 3, 1967, pp. 415–426.

11   Daniel Bell, *The Cultural Contradictions of Capitalism*, New York: Basic Books 1976, p. 250.

12   On the political functions of inflation and the way they were taken over, in part, by public debt in the 1980s, see chapter two of the present volume and Streeck, *Buying Time*.

13   That is, it was *not* a matter of growing demands for public handouts by spoiled citizens. However, unemployment insurance has undoubtedly become essential for the legitimation of the capitalist economic system, and citizen entitlements for support in times of economic stress can be curtailed only at high political risk, at least outside the United States.

momentum to calls for 'tax reform', meaning tax cuts that typically most benefited the payers of high taxes – like the Reagan tax cuts of the early 1980s.

Overall, the 'fiscal crisis of the state' turned out to be caused less by an increase in citizen entitlements than by a general decline in the taxability of democratic-capitalist societies (see above, Figure 1.5, p. 54). While tax revenue had kept pace with public spending by and large until the mid-1970s, by the mid-1980s it began to stagnate until, after a short recovery, it started declining at the end of the century. By 2007, taxation levels were back where they had been twelve years earlier, only to decline further in the course of the financial crisis. A contributing factor was the 'globalization' of the capitalist economy, which led to increased tax competition among countries, resulting in tax cuts for corporations and earners of high incomes.[14] It also extended the opportunities for owners of capital to evade taxation by moving assets between countries or into international tax havens.[15] If, in other words, the increasing fiscal problems of the rich capitalist democracies after the 1970s were due a revolution of rising demands, that revolution occurred not among ordinary citizens, but among capital and those in command of it.

Another respect in which early theories of fiscal crisis had failed to anticipate what was coming was that they underestimated the possibilities of capitalist states to finance deficits for a protracted period of time by borrowing. Actually, the rise of public debt in the final third of the twentieth century and beyond was linked to the financialization of the capitalist economy, which in part consisted of an explosive growth of its financial sector and of the amount of credit money it produces. Credit enabled states under capitalism to live with a widening gap between citizen demands and capitalist needs for infrastructural support on the one hand, and the increasingly powerful resistance by taxpayers – individual as well as corporate – to pay the bill on the other. Financialization made it possible for governments to push back the moment when they had to do something about the increasing inadequacy of their fiscal means. Low nominal interest rates, made possible by the return to sound money, helped as they made rising debt levels more manageable; in fact, they soon began luring governments into substituting credit for taxes as the latter became more difficult to collect. There also was an international dimension to the debt state. In particular, the United States began to sell its

---

14   Philipp Genschel and Peter Schwarz, 'Tax Competition and Fiscal Democracy'. In: Schäfer, Armin and Wolfgang Streeck, eds, *Politics in the Age of Austerity*, Cambridge: Polity 2013.

15   OECD, *Addressing Base Erosion and Profit Shifting*, Paris: OECD 2013.

public debt abroad to sovereign investors, especially to the governments of oil-producing countries looking for opportunities to 'recycle' their surpluses and in return gain military protection against regional adversaries and their own peoples.

In subsequent years 'financial services' became the most important growth industry by far in both the United States and the United Kingdom.[16] After the end of the Bretton Woods monetary regime, with the dollar continuing to be the leading global reserve currency, the United States enjoyed the 'exorbitant privilege' (Giscard d'Estaign) of being able to indebt itself internationally in its own currency and repay its debt, if need be, by printing basically unlimited amounts of it. The rich supply of fiat dollars that ensued nourished an expanding financial industry about to turn into the financial sector of capitalism worldwide. Aggressive deregulation of financial institutions allowed for unprecedented 'financial innovations' that attracted capital from all over the world and became a major instrument for governments not only looking for new economic growth but also desperately seeking access to credit. Indeed, as the overall credit supply expanded, it was not just states that became increasingly 'leveraged' but also corporations and, later, private households. Thus the rise of the debt state became embedded in a movement of advanced capitalism as a whole towards higher and higher indebtedness across the board – with public debt in fact amounting to no more than a small share of overall debt (for six selected countries see Figure 4.1, p. 118).[17]

How closely the management of the debt state came to be connected to the leveraging of capitalism in general became particularly visible in the 1990s when the first attempts were made at fiscal consolidation. In the United States, Clinton had won the presidency in 1992 by promising to do something about 'the double deficit' in the federal budget and the balance of trade. The 'peace dividend' after 1989 seemed to open a window of opportunity for spending cuts, and that a country like Sweden experienced two successive fiscal crises (1977ff. and 1991ff.) was seen as a general warning signal. Orchestrated by the United States through international organizations like the OECD and the IMF, capitalist democracies made an effort to break the upward trend in their indebtedness by returning to balanced budgets through spending cuts and

---

16 Krippner, *Capitalizing on Crisis:*.

17 Figures become even more impressive if the liabilities of the financial sector are added. In the United States, they are today as high as the liabilities of the three other sectors together. Total liabilities, including all sectors, increased from roughly 400 per cent of GDP in 1974 to more than 800 per cent after 2010.

Figure 4.1: Liabilities (excluding financial corporations) as a percentage of GDP, by sector, six countries, 1995–2011

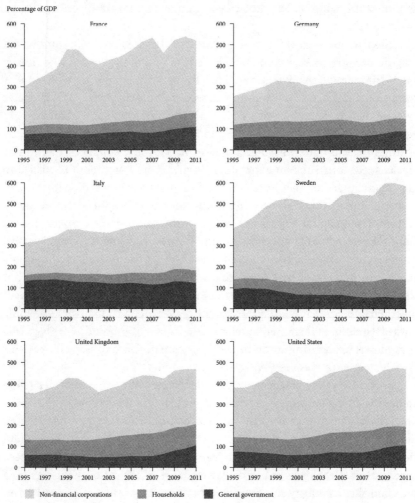

Source: OECD National Accounts, non-consolidated data.

reforms of their budgeting institutions.[18] Indeed, countries succeeded in the 1990s in bringing down public expenditure to levels that more closely matched their stagnant revenue (see above, Figure 1.5, p. 54).

In the United States, this went as far as producing a budget surplus by the end of Clinton's second term. It should be noted, however, that this was due to

---

18   James M. Poterba and Jürgen von Hagen, eds, *Fiscal Institution and Fiscal Performance*, Chicago: University of Chicago Press 1999.

a large extent to low interest rates made possible by monetary expansion, to savings on defence spending in the wake of 1989 (soon to prove short-lived), to economic growth (especially in the financial sector) inflating the denominator of the debt equation, and to savings on social security (as a result of both low unemployment and cuts in entitlements).[19]

The consolidation attempts of the 1990s responded to, perhaps misinformed, concerns among American voters about high public debt. But one can also assume creditors were concerned about the long-term solvency of sovereign borrowers. In any case, in an era of financial deregulation and expansion, pressures for fiscal consolidation presented an opportunity for cutting back the state in favour of the private sector, by referring citizens to private credit as a substitute for previously free public services. Thus, financialization not only *required* fiscal retrenchment – to ensure the further creditworthiness of sovereign borrowers – it also made it possible, and with it the retrenchment of the state. As households indebted themselves to compensate for cuts in public provision, aided by low interest rates furnished by obliging central banks, they opened the door for the private sector to move into fields that had previously been the domain of government. They also filled the gap in aggregate demand caused by cuts in public spending – an effect referred to as 'privatized Keynesianism'.[20]

Far from being unsuccessful, the first wave of consolidation managed to bring down public debt during the decade from the mid-1990s to the eve of the Great Recession (see above, Figure 1.4, p. 54) – helped in Europe by the Maastricht Treaty on European Monetary Union with its debt limits, while hindered in the United States after 2001 by the Bush tax cuts and rapidly rising defence spending. However, all of this was undone when the pyramid of private debt that had grown alongside public debt – all the more so after the increase of the latter had temporarily been halted – collapsed in the financial crisis of 2008. Here again, the close interconnection between the debt state and the financialization of modern capitalism became apparent, as states found themselves forced to absorb the bad debt created by the private sector under

---

19   Between 1993 and 2000, public expenditure in the United States declined by 4 per cent of GDP while tax revenue increased by 2 per cent. The 1993 federal deficit of 4 per cent of GDP turned into a surplus of 2 per cent in 2000.

20   Crouch, 'Privatised Keynesianism: An Unacknowledged Policy Regime'; Colin Crouch, *The Strange Non-Death of Neoliberalism*. See in addition, among others, Monica Prasad, *The Land of Too Much: American Abundance and the Paradox of Poverty*, Cambridge, MA: Harvard University Press 2012; Raghuram J. Rajan, *Fault Lines: How Hidden Fractures Still Threaten the World Economy*, Princeton, NJ: Princeton University Press 2010; and Gunnar Trumbull, 'Credit Access and Social Welfare: The Rise of Consumer Lending in the United States and France', *Politics and Society*, vol. 40, no. 1, 2012, pp. 9–34.

financial deregulation. In fact, they had to take up additional debt for stimulus spending to prevent a complete breakdown of their national economies. Ironically, it was the debt that states incurred to protect societies from the fallout of speculative lending and borrowing – encouraged by government policies of deregulation and cheap money – that made 'financial markets' suspicious about states' capacity to live up to their obligations as debtors. When declining creditor confidence showed itself in rising risk premiums on government bonds from a number of countries (Figure 4.2), it was time for the *debt state* to be rebuilt into a *consolidation state*.[21]

Figure 4.2: Long-term interest rates on government bonds, selected OECD countries,* 1998–2014

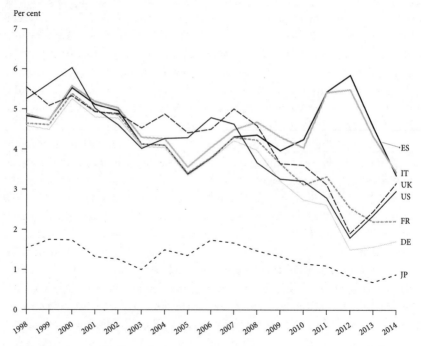

*Including Greece would have distorted the scale and made changes in the interest rates for other countries invisible.
Source: OECD Economic Outlook No. 95.

----

21   Figure 4.2 documents that there is no one-to-one relationship between a country's level of indebtedness and the risk premium it has to pay in capital markets – Japan, for example, refinances its huge national debt at record-low interest rates. The figure also shows that sudden jumps in interest rates for just a few countries (one could add Greece, Ireland, Portugal and others for the post-2009 period) are capable of setting in motion a general effort at regaining market confidence by 'reform', as in the European Union. See the next section.

CONSOLIDATION IN HARD TIMES

Understanding the politics of the consolidation state requires a look at the political economy of the debt state. The rise of the debt state took place simultaneously with a general increase in economic inequality and was closely linked to it. The declining taxability of capitalist economies in the course of 'globalization' produced a rising demand for credit on the part of governments, while tax cuts for the increasingly rich increased the corresponding supply. As a result, the debt state found it convenient to substitute credit for ever more difficult-to-collect taxes, to the extent that citizens remained willing to consider government bonds a safe investment. States going into debt allow citizens with high incomes to keep their money instead of having it confiscated, invest it safely, collect interest on it, and pass it on to their children. Unlike what is sometimes suggested in the literature,[22] the rich in rich democracies are not necessarily opposed to government debt since the alternative may be higher taxes, especially for them. What they must be concerned about, however, is too much debt compromising the capacity of governments to service it.

How much is too much debt cannot be answered generally. States default if they cannot repay old debt by taking up new debt. At what level of indebtedness financial markets will cease to extend credit to states differs, because it depends not on the magnitude of the existing debt as such, but on the confidence of the markets in it being repaid. As debt levels rise, therefore, debt states must intensify their efforts to secure that confidence to avoid rising risk premiums and at some point losing their ability to borrow. Normally, states can be expected to do their utmost *not* to default, as this may for a long time exclude them from borrowing. One advantage they have in this respect is that they may use force – on their citizens – to raise the funds they need to pay their creditors.[23] Governments may also oblige some of their subjects, especially financial firms under prudential supervision, to invest part of their capital in government bonds, on the premise that these are particularly safe. On the other hand, a sovereign government cannot be forced to pay back its

---

22   Uwe Wagschal, *Staatsverschuldung: Ursachen im internationalen Vergleich*, Opladen: Leske + Budrich 1996.

23   As has often been noted, the rise of democratic constitutionalism, by making 'the people' the sovereign, turned sovereign debt into debt of the people. Unlike a king, a people never dies, and in a democracy, government debt can be construed as debt incurred by the people themselves, who can therefore be held morally responsible for it (Marion Fourcade, Philippe Steiner, Wolfgang Streeck and Cornelia Woll, 'Moral Categories in the Financial Crisis', *Socio-Economic Review*, vol. 11, no. 4, 2013, pp. 601–627). The probability that public debt would be conscientiously served was highest after the first wave of democratization, when the king in Parliament took the place of the king in person, and the parliament consisted basically of holders of property, including state papers. However, a popular-redistributive democracy may potentially be as predatory in relation to its creditors as a personal ruler.

debt as there is no way for creditors to take possession of a state's assets, except by war. Sovereign governments are in principle free to repudiate their debts or repay them only in part. Attempts to establish an international bankruptcy regime for states that would regulate the rights and obligations of debtors and creditors and establish some form of international jurisdiction have been unsuccessful so far.

Fiscal consolidation, then, is essentially a confidence-building measure. Its objective is to make a state attractive for financial investment by making it clear to the financial markets that the state is in a position to service its debt. Consolidation is rarely about states ceasing to borrow altogether. Even after a state's accumulated debt has begun to shrink, there will long remain old debt that has to be refinanced on a revolving basis. Regardless of whether their debt is growing or declining, states thus continue to have a vital interest in low-risk premiums on government bonds, since even a minor increase in the average rate of interest they have to pay may wreak havoc on their finances.[24]

Today's emerging consolidation state is a political-institutional response to financial market demands for a break in the trend towards ever higher public indebtedness, at a time when debt levels were rising dramatically, annihilating all gains from the first wave of consolidation that began in the 1990s. To continue lending, financial markets want to be assured that public debt is under political control, certified by a demonstrated capacity of governments to halt and indeed reverse its long-term growth. Creditors' calls for consolidation reflect the experience of the last four decades that the Keynesian promise of governments deleveraging in good times to be able to incur new debt in bad times had not been kept: that fiscal reflation had a ratchet effect producing ever higher debt levels, in effect continuously expanding public expenditure. Consolidation is to reverse what had increasingly seemed like a one-way street towards insolvency and make governments return once and for all to fiscal solidity and sustainability.

Debt containment or reduction may be achieved by not replacing paid-back debt or, failing that, by 'fiscal repression': a combination of low interest rates with higher rates of inflation, or nominal growth, over a longer period of time, by which existing debt is slowly devalued. Lowering or at least stabilizing public debt by fiscal repression may be an acceptable way of restoring

---

24 An increase in the average interest rate on a state's accumulated debt by two percentage points would mean an increase in public spending by five percentage points in a country with a total debt of one hundred per cent of GDP and a government share of 40 per cent of GDP. Total defence spending for most NATO countries is far below 2 per cent of GDP.

financial credibility, as long as the resulting 'haircut'[25] remains moderate and big investors are given early enough warning. In practice, consolidation as a confidence-building measure proceeds, almost as a matter of course, *not by raising revenue but by cutting expenditure.* Exceptions may be higher sales taxes, user fees and social security contributions making tax regimes more regressive. Much-publicized efforts to close tax loopholes and prevent international base shifting, most recently at the G20 level, have yet to produce results; in any case, they would seem capable at most of slowing down the decline of tax revenue, not of ending or reversing it. A budget surplus, including one owed to lower interest rates or unexpected increases in tax revenue, is preferably used to pay off debt or cut taxes, to suppress political temptations to restore previous spending cuts.

An established consolidation state is one that has managed to institutionalize a political commitment and build a political capacity never to default on its debt, projecting an uncompromising determination to place its obligations to its creditors above all other obligations. It features a general configuration of political forces that makes spending increases difficult while making spending cuts, on everything except debt service, easy. Countries with a small state, like the United States and Japan, are more likely to be recognized as consolidation states since a small government share in the economy can be taken to indicate both an entrenched aversion to state spending and the possibility for tax increases as *ultima ratio* in financial emergencies.[26]

A country that comes close to the ideal is the United States, which combines powerful anti-taxation politics with a sacrosanct constitutional commitment never to compromise its 'full faith and credit'.[27] In fact, in the United States, as in no other country, it is understood across the political board that properly servicing the public debt must take precedence over everything else, including public pensions. Even the Tea Party movement contributed – unintentionally – to the perception of the United States as a solid debtor when it was defeated in 2011 and 2013 over the national debt ceiling by a coalition between the president and the Republican leadership – who at the time could not agree on anything except that the United States must in all circumstances service its debt, if necessary by incurring more debt.

---

25 A colloquial expression for a sovereign debtor unilaterally changing the terms of a loan in a fiscal crisis at the expense of its creditors.

26 Thus, Japan could in principle resolve its huge public debt problem by introducing a higher sales tax, and the United States could do the same with a federal gasoline tax, even one remaining clearly below European levels.

27 Article IV, Section 1 of the United States Constitution, which has come to be interpreted as applying to U.S. treasury bonds and similar financial commitments.

I have described the debt state elsewhere[28] as having two constituencies, citizens and creditors – or two peoples, a *Staatsvolk* and a *Marktvolk*. Debt states have to be loyal to both, with the two struggling over who is to be the principal stakeholder and who, in a fiscal crunch, has to give. The consolidation state settles that struggle in favour of its second constituency, its *Marktvolk*, by firmly internalizing the primacy of the state's commercial-contractual commitments to its lenders over its public-political commitments to its citizenry. In a consolidation state, citizens lose out to investors, rights of citizenship are trumped by claims from commercial contracts, voters range below creditors, the results of elections are less important than those of bond auctions, public opinion matters less than interest rates and citizen loyalties less than investor confidence, and debt service crowds out public services (for an ideal-typical representation of the relations between debt states and their two constituencies see Table 4.1). One could also speak of two kinds of public debt: *explicit* in relation to 'the markets' and *implicit* in relation to citizens, the latter downgraded in comparison to the former – or of two classes of property rights or entitlements: *capitalist* and *civic*, the former rising above the latter. In short, a consolidation state may be described as one whose *commercial market obligations* take precedence over its *political citizenship obligations*, where citizens lack access to political or ideological resources with which to contest this.

Table 4.1   The democratic debt state and its two peoples

Staatsvolk	Marktvolk
national	international
citizens	investors
civil rights	contractual claims
voters	creditors
elections (periodic)	auctions (continual)
public opinion	interest rates
loyalty	'confidence'
public services	debt service

Converting a popular democracy into a consolidation state takes time since it requires disempowering democratic-egalitarian politics in favour of solid

---

28   Streeck, *Buying Time*.

customership in financial markets. The goal is to resolve the basic *ambivalence of democracy* as a depersonalized and therefore less capricious, longer-lived, and more reliable debtor, on the one hand, and a sovereign agent of wealth allocation and redistribution, on the other. This involves tying the hands of the state by redefining its sovereignty into a guarantee of its ability to repay its debt, for example by making balanced budgets an enforceable constitutional requirement. While a balanced budget or a budget surplus may be presented by governments to citizens as a step on the way to governmental independence from financial investors,[29] the immediate purpose is to reassure lenders that their investment is safe and that they can at any time be paid and repaid. Lower risk premiums may also be achieved by other institutional reforms, to the extent that these credibly prevent future governments from once again mitigating capitalist distributional conflicts by public spending and thereby jeopardizing the state's reliability as a debtor.

Preventing the debt state from predating on its lenders may also be done by international means. States have a collective interest to ensure that the reputation of sovereign debtors is not jeopardized by wayward governments using their sovereignty to expropriate their lenders. International institutions like the IMF, the World Bank and the European Union help potentially insolvent states with loans, on the condition they reform themselves so that they can credibly promise not again to overdraw their accounts. Discipline may also be exercised by hegemonic countries aligned with global financial markets, such as the United States. The latest case here is Argentina. Having borrowed in New York, the country unexpectedly found itself under the jurisdiction of an American court, which declared the restructuring in 2002 of part of its debt to be illegal.[30] As all major banks have, by necessity, subsidiaries in the United States, any government using the banking system to handle its financial transactions may be exposed to American legal action defending the property rights of investors in public debt, should the current rulings stand.

Turning the debt state of the late twentieth century into a consolidation state is not an easy undertaking, especially as it takes place in hard economic times. With economic inequality growing everywhere, debt-financed social expenditure

---

29   See, for example, the various interview statements by the former Swedish prime minister, Göran Persson, reported by Philip Mehrtens, *Staatsschuldung und Staatstätigkeit: Zur Transformation der politischen Ökonomie Schwedens*, Frankfurt am Main: Campus 2014.

30   This followed years of inventive attempts by American 'vulture funds' to mobilize the civil laws of several countries to make the Argentine state deliver on the original conditions of the loan. Essentially what this was about was substituting national commercial law for the still non-existent international sovereign bankruptcy law. See Pola Oloixarac, 'Argentina vs. The Vultures', 18 September 2014, topics.nytimes.com, accessed 24 September 2014.

helped states maintain an appearance of egalitarian even-handedness. Budget-balancing by cutting social benefits and social services risks a democratic backlash unless political institutions are rebuilt to insulate economic policies from popular-electoral pressures, in a Hayekian[31] or post-democratic way.[32] Moving towards a consolidation state is also made difficult by the fact that it is taking place at a time of low growth, if not secular stagnation,[33] with austerity likely to cause further economic contraction.[34] (It is also made more urgent by the additional debt accumulated as a result of the financial crisis of 2008.) To investors in public finance seeking reassurance that their investment is safe, economic growth is as important as balanced budgets; both at the same time are, however, difficult if not impossible to obtain. Politically, institutional reforms and fiscal austerity are hard to impose under conditions of low growth and rising inequality on a society that still has recourse to democratic elections, while economically they may further impair aggregate demand and produce a deflationary downward spiral. Although the reigning neoliberal doctrine promises growth as a future reward for present austerity, for investors waiting to be paid that promise may be too uncertain, and the future too far away, to make them feel better.

The transformation of the debt state into a consolidation state is under way, but it is far from smooth. While interrelated through global financial markets, its local manifestations differ, although the logic is the same. Some institutional reforms have been implemented, but many are still works in progress. In Europe especially, consolidation is politically contested, in particular in countries like France and Italy. As creditors worry about consolidation subverting economic growth, and governments about austerity undercutting political stability, public debt has further increased in most countries and was still rising in 2014 – even though nobody believes present levels to be sustainable. Currently much of the refinancing of debt states is provided by central banks, in the United States and Japan directly, in Europe indirectly by the European Central Bank lending to national banking systems which, in turn, lend to their national states.[35] But although the balance sheets

---

31   Streeck, *Buying Time*.

32   Crouch, *Post-Democracy*.

33   As suggested by none other than Lawrence ('Larry') Summers, in a now legendary presentation at the IMF Economic Forum on 8 November 2013. See also his essay 'Why Stagnation Might Prove to be the New Normal' in the *Financial Times* on 15 December of the same year, where he proposes that even before the crisis of 2008, 'bubbles and loose credit were only sufficient to drive moderate growth'.

34   Mark Blyth, *Austerity: The History of a Dangerous Idea*, Oxford: Oxford University Press 2013.

35   The European Central Bank (ECB) is not allowed under the Maastricht Treaty to lend to member countries, which is why it had to devise ways to circumvent the treaty.

Figure 4.3: Total central bank assets

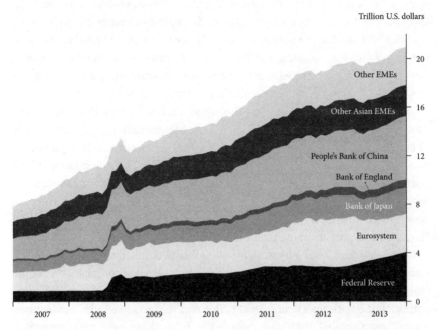

Source: Bank for International Settlements, *84th Annual Report* (2013/14), statistical data.

of the leading central banks have rapidly expanded since 2008 (Figure 4.3), historically low interest rates and unprecedented infusions of liquidity into the world economy have as yet failed to stimulate economic growth, thereby making market-conforming reforms more palatable and helping states pay their lenders. Like public debt, there is agreement among economic elites that the policy of cheap money cannot be continued forever. What is being debated is how long it can still be relied upon and how it can be ended without causing a new political-economic mega-crisis.

THE EUROPEAN CONSOLIDATION STATE

The emerging consolidation state in Europe differs in several respects from the U.S. model. Western European countries do not have command of a hegemonic currency, and redistributive democracy has not yet lost its popular support. Nor is the primacy of states' explicit debt to capital markets over their implicit debt to their citizens as well established as in the United States, and the same applies to austerity as a principle of domestic state activity, except perhaps in Britain and post-communist Eastern Europe (which, however, did not have enough time to build up potentially critical amounts of public debt). Also, in the Europe of the European Monetary Union (EMU), consolidation takes on a peculiar form as it proceeds under an international regime governing the fiscal and financial policies of a collection of formally sovereign nation states, so as to secure their compatibility with a common supranational monetary policy. Unless otherwise indicated, the following discussion will focus only on the Eurozone, or *Euroland*, and its member states.

The construction of the euro monetary regime betrays its origin in the first global consolidation wave in the 1990s. Member states were not allowed to run budget deficits above 3 per cent of Gross Domestic Product, and accumulated debt was not to exceed 60 per cent of GDP. The sole mission of the European Central Bank (ECB) was to defend monetary stability, and extending credit to member states was explicitly forbidden. Like the German Bundesbank, the ECB is independent from elected government and insulated from political pressures; in fact it is even more independent as it does not have a unified supranational government as a political counterpart but faces only a council of heads of national governments. Member-state compliance with the rules of Euroland is to be enforced by another nonpolitical supranational authority, the European Commission. This regime, fashioned after the German model, soon proved unable to enforce fiscal discipline even on Germany. It also failed to prevent the post-2008 Eurocrisis, when public and private debtors in a number of EMU member countries suddenly appeared over-indebted and lost the confidence of their creditors, especially as their national economies became locked into stagnation, with a possibility of debt deflation. As a consequence, risk premiums on public debt in several EMU member countries began to rise; in countries like Italy, Greece, Spain and Ireland they reached an unmanageable level.

As indicated, there are no general economic limits to public debt, which requires strictly individualized, case-by-case risk assessment on the part of creditors. Under EMU, financial markets had freely lent to weaker member countries at historically low interest rates, apparently on the assumption that, regardless of the treaty, their debt would somehow be mutualized should they become insolvent. After 2008 this turned out to have been an illusion, probably inspired by integrationist forces in the Commission, and lending to Mediterranean countries became an international counterpart to subprime lending in the U.S. housing market. Since servicing the accumulated debt remained a national responsibility, it became apparent that the decoupling of fiscal and financial policy from national democracy, as demanded by financial markets, had not gone far enough. Democratic resistance to austerity in the South and to a 'transfer union' in the North stood in the way of restoring investor confidence in Southern member states. Hopes that growth would return as a result of neoliberal 'reform' – of fiscal policies and institutions, as well as of labour markets and social security systems – were either disappointed or remained untested, as reform got stuck in domestic politics. In the resulting stalemate, the ECB bought time for the euro by flooding the markets with money, as ersatz debt mutualization, to keep interest rates low and member states solvent. At the same time, the ECB insists that this cannot continue forever and that national governments have in return to push through institutional and economic reforms, so as to make European capitalism, as organized in EMU, more 'market-conforming' (Angela Merkel).

The rebuilding of the EMU state system into a *European consolidation state* proceeds slowly and fitfully, punctuated by national and European elections that force governments to make themselves appear responsive to citizen concerns, including those they otherwise discredit as 'populist'. While the emerging European consolidation state amounts to a novel kind of political-economic regime, it is being developed out of EMU in a gradual, path-dependent institutional reform process. Its outstanding characteristic is a unique amalgam of national, international and supranational rules and institutions, of constitutions and treaties, and of national politics and international relations. The result is *a state consisting of states*, with domestic politics that combine diverse national politics, foreign relations between nation states, and supranational authority wielded over them in their collective name by bureaucratic agencies. As a fiscal consolidation regime, the EMU in its evolving form as an international consolidation state may be characterized as follows.

1. In a first approximation, the emerging European consolidation state is a mutual surveillance and control arrangement among what are still formally sovereign nation states. It is founded on a shared interest in states' collective reputation in financial markets and on the recognition that the default of one state may have adverse effects on all others, for example in the form of higher interest rates or repercussions on national banking systems. The transformation of the EMU into an international consolidation state on top of a set of national welfare states is to secure an ever tighter coupling of their economic behaviour through mutual observation, supervision and discipline. Institutional development starts from the original structure of the EMU as established in the 1990s, which is being gradually expanded and strengthened in the course and in the aftermath of the post-2008 fiscal crisis, among other things through new regulations, in particular the so-called

Six-pack, and new treaties, like the Fiscal Compact passed in late 2011 and early 2012, respectively.[36]

2. As an international regime not directly exposed to traditional class politics and popular democracy, the European consolidation state is in a better position than a nation state to impose on unreliable electorates a market-conforming fiscal policy, a policy of austerity and the primacy of debt service over public services. Disempowering the *Staatsvolk* in favor of the *Marktvolk* (Table 4.1) by institutionally decoupling popular democracy from the management of the economy[37] is more easily done by means of international than by national politics. As the community of states gains power over its members, vested in both horizontal international agreements and vertical supranational institutions, it can even recall elected national governments and install representatives of the international financial industry as national heads of government, as was done by the European Council in Greece and Italy in November 2011.[38] The objective is to wrest what is left of national sovereignty over economic policy from notoriously difficult national electorates through aggressive institutional reform at international as well as national level.

3. More than in any nation state, the EMU's central bank, the ECB, can act as an external force in relation to democratic governments. Administering the monetary policy of eighteen nation states, it is sufficiently far away from the domestic politics of each of them to make monetary policy support for national governments conditional on

---

36 Details of rules and procedures are, as always in the European Union, extremely complex and fully comprehensible only for experts. In essence, the updated macroeconomic regime of the EMU involves binding obligations on member states to commit themselves constitutionally to balanced budgets. It also institutes comprehensive current surveillance of member states' fiscal policies by the European Commission. Under the so-called Excessive Deficit Procedure, states may be subject to heavy automatic fines if they fail to keep their public deficits below specified limits. Moreover, under the Excessive Imbalance Procedure, countries may be specifically ordered by the Commission to revise their macroeconomic policies and change relevant institutions, such as their national collective bargaining regimes and their social policies, so as to make them compatible with supranational coordination. Individual policy directives may extend to a wide range of issues not hitherto under European Union jurisdiction. For more see Martin Höpner and Florian Rödl, 'Illegitim und rechtswidrig: Das neue makroökonomische Regime im Euroraum', *Wirtschaftsdienst – Zeitschrift für Wirtschaftspolitik*, vol. 92, no. 4, 2012, pp. 219–222; Fritz W. Scharpf, 'Monetary Union, Fiscal Crisis, and the Disabling of Democratic Accountability'. In: Schäfer, Armin and Wolfgang Streeck, eds, *Politics in the Age of Austerity*, Cambridge: Polity 2013, pp. 134–136; and Streeck, *Buying Time*, pp. 107–9.

37 I have described this as the imposition of a Hayekian regime on the European political economy (Streeck, *Buying Time*).

38 When the prime minister of Greece, Andreas Papandreou, was replaced with the central banker Lukas Papademos, and the Italian prime minister Silvio Berlusconi had to resign in favour of the former European Commissioner and Goldman Sachs functionary, Mario Monti.

their cooperation with respect to fiscal policy and institutional reform. Together with other international organizations, in particular the International Monetary Fund and the European Commission, the ECB has deeply intervened into the domestic politics of formally still sovereign member states, among other things prescribing to the Greek government how many civil servants it had to dismiss and when. Since the ECB must be concerned above all about the confidence of financial markets in the currency that it administers, the reforms it demands from member states can only be of a market-conforming kind. In particular, the ECB cannot be supportive of any egalitarian-redistributive ambitions of national governments. The ECB's unprecedented political independence translates into an unprecedented capacity to cater to the interests of financial markets and into unprecedented dependence on these.

4. The international relations embedded in the EMU consolidation state are highly asymmetrical. Economically weak countries, while in the majority, face a small number of economically strong countries in a position effectively to dictate to them, by threatening to withhold financial support. Germany, on account of its regained economic power after 2008 and as the main beneficiary of EMU due to its export strength and to currently low European interest rates,[39] *de facto* governs the EMU as a German economic empire. In the form of the euro, it imposes a hard currency of the kind Germany has become used to since the war on the rest of Europe, including on countries like France and Italy that have long relied on a soft currency as a means of managing domestic distributional conflict while intermittently relying on devaluation to restore temporarily their international competitiveness.[40] There is no provision in the treaties for turning the EMU into an

---

39 This was different in the early 2000s when euro interest rates, set to combat inflation in the South, were too high for low-inflation Germany (Scharpf, 'Monetary Union, Fiscal Crisis, and the Disabling of Democratic Accountability').

40 There is now a large body of literature on the frictions caused by differently organized national political economies being forced under a common monetary regime. See, for example, Klaus Armingeon and Lucio Baccaro, 'Political Economy of the Sovereign Debt Crisis: The Limits of Internal Devaluation', *Industrial Law Journal*, vol. 41, no. 3, 2012, pp. 254–275; Charles B. Blankart, 'Oil and Vinegar: A Positive Fiscal Theory of the Euro Crisis', *Kyklos*, vol. 66, no. 3, 2013, pp. 497–528; Peter Hall, 'The Economics and Politics of the Euro Crisis', *German Politics*, vol. 21, no. 4, 2012, pp. 355–371; Alison Johnston and Aidan Regan, *European Integration and the Incompatibility of Different Varieties of Capitalism: Problems with Institutional Divergence in a Monetary Union*, MPIfG Discussion Paper 14/15, Cologne: Max Planck Institute for the Study of Societies 2014; and Martin S. Feldstein, *The Euro and European Economic Conditions*, Working Paper 17617, Cambridge, MA: National Bureau of Economic Research 2011.

arrangement for international redistribution, also known as a 'transfer union' – quite apart from the fact that even Germany and France together are far too small to provide the weaker countries with more than symbolic economic assistance.[41] To the extent that some redistribution from the strong to the weak is required for keeping over-indebted states solvent and monetary union together, it must be accomplished through covert channels, also because of certain voter resistance in the European North. Serving as an invisible conduit for money transfusions is another function today performed by the ECB.

5. The institutional reforms imposed by the EMU on its over-indebted member states would, if carried out to their end, result in a deep restructuring of national political economies, especially in the Mediterranean countries. Based on the 'German model' as it is understood today,[42] such reforms would in particular undo the historical class compromise in countries like Italy and France which accepted high rates of inflation and high public spending, including frequent public deficits, as a price for social peace.[43] High inflation made high public debt bearable because it devalued the debt on a current basis; low interest rates and high state subsidies provided for stable employment; and negative effects on external competitiveness were compensated from time to time by devaluation. To the extent that this system supported 'rigid' labour markets, short working hours, costly public services, high and early pensions, and high and regular nominal wage increases, it was a thorn in the eye of a growing middle class, as well as of technocratic-nationalist elites bent on 'modernizing' their countries. To them, the EMU promised to break institutionally entrenched resistance to capitalist modernization by undoing the various economic fixes on which their national class compromise depended. By having the bitter medicine of austerity and flexibility forced on their countries from the outside, they hoped they would ultimately become able to 'stand on their own feet,' get ready for 'globalization,' and compete successfully with Germany.

EMU and the international consolidation state growing out of it represent a unique opportunity for the capitalist rationalization of 'backward' economies,

---

41   Wolfgang Streeck and Lea Elsässer, *Monetary Disunion: The Domestic Politics of Euroland*, MPIfG Discussion Paper 14/17, Cologne: Max Planck Institute for the Study of Societies 2014.

42   Some two decades ago, the 'German model' was known for relatively low inequality and high social protection under a negotiated social compact between capital and labour. Today, Germany is identified with wage restraint, zero inflation, surplus exports, budget balancing, and 'welfare reform'.

43   Hall, 'The Economics and Politics of the Euro Crisis'; Blankart, 'Oil and Vinegar'.

states and societies. Nevertheless, because of the danger of democratic obstruction, change towards market-conforming democracy can be administered only slowly. Both national and international politics around fiscal consolidation are complex and convoluted; see the agonies of the Hollande government in France, originally elected to replace *Merkozy*, in the face of German pressures to accede to German-European international consolidation policies. See also the rise in Germany of the anti-euro party, AfD, which expresses and indeed cements German resistance to a 'transfer union', or the growing international tensions between France and Italy on the one hand and Germany on the other. At the end of 2014, the discussion was about a managed devaluation of the common currency as a substitute for national devaluation; about moving the consolidation deadlines of the Fiscal Compact forward; and about 'growth programs' for the South and for France, to be funded by new debt, even though debt is already at a historical high and adding to it has not produced growth for more than half a decade now.[44] Given the unsustainability of further debt accumulation, these are rear-guard battles on the collective march towards balanced budgets, enforced by pressures from financial markets on the one hand and by German hegemony on the other.

A NEW REGIME

Rebuilding a debt state into a consolidation state – one in which financial markets can again have confidence, and for longer than just for the moment – is a long-drawn process. At its conclusion stands a new fiscal regime with public austerity as a fundamental principle governing the relationship between state and society: a reformed 'configuration of political interests, institutions, and policy arrangements that structure conflicts over taxes and spending . . . a particular political context of institutions, powerful organizations, public policies, and dominant ideas'.[45]

Ending the secular build-up of public debt and regaining the confidence of financial markets requires deep changes in political institutions and social structures. Already the gradual cutting down on new debt towards a balanced budget, which tends to take several years, would be unsustainable unless

---

44 In fact, at high levels of indebtedness even otherwise auspicious conditions may not make borrowers incur additional debt, for fear of bankruptcy. European growth rhetoric is to pacify voters, social-democratic parties, and Southern member states. It also plays on the ambivalence of creditors who want consolidation and growth at the same time. Experience tells them, however, that additional debt, if allowed, will simply be added to existing debt, rather than being used to advance consolidation.

45 Paul Pierson, 'From Expansion to Austerity: The New Politics of Taxing and Spending'. In: Levin, Martin A., et al., eds, *Seeking the Center: Politics and Policymaking at the New Century*, Washington, DC: Georgetown University Press 2001, pp. 56–57.

accompanied by a redefinition of the responsibilities of government and the purposes of public policy, in the direction of a smaller state and an expanded market, less public and more private provision, privatization of state activities and assets, and a substitution of individual effort for collective solidarity. Ultimately, the construction of a consolidation state embedded in a consolidation regime implies a far-reaching rationalization, or 'economization', of politics and society. In the process, states become less like sovereigns and more like firms: instead of overriding markets, they are to be responsive to them. Whereas the politics of democratic capitalism was to protect society from the 'vagaries of the market' (Polanyi), the politics of the consolidation state protects financial markets from what are for them the vagaries of democratic politics.

Consolidation is to turn the activist-interventionist state of post-war democratic capitalism into a lean state receptive to market pressures. To be credible and effective, fiscal discipline must be anchored in the political institutions that control the social production of collective demands. In the final analysis, the transformation of the debt state into a consolidation state is to end the tendency, envisaged under both 'Wagner's Law' and the Marxian conjecture of an increasing socialization of production, for a maturing capitalist-industrial society to require ever-rising levels of public support – of infrastructural investment and all sorts of collective repair work and compensation – up to a point where capitalist industrialism would become incompatible with private ownership in the means of production. Imposing public austerity on the debt state of the late twentieth century may be interpreted as an effort to escape this trend, in response to the growing resistance of capitalist society against being taxed for public provision. What results is a large-scale political experiment turning over to private enterprise the tasks of insuring against social risks, providing welfare, education and health, building and maintaining physical infrastructures, and even parts of government itself (warfare, the collection of intelligence). In this way, the establishment of the consolidation state would represent the final stage of the (neo-)liberalization process that began with the end of the 'roaring seventies'.[46]

As indicated, the model of a consolidation state is the United States after it imposed an austerity regime on itself in the 1990s.[47] An important step along the way was 'the end of welfare as we have come to know it' under the Clinton presidency.[48] The fact that the reform was pushed through by a Democratic president

---

46   Streeck, *Buying Time*.

47   Paul Pierson, 'The Deficit and the Politics of Domestic Reform'. In: Weir, Margaret, ed., *The Social Divide: Political Parties and the Future of Activist Government*, Washington, DC: Brookings Institution Press and Russell Sage Foundation 1998, pp. 126–178.

48   This refers to the passage of the Personal Responsibility and Work Opportunity Act in 1996.

only reinforced its confidence-building effect. Further contributing to it was that the gradual progress towards a balanced budget, and then towards a budget surplus at the end of Clinton's second term, was achieved through spending cuts rather than revenue increases. In fact, shrinking the deficit by shrinking public spending was accompanied by substantial tax cuts which, while repeatedly renewing the deficit, created pressures for more spending cuts once 'fighting the deficit' had been established as the supreme principle of the new regime.[49]

Clinton's successor immediately squandered the Clinton surplus on tax cuts, advertised by George W. Bush during his presidential campaign in 2000 as 'returning to citizens what is rightfully theirs'. Yet neither this nor the wars in Afghanistan and Iraq did anything to diminish the confidence of financial markets. The United States has more than one way to reassure its creditors, including its capacity to produce unlimited amounts of a global reserve currency out of thin air. That the American government nevertheless administered the bitter medicine of domestic austerity to its already anaemic welfare state in the 1990s can only have added to financial markets' trust in its 'full credit', on top of the culturally established primacy of financial market obligations over citizen entitlements. Moreover, to the extent that the United States runs a deficit to finance its military and its wars, it can ask resource-rich allies to buy treasury bonds in return for protection, making it unnecessary for the latter to maintain military forces of their own. Also, spending on warfare is discretionary and temporary; and like tax cuts and tax expenditures, it may also be used to justify spending cuts in other areas. Even major increases in public deficits, which would make borrowing unaffordable for other countries, cannot therefore detract from the United States' standing in financial markets.

European countries, less privileged than the United States, began a decade later to reinvent themselves as consolidation states. Their efforts at installing an austerity regime as a credible commitment to market conformity had to go further than American efforts, given their competitive disadvantages in capital markets: no global currency, no military capabilities worth paying for, generally higher state shares in their economies, and citizens more insistent on social rights and entitlements. Anchoring national pledges to fiscal austerity in international law – like in the Fiscal Compact – helped, as did the emerging hegemony of a country like Germany, which has historically thrived on export-driven growth and a hard-currency regime.[50] Growing debt burdens after 2008 increased the pressure for a second, even more determined round of

---

49   Pierson, 'From Expansion to Austerity'.

50   Or, in Mertens' term, an export-and-saving regime (*Privatverschuldung in Deutschland: Institutionalistische und vergleichende Perspektiven auf die Finanzialisierung privater Haushalte*, Dissertation, Cologne: University of Cologne 2014).

consolidation efforts, aimed at reducing state shares and freeing up capacities to service the remaining public debt. As elsewhere, consolidation in Europe does not have to be accomplished overnight; phasing in spending cuts over time even seems preferable, as it allows for the gradual settling in of an austerity regime as a permanent feature of political economy.

How austerity may become permanent as a country moves from budget deficits to a stable surplus has recently been shown by Lukas Haffert.[51] Haffert debates what he calls the 'symmetry hypothesis', which is that a state, once it has overcome a chronic deficit, may use its regained fiscal capacity to return to political activism and restore the programmes it had temporarily cut. In fact, as Haffert shows, this is often the promise made by social-democratic governments when embarking on public austerity. In reality, however, spending patterns after consolidation remain dedicated to austerity, which becomes the central virtue distinguishing a neoliberal consolidation state from its debt-state predecessor. Haffert explains this by the fact that the transition from rising to declining debt levels is associated with and can only be accomplished by deep changes in political and institutional routines, in the configuration of vested interests, and in power relations and ideologies that are impossible to reverse on short order.

What are the lasting political-economic consequences of states devoting themselves to fiscal consolidation, in order to reassure financial markets that they will consider their debt obligations sacrosanct and do whatever it takes to remain fit for debt service? Four such consequences have been established by recent research.

1. Budget balancing, if achieved by spending cuts rather than tax increases, and even more so if accompanied by tax cuts, comes at the expense of discretionary as distinguished from mandatory spending.[52] As public budgets approach a balance, a growing share of government expenditure goes to cover comparatively rigid, legally fixed expenditures, such as wages for public sector workers, public pensions and, of course, debt service. As the latter is sacrosanct in a consolidation state, it is public investment, both in the physical infrastructure and in education, families, active labour market policy and the like – what has

---

51   Lukas Haffert, *Freiheit von Schulden – Freiheit zur Gestaltung? Die politische Ökonomie von Haushaltsüberschüssen*, Dissertation, Cologne: University of Cologne 2014.

52   Wolfgang Streeck and Daniel Mertens, 'Politik im Defizit: Austerität als fiskalpolitisches Regime', *Der moderne Staat*, vol. 3, no. 1, 2010, pp. 7–29; Wolfgang Streeck and Daniel Mertens, *Fiscal Austerity and Public Investment: Is the Possible the Enemy of the Necessary?* MPIfG Discussion Paper 11/12, Cologne: Max Planck Institute for the Study of Societies 2011.

been called 'soft'[53] or 'social'[54] investment – that must give. Over a longer term, this will produce pressures also on 'entitlements' like social security, making them more politically vulnerable and less mandatory in effect. Complaints about old commitments suffocating spending for the future and strangling 'fiscal democracy' by denying governments political discretion[55] may also result in less generous benefits for subsequent generations, while the benefits of existing claimants are frozen under so-called 'grandfather clauses'. This is likely further to delegitimize social policies.

2. Budget balancing allows no new debt, and this holds all the more for debt reduction by fiscal surplus. Public investment will therefore have to be paid for out of what will very likely be shrinking current revenue. Regaining and retaining the confidence of financial markets may therefore require governments to cut public investment even if real interest rates on government debt approach zero. Resulting deficiencies in physical and social infrastructures must be attended to by private investors assuming what had previously been public responsibilities. One effect is likely to be public–private partnerships (PPPs) of various sorts, with private investment backed by the public, and governments or individual citizens paying user fees to private firms. Indications are that states and citizens will tend to be paying more under such arrangements than they would have paid had the investment remained in public hands. This seems to hold especially for local communities, which often lack the expertise to negotiate as equals with the legal departments of international investors.

3. Cutting discretionary expenditure inevitably involves cuts in social services such as education and especially in universal services benefiting all citizens. As the range and quality of state-provided services consequently deteriorate, the middle class will look for complementary or alternative private provision, and governments will be urged to allow private firms to compete with public authorities. In the process, the better-to-do will get habituated to more customized provision, which will make them demand (further) tax cuts so they can pay for them – tax cuts that will drive further spending cuts. As the welfare state then loses growing segments of its middle-class constituency,

---

53   Streeck and Mertens, *Fiscal Austerity and Public Investment*.

54   Nathalie Morel, Bruno Palier and Joakim Palme, eds, *Towards a Social Investment Welfare State?* Bristol: Policy 2012.

55   Richard Rose, 'Inheritance Before Choice in Public Policy', *Journal of Theoretical Politics*, vol. 2, no. 3, 1990, pp. 263–291.

public programmes will turn into programmes for the poor which, according to an American adage, will make them poor programmes.

4. Privatization of investment in physical and social infrastructures gives rise to a growing private industry operating in what used to be the public sector. While typically subject to regulation, private providers are likely soon to become powerful players in the political arena where they will ally with the upwardly mobile middle class and its liberal-conservative political parties. The evolving connections of the new firms with the government, often taking the form of a revolving-door exchange of personnel, and their campaign contributions will further cement the shift from a redistributive towards a neoliberal state that abandons to civil society and the market its responsibility to provide for social equity and social cohesion.

The most advanced case of a consolidation state with a firmly established austerity regime is, surprisingly, the former model country of social democracy, Sweden.[56] Here the departure from the post-1970s debt state was much more thorough and went much farther than in the United States, where consolidation was and is made less compulsory by the competitive advantages the country enjoys in global capital markets. It is also interesting to note that Sweden is not a member of the EMU and still has its national currency, meaning that it was not forced to consolidate by international treaties. Sweden is, however, deeply traumatized by the experience of its two fiscal and financial crises in 1977 and 1991, crises far more severe than in most European countries after 2008.[57] The lesson learned at the time across the entire Swedish political spectrum was that international financial markets would not hesitate to punish the country mercilessly if they were to lose confidence in it, and that restoring and preserving that confidence had to be the foremost objective of national economic policy.

Sweden's consolidation state operates an austerity regime based on two fundamental principles: an ironclad commitment to a fiscal surplus generated

---

56 Lukas Haffert and Philip Mehrtens, *From Austerity to Expansion? Consolidation, Budget Surpluses, and the Decline of Fiscal Capacity*, MPIfG Discussion Paper 13/16, Cologne: Max Planck Institue for the Study of Societies 2013, Mertens, *Privatverschuldung in Deutschland*.

57 Between 1977 and 1983, Swedish total public debt more than doubled, from 30 per cent of GDP to 70 per cent, with a peak deficit of 7 per cent of GDP in 1982. After four years of a budget surplus around 4 per cent, public debt increased again, from 48 to 84 per cent between 1990 and 1995, with a peak deficit of 11 per cent in 1993. Beginning in 1998, it was gradually reduced to 50 per cent in 2007, the year before the global financial crisis (Mehrtens, *Staatsschuldung und Staatstätigkeit*, p. 70). From 1998 to 2008, the Swedish state ran a budget surplus; with cyclical adjustment the surplus has continued up to the present (Haffert and Mehrtens, *From Austerity to Expansion?*, p. 24).

and continuously renewed by spending cuts, to bring down the accumulated debt; and regular tax cuts to renew the pressure for spending cuts and enable the middle classes to replace public benefits and services by self-provision in free markets. Combining a surplus policy with lower taxes makes for a shrinking state share in the national economy, producing a leaner state increasingly in line with neoliberal prescriptions of a non-activist public policy. Obviously, Swedish neoliberal reform was and is facilitated by the fact that it started at a very high level of government activity, so that a national austerity regime has a lot of state activity to feed upon for a protracted time. While the Swedish landing path can therefore be a particularly long one, however, the country's consolidation regime has become so deeply engrained over time that it is hard to imagine how it could be displaced in any foreseeable future.

By the end of 2014, roughly two decades of neoliberal reform had, incrementally but all the more effectively, changed the Swedish political economy almost beyond recognition.[58] Since the peak of the second crisis in 1993, total government expenditure was brought down from 70 to 50 per cent of GDP, and total revenue from 60 to 50 per cent (2012). This process is expected to continue, assisted by deep changes in political-economic institutions which, for example, prevent the central bank from accommodating an expansionary fiscal policy:

> The medium-term financial forecast of the Swedish government for the years 2013–2015 projected surpluses of up to three percent of GDP . . . The estimated annual surplus is up to three percent of GDP. The improvement of the budget balance would be achieved solely by expenditure cuts and not by revenue increases.[59]

The economic downturn after 2011 did not cause a rethinking of fiscal priorities. Transition from high to low taxing and spending was accomplished, among other things, by a pension reform (1994/1998) that has made the pension system 'completely independent financially from the budget. There is no longer any cross-subsidization from the public purse to the pension funds' (ibid.: 17). In spite of the fiscal surplus, pensions were cut in 2010 and will be further cut in future, in line with expected shortfalls in revenue due to demographic change. There also was what was called the 'tax reform of the century' in 1990 and 1991, which contributed to the fiscal

---

58 Haffert and Mehrtens, *From Austerity to Expansion?*; Philip Mehrtens, *Staatsschulden und Staatstätigkeit.*

59 Haffert and Mehrtens, *From Austerity to Expansion?*, p. 21.

crisis of the early 1990s and helped justify the subsequent cuts in public expenditure. Taxes were further lowered in 2006 and 2008, as well as in several subsequent years. The reform made the tax system more regressive as capital incomes were taxed much lower than incomes from labour, property taxes were abolished and the value-added tax remained one of the highest in the world.

Fiscal consolidation, in Sweden no less than elsewhere, was associated with a steep decline in both 'soft' and 'hard' public investment.[60] Among other things, spending on active labour market policy was more than halved. Simultaneously, unemployment stabilized at around 8 per cent, a radically new normal in the Swedish labour market that would have been completely unimaginable before the first fiscal crisis and the monetarist turn under the Social-Democratic Carlsson Government. Consolidation was also accompanied by a steep increase in income inequality, steeper than in almost all other advanced capitalist societies. Moreover, from 1998 to 2010, the share of students in private schools below the university level increased from 2 to 12 per cent, exceeding the respective ratio in the United States.[61] Privatization is rapidly proceeding also in the large Swedish healthcare and childcare sectors. Further adherence to the policy of combining tax cuts with debt repayment, thereby shrinking the state, seems assured as the new consolidation regime has become firmly entrenched in the Swedish political economy in the past two decades.

THE CONSOLIDATION STATE AND DEMOCRACY

The regime of the consolidation state involves a deep transformation of democracy as we know it, away from traditional institutions of popular political participation designed to stand up for social equity against the laws of the market.[62] Where there are fewer public goods due to privatization, there is less to decide politically, and the economic democracy of capitalism – one dollar, one vote – begins to replace political democracy. With markets becoming the principal mechanisms of collective decision-making – by aggregation instead of deliberation – there is even less 'fiscal democracy' left than in the rigidified debt state of old. This is also because, at the macro-level, public finances are increasingly constrained by constitutionally enshrined debt limits and

---

60   Streeck and Mertens, *Fiscal Austerity and Public Investment*.
61   Mehrtens, *Staatsschuldung und Staatstätigkeit*, p. 220. At the secondary school level, the ratio was already at 50 per cent in 2010, with roughly 90 per cent of private school operators being profit-oriented corporations (Mehrtens, *Staatsschulden und Staatstätigkeit*, p. 223).
62   Streeck, *Buying Time*, pp. 58ff.

balanced-budget rules. In the European case, there are also international agreements on fiscal austerity from which countries can break away only at high political and economic cost.

Institutional restructuring towards a consolidation state abandons democratic principles in several other respects as well. Public–private partnerships are often based on complex commercial contracts, large parts of which have to remain confidential to protect trade secrets. As independent central banks rise to become the principal agents of economic policy, political decisions with far-reaching social consequences move out of the purview of parliaments and elected governments. Central banks are run by small bodies deliberating in secrecy, and given the significance of their decisions for the rational expectations of economic agents this cannot be otherwise. Also, whether or not economic policies conform to the needs of the markets cannot be decided by political debate but only by the markets themselves, and whether economic policies are 'right' is for the technocratic experts to determine who are charged with applying the rules by which policies are to be bound. All of this requires and advances a decoupling of the management of the economy from democratic politics – backed ideologically by newly fashionable elitist theories claiming democracy to be irrational, incapable of dealing with complex problems, too slow to respond to changing conditions in a global economy and too vulnerable to popular pressures for economically inefficient intervention in free markets.[63]

Turning the economy over to a combination of free markets and technocracy makes political participation run dry.[64] Where national democratic institutions are neutralized by international 'governance', as under European Monetary Union, their de-politicized empty spaces are likely to be filled with new content, which may be public entertainment of the 'post-democracy' kind[65] or some politically regressive sort of nationalism. Under the auspices of the emerging consolidation state, politicization is migrating to the right side of the political spectrum where anti-establishment parties are getting better and better at organizing discontented citizens dependent upon public services and insisting on political protection from international markets.

---

63   Daniel A. Bell, *Beyond Liberal Democracy: Political Thinking for an East Asian Context*, Princeton, NJ: Princeton University Press 2006.

64   Schäfer and Streeck, *Politics in the Age of Austerity.*

65   Crouch, *Post-Democracy.*

CHAPTER FIVE

Markets and Peoples: Democratic Capitalism and European Integration

Hopes that the resolutions of European heads of state would stabilize the financial markets and solve the Eurozone debt crisis, once and for all, have risen with each new summit over the past two years, only to be dashed again once the fine print comes to light.[1] Would investors really join in on the 'voluntary haircut'? Was the bazooka, after all, not more of a water pistol? No one could say with any degree of certainty what should be done to repair the crashed global financial system. Some demand strict austerity, others growth; everybody knows that both are necessary, but cannot be had at the same time. The technocrats' rescue packages alternate between the horns of ever-new dilemmas; ingenious patent remedies are offered by the score, but have an ever-shorter life span. If, the British veto notwithstanding, European leaders were able to sleep free of nightmares after December 2011's summit agreement on a twenty-six-nation treaty, and the ECB's long-term loans of half a trillion euros to the banks at 1 per cent, soon after it was back to business as usual. One thing is for sure: 'the markets' will calm down when they calm down; but they remain silent about when that will be and what they will next demand. Will they attack France? If need be, of course. They will only be satisfied once they are guaranteed to get their money back, through national austerity packages, international deposit-protection agreements or, ideally, both.

As I have argued before,[2] that post-war 'democratic capitalism' involved a fundamental contradiction between the interests of capital markets and those of voters; a tension that had been successively displaced by an unsustainable process of 'borrowing from the future', decade by decade: from the inflation of the 1970s, through the public debt of the 1980s, to the private debt of the 1990s and early 2000s, finally exploding in the financial crisis of 2008. Since then, the dialectic of democracy and capitalism has been unfolding at breathtaking speed. Only a few months ago, reports of jokes in Brussels' corridors regarding the desirability of a military putsch after Papandreou's suggestion of a referendum were followed by the replacement of first the Greek and then the Italian government. Accompanied by collective sighs of relief, power was passed to

---

1   This chapter was first published in: *New Left Review*, vol. 73, January/February 2012, pp. 63–71.
2   See Ch. 2, this volume.

highly regarded economist-technocrats, who, it is now hoped, will finally enforce the logic of 'the markets'. Such confidence is, at face value, not unwarranted. Mario Monti, Italy's new prime minister, was the EU Commissioner for Competition who broke up the German state banking system (whereupon it attempted a fruitless restructuring exercise, through the purchase of American junk bonds). When his Brussels tenure came to an end Monti earned his living as an advisor to, among others, Goldman Sachs, the greatest junk-bond producer of them all. Lukas Papademos, now prime minister of Greece, was president of the Greek Central Bank when the country secured, through falsified statistics, its access to the monetary union and thus to unlimited credit at German rates of interest. Help with the creative accounting of the Greek national balance sheet was provided by the European division of none other than Goldman Sachs – to be headed shortly thereafter by Mario Draghi, who is now of course president of the European Central Bank. The three of them should get along well.

CONTINENTAL IMBALANCES

Meanwhile, it is now quite clear that the democratic states of the capitalist world have not one sovereign, but two: their people, below, and the international 'markets' above. Globalization, financialization and European integration have weakened the former and strengthened the latter. The balance of power is now rapidly shifting towards the top. Formerly, leaders were required who understood and spoke the language of the people; today it is the language of money that they have to master. 'People whisperers' are succeeded by 'capital whisperers' who, it is hoped, know the secret tricks needed to ensure that investors receive their money back with compound interest. Since investor confidence is more important now than voter confidence, the ongoing takeover of power by the confidants of capital is seen by centre left and right alike not as a problem, but as the solution. In northern Europe, exotic anecdotal accounts of Greece and Italy's endemic clientelism make it easier to retreat into platitudes about how democracy cannot entail the right to live beyond one's means or not repay one's debts, all the more so when it involves 'our' money.

Things are not so simple, though. It is not 'our' money but that of the banks which is at stake, and not solidarity with the Greeks but with 'the markets'. As we know, the latter had virtually thrust their money at the former, in anticipation of being paid back, if not by them, then by other Eurozone states, if necessary by means of the 'too big to fail' blackmail of 2008. Governments have not contradicted these expectations, even though the giant surveillance apparatuses of the large nation states and international organizations cannot have failed to notice how countries like Greece saturated themselves with cheap credit after their accession to the Eurozone. Indeed, it seems in retrospect that this outcome – shoring up the money supply of the southern states with private credit, to substitute for the dwindling subsidies from strained EU regional and structural funds, in an era of worldwide budget consolidation – was one of the chief reasons for letting the Mediterranean late-comers to democratic capitalism join the European Monetary Union. That way, not only did banks make profitable, seemingly secure deals, but the export industries of the northern states could profit from the steadily renewed purchasing power of their southern customers, without having to fear that countries such as Portugal, Spain, Italy and Greece would protect themselves from the higher productivity of the northern economies through periodic currency devaluations.

The feigned astonishment of the North's political elites at their Mediterranean neighbours' use of loans and subsidies for fuelling speculation and corruption – rather than 'honest' Anglo-Saxon growth – must count as one of the most brazen feats of political PR-history. Anyone half-way informed knew about the impossibly large Greek olive harvests subsidized twice by the EU: first for their production and then for their equally virtual transformation into machine oil – just as the intimate connections in post-war Italy between Christian Democracy and the mafia, with a figure such as Giulio Andreotti acting as the nerve centre of a powerful network connecting state apparatus, political parties, armed forces, organized crime and intelligence services were anything but a state secret. As far as Greece is concerned, European politicians were well aware of the outstanding historical bills that had accrued since the end of the military dictatorship: a distribution of wealth reminiscent of Latin America; a practically tax-exempt upper class; and a democratic state that had no choice but to borrow the resources that its rich citizens had stashed abroad from 'the markets' or other states, so that the 'old money' could peacefully remain 'old money', and the new money could be used to buy the support of a growing middle class with its increasingly northern-oriented consumption norms.

That no one took exception to this at the time may be due to the fact that the sole alternative, after the end of military rule in 1974, would have been a radical remodelling of Greek society, perhaps along the lines of Emilia–Romagna, then under Eurocommunist rule. However, no one in northern Europe nor the US was prepared to risk this, any more than in Portugal after the Carnation Revolution, in Spain after Franco, and least of all in 1970s Italy,

where the Communist Party under Enrico Berlinguer abstained from participating in the government so as not to provoke a military coup like in Chile.
And so the EU admitted anything resembling a post-fascist democracy, in the
hope that economic growth would eliminate the archaic social and class structures which had been responsible for both military dictatorships and stalled
capitalist modernization.

CONVERGENCE, ITALIAN STYLE?

As for organized Europe, today torn between the North and the South, we may
have to brace ourselves for another round of integration. This may seem astonishing, given the commonly diagnosed deterioration of a 'European
consciousness'. But the new drive will once more operate through the proven
neo-functionalist model, without the participation – and possibly even against
the will – of the populace. Neo-functionalist integration relies on a 'spill-over'
from already integrated fields into other, functionally associated areas, set off
by causal connections which present themselves politically as factual
constraints (*Sachzwänge*) that merely require ratification. This was how Jean
Monnet envisaged the European integration process, and how a whole generation of political scientists wrote it on the blackboards. By the 1990s, however,
this mechanism appeared to be exhausted. As integration advanced into core
areas of the nation states and their social orders it became commensurately
'politicized' and ground to a halt. New steps towards integration became more
difficult and could only be achieved, if at all, through the European Court of
Justice. A spectre was haunting Brussels' Europe: would the disempowerment
of the nation states henceforth have to depend upon the 'European consciousness' of its peoples – or even upon the mobilization of a *democratic* European
consciousness?

The Eurozone crisis has resolved this question by once again sundering
the integration process from the will of the people. Monetary union, initially
conceived as a technocratic exercise – therefore excluding the fundamental
questions of national sovereignty and democracy that political union would
entail – is now rapidly transforming the EU into a federal entity, in which the
sovereignty and thereby democracy of the nation states, above all in the
Mediterranean, exists only on paper. Integration now 'spills over' from
monetary to fiscal policy. The *Sachzwänge* of the international markets –
actually the historically unprecedented empowerment of the profit and
security needs of financial-asset owners – is forging an integration that has
never been willed by political-democratic means and is today probably
wanted less than ever. The legal forms within which this takes place are

secondary: whatever happens, the European Central Bank will buy endless quantities of bonds that private investors no longer want; and Frankfurt, Brussels, Berlin, maybe also Paris, will 'clamp down' (Angela Merkel) on the households of debtor nations for decades, with or without treaty change. Unlike the farce over the 2005 'Constitutional Treaty', there will be no referenda this time. The North will pay for the South so that the South can pay the banks and the North does not *have* to. The power of European institutions immune to democratic pressure, especially the ECB, is reaching heights previously unimaginable, backed and buttressed by a directorate of two hegemonic nation states – which would long since have become a directorate of one, if the new supreme power were not obliged for historical reasons to obscure the true circumstances as much as possible.

True, the 'ever-closer union' this entails will be anything but an idyll; it will have come to pass in the style of a shotgun wedding, necessitated by an unplanned pregnancy and enforced by parental authority – not usually a recipe for happiness. The 'transfer union' currently emerging may best be compared to unified Italy, whose rich northern regions have subsidized the backward South throughout the post-war period, without much effect. What began as a way of completing national unity quickly turned into a system of institutionalized corruption. The aid money of the Cassa del Mezzogiorno flowed not to dynamic local entrepreneurs – who barely existed and in any case lacked any breathing space – but to the entrenched post-feudal upper class, which in return delivered the votes of the rural population it controlled to Christian Democracy; whereupon the national government abstained from any attempt to disturb their domain. And so, true to the ways of *The Leopard*, things could stay the same.

Nationalism – and European regional funds – have helped to make the burden of the South bearable for the Italian state, and hence to keep it together. Since the 1990s, however, with capitalist development of the South still remote and money from Brussels having to be shared with Eastern Europe, a growing fraction of the northern Italian electorate has become increasingly secessionist. For a while, as in Greece, the cheap credit instantly available after entry into the monetary union helped the central government to sedate the Mezzogiorno without having to tax the North. But these loans are no longer available. No one today expects an economic upswing in southern Italy, whether of its own making or through some EU magic. The malaise under Berlusconi was due not only to his peculiar use of his spare time, but also to the fact that no one could answer the question of how Italy should safeguard its national unity in face of the gaping inequalities between a rich North and a stagnant South, which seem insurmountable without deep social upheaval.

If Lombardy has not succeeded in generating the capitalist modernization of the Mezzogiorno over the course of half a century, what hope is there that northern Europe's transfer payments to the Mediterranean will ever be anything more than a levy on northern taxpayers for the higher productivity of their countries' corporations? Greeks and Finns do not have a joint memory of a shared national revolution; nor is there any prospect of regional develop- ment subsidies being paid for by a third party. Why then should northern Europeans be more patient with southern Europe than northern Italians with southern Italy? An often overlooked yet ominous parallel exists since the introduction of the euro, which in Europe, as in Italy, has blocked the possibil- ity of devaluation for the economically weak regions of the South. The result could be the same: permanent backwardness, insurmountable dependency on transfer payments, and growing disenchantment among both recipients and providers of economic assistance.

Northern Europe allowing Greece to remain in the currency union appears like something of a Trojan Horse – this time the Greeks not bearing gifts but receiving them. The Greek state and parts of the Greek bourgeoisie still seem to prefer a bird in the hand – in the form of occasional European subsidies – to two in the bush: self-determined economic and social develop- ment after a return to a national currency. The nexus of interests at stake is extremely complex and cannot be disentangled here in detail. But it is worth noting that IG Metall, the German trade union, bluntly justifies its support for 'international solidarity' with Greece in terms of securing German exports to the Mediterranean on a long-term basis.[3] Since 'solidarity' could not be a 'one-way street', however, Greece's fiscal and social policies would have to be placed under supervision, not least to make the price the North has to pay for the cohesion of the Union more palatable to a general public that is itself suffering from intensified austerity policies. Monetary union thus 'spills over' into a form of political union, at the cost of democracy in the South – where the budget-making power of parliaments is transferred to the supervisory

---

3   See IG Metall, '10 Gründe für den Euro und die Währungsunion' (10 Reasons for the Euro and the Currency Union), Press Release, 18 November 2011. 'The German economy lives like no other national economy from exports. Our customers abroad account for millions of jobs in Germany. The most important buyers of German products are the Europeans . . . the joint currency has enormously contributed to the competitiveness of German products. If the debtor countries are thrown out of the common currency, they will devalue their currencies to increase their competitiveness. The remaining Euro, which will be the currency only of the economically strongest European Union countries, will then come under massive pressure to revalue. A return to the deutschemark would mean a revaluation of no less than 40% . . . eurobonds, rescue funds and other support for the deficit countries should be tied to conditions aimed at reducing debt . . . debts and surpluses of individual countries should be monitored by a European Currency Fund. Excessive debts or surpluses should result in proceedings for the correction of imbalances.'

apparatus of the EU and the IMF – as well as in the North, where the people and their parliamentary representatives can read almost daily in the newspapers which bailout fund has once again been leveraged overnight in what way.

Meanwhile, governments and public opinion in northern Europe impress upon the debtor nations their self-righteous utopia of a market-conforming life, notwithstanding that they themselves have become addicted to what Ralf Dahrendorf dubbed *Pumpkapitalismus* – capitalism on tick – based on cheap money provided by financial markets running amok. It might be more productive to ask how the social contract of democratic capitalism should be rewritten, in order to dispense with the increasingly dangerous habit of conflict-pacification through advance payments. How should we imagine a capitalism which is not dependent, for the sake of social cohesion, on a bloated credit system that promises to underwrite unlimited consumption standards of which everybody knows by now that they are not generalizable? A credit system, for that matter, whose promises seem increasingly irredeemable and that ever fewer creditors believe in. These questions have been addressed in various ways by conservatives, like Meinhard Miegel, or progressives such as Amartya Sen and Jean-Paul Fitoussi. But we know – or ought to – that a break with the self-destructive mass consumerism that currently has the world in its grip will only be possible if greater sacrifices can be extracted from those who have profited most from the recent transformations of the capitalist economy, as opposed to those who have seen their life chances decline during decades of liberalization and globalization.

A democratic departure from the life-threatening sedation provided by cheap-money capitalism would require new solutions to the problems which the latter has only worsened. Consumer credit as compensation for stagnating wages and a growing gap between top and bottom could become superfluous if all earned a decent wage. Better living and working conditions for the great majority would alleviate the need for yet more consumer toys to compensate for status anxiety, competitive pressure and increasing insecurity. This will not be possible without a revitalized trade-union movement that would help to end the ever more destructive exploitation of the human capacity to work and nurture families. At the same time, debt financing of public expenditure would have to be replaced by more effective taxation of the incomes and assets of liberalization's winners. States should no longer have to carry out the tasks mandated by their citizens for society as a whole with borrowed money, which then has to be repaid with interest to the lenders, who in turn bequeath what has remained of their wealth to their children. Only if the trend towards deepening social division – the signature of capitalism in the late twentieth and early twenty-first centuries – were reversed would it be conceivable that modern society could free itself from the compulsion to assure domestic peace through the unchecked production of toxic assets to engineer synthetic growth.

This theme is anything but new. What should worry us is not the fact that it suddenly occurred – or recurred – but that its democratic solution appears so impossible today that we shy away even from naming it, so as not to seem stuck in the past. 'Just as ancient peoples had above all need of a common faith to live by, we have need of justice', Emile Durkheim wrote in his seminal work on the division of labour.[4] Since the end of the post-war era, it is all water under the bridge, much of which has flowed down the Hudson River, past the southern tip of Manhattan from where the world is governed these days. Trade unions are disappearing, capital listens only to presidents of central banks, not to political parties; and the money of the rich is everywhere and nowhere, gone in an instant when strapped tax states reach for it. We can only wonder what form of opiate of the people the profiteers of late capitalism will come up with, once the credit doping of the globalization era stops working and a stable dictatorship of the 'money people' has yet to be established. Or may we hope they will have run out of ideas?

---

4   Emile Durkheim, *The Division of Labour in Society*, Basingstoke: Macmillan 1984 [1893], p. 322.

CHAPTER SIX

Heller, Schmitt and the Euro

Hermann Heller's penetrating discussion[1] of Carl Schmitt's project of an 'authoritarian state'[2] provides us with an object lesson on the nature of liberalism and its relationship to democracy – one could also say: on the deep tensions between democracy and capitalism.[3] What we can learn here is not at all limited to the *Weltwirtschaftskrise* and the final years of the Weimar Republic. Liberalism, Heller finds in Schmitt, exists in a strange, paradoxical relationship with the state and the public power. The freedom of the market from state interference that defines a liberal and indeed a liberal-capitalist economy is not a state of nature but is and needs to be politically constructed, publicly instituted and enforced by state power. The depoliticized condition of a liberal economy is itself an outcome of politics, in the sense of a specific use of the authority of the state for a specific political purpose – it is a political construction that must be politically defended against the possibility of political authority falling into the hands of social forces that might use it for non-liberal, market-subverting objectives.

This is where the state and its institutions come in, as reflected in Schmitt's distinction between a 'total' and an 'authoritarian' state. In 1932, on the eve of Hitler's *Machtergreifung*, when Schmitt presented his project to the *Langnamverein* of Rhineland industrialists, the 'total state' was still identified with the 'pluralist democracy' of Weimar, a state penetrated by a variety of social groups, including the organized working class, all of which trying to make it serviceable to their particular interests. To Schmitt this state was a weak state even it might have looked strong on account of its omnipresence and its deep interpenetration with society and economy. From the perspective of the latter, such interpenetration entails an ever-present danger of a 'distortion' of market outcomes in the name of democratic-popular – today one would say: populist – concepts of 'social justice', detracting from efficiency as well as curtailing basic rights of property. The 'total state', that is to say, is in

---

1 Hermann Heller, 'Autoritärer Liberalismus?', *Die Neue Runfschau*, vol. 44, 1933, pp. 289–298.

2 Carl Schmitt, 'Gesunde Wirtschaft im starken Staat. Mitteilungen des Vereins zur Wahrung der gemeinsamen wirtschaftichen Interessen in Rheinland und Westfalen (Langnamverein)', *Neue Folge*, vol. 21, no. 1, 1932, pp. 13–32.

3 This chapter was first published in: *European Law Journal* 21(3), 2015, 361–370. I am grateful to Martin Höpner for constructive advice.

Schmitt's dictionary of 1932 nothing else than the democratic, or more precisely, social-democratic interventionist welfare state. It is not yet the Behemoth,[4] then waiting in the wings, the fascist total state, the *Führerstaat* with its *Neuordnung der Wirtschaft*, its Five-Year Plans, and its war economy – the total state preparing for total war and taking its economy into its own hands, at least for the time being.

Of course, when the real total state arrived, the concern Schmitt had in 1932 had become void: that its complex extensions into economy and society might be utilized by the democratic organizations of the working class to correct the distribution of wealth and income as produced by capitalist markets. Before Hitler sent the leaders of the Left to the camps, the total state still bore the risk that it might become democratic, or at least be occasionally used for democratic purposes. This was why the authoritarian state was to be preferred as long as there was still a potentially viable Left. Obviously what Schmitt called the authoritarian state was a liberal state, but calling it thus might have been misunderstood by his audience to mean a state that would also be democratic. This was definitely not what German industrialists had in mind at the time. Schmitt's authoritarian state, as Heller rightly notes, was a *liberal-authoritarian* state, one that was, in the classical liberal way, strong and weak at the same time: strong in its role as protector of 'the market' and 'the economy' from democratic claims for redistribution – to the point of being able to deploy the public power to suppress such claims – and weak in its relationship to the market as the designated site of autonomous capitalist profit-seeking, which government policy was to protect and if necessary expand without, however, entering it.

In an interesting way, the strong-and-weak state of liberalism – keeper of the capitalist market economy while staying out of its everyday operation – resembles how deist theology, in its Leibnizian version, imagined God: as an all-powerful clockmaker limiting himself to watching the operation of the perfect clock he has made, without intervening in it.[5] After all, if he had to intervene, the clock would not be perfect. The modern state, having made space for self-equilibrating markets in accordance with the rules of economic science, cannot do better than let them run their course. Action is required only if ignorant or malicious outsiders try to break into the protected zone of

---

4   Franz Neumann, *Behemoth. The Structure and Practice of National Socialism*, 2nd, revised edition, New York: Oxford University Press 1944.

5   For a much more profound exploration of the theological dimension of German anti-liberal liberalism, see Philip Manow, 'Ordoliberalismus als ökonomische Ordnungstheologie', *Leviathan*, vol. 29, 2001, pp. 179–198.

market freedom, threatening to upset the benevolent free play of market forces. It is in such critical moments that the authoritarian state must show that it deserves its designation and that it has the power and the determination to ensure that the rules of a liberal economic constitution will not just exist on paper.

Another general observation that comes to mind reading Heller and Schmitt concerns the similarities between Schmitt's 'authoritarian liberalism' and the 'ordoliberalism' of post-war Germany. What Heller and Schmitt make apparent, from opposite political positions, is the statist-authoritarian element in what was and still is normally advertised as the liberal antipode to the strong state of National Socialism.[6] Both Schmitt and the ordoliberals[7] differ from Anglo-American liberalism in that they never believed in a market economy independent from state authority.[8] To them Leviathan was and had to be there first. They also have in common that they regard the economy, the market and capitalism as a self-driving and self-equilibrating machinery put in place by an act of politics and the state and then let go – a machinery in need of protection from uninformed or corrupt outside interference and, perhaps, of being repaired once in a while from its wear and tear. The competitive advantage of ordoliberalism after 1945 was that it could be sold as a lesson learned the hard way from the statist-dictatorial Nazi regime and its war economy: from the failure, political, moral and economic, of the Behemoth. Authoritarian liberalism, which to Schmitt might still have been the second-best solution, given that a 'total state' was still too closely associated with pluralist democracy, could now, after the disaster of the dictatorial total state, become the first-best choice from the perspective of capitalism and its resurrection, given capitalism's damaged reputation after the disasters of the first half of the twentieth century.

---

6   On the complex relationship between ordoliberalism and National Socialism, as mediated by the ambivalent attitude of German Protestantism towards the Third Reich, see the masterful analysis by Philip Manow ('Ordoliberalismus als ökonomische Ordnungstheologie').

7   Who incidentally were more closely connected historically than one would perhaps expect. Schmitt's November 1932 lecture, 'Starker Staat und gesunde Wirtschaft' (A Strong State and a Healthy Economy), on which Heller commented, was preceded by a lecture by one Alexander Rüstow, economist and sociologist, titled 'Freie Wirtschaft, starker Staat' (Free Economy, Strong State), which was held in September of the same year. There, Rüstow referred to Schmitt having earlier characterized the 'total state' as a weak state: '. . . not total power, but total powerlessness . . . a weakness that is unable to defend itself against the united assault of organized interests (Interessentenhaufen). The state is torn apart by greedy interests . . .' Rüstow had set out in 1918 on the radical Left but then moved to the conservative Right during the Weimar Republic. Unlike Schmitt, he had to emigrate in 1933 to escape Nazi persecution. After 1945 he became one of the leading figures of German ordoliberalism. He died in 1963.

8   For a perceptive discussion of the relationship between ordoliberalism and neoliberalism see Mark Blyth, Austerity.

As indicated, German ordoliberalism, having inherited from Schmitt a keen awareness of the crucial role of the state in designing and protecting a capitalist economy, as well as of the risks associated with state intervention in a democracy, played a special role in the post-war political economy, both ideationally and practically. New Deal Keynesianism and the residues of the war economy in the United States were much less about 'free markets' than West German ordoliberalism which had managed to take over the Ministry of Economics for the two decades of *Wirtschaftswunder*. In a capitalist world fascinated with demand management and planning, the German Economics Ministry was the one place where market liberalism was more than a sectarian memory from a distant past cut off from policy. This made Germany an interesting address for 'Austrian' economists then hibernating, as an exotic sect, in the United States and Britain. The most important liaison between the two was, of course, Friedrich von Hayek, who for a few years occupied a chair at Freiburg, the academic home of the German ordoliberal school.[9] Michel Foucault's analysis of the rise of neoliberalism rightly focuses on Germany rather than Anglo-America.[10] In anchoring ordoliberalism in the German state tradition and the politics of post-war and post-Nazi Germany, Foucault might have gone back further to Schmitt and Heller, where he would have found the basic figure of thought that informed and informs liberal ideas of the economic role of state authority under capitalism – the idea, in the words of the title of a 1980s book on Margaret Thatcher, of the need of a 'free economy' for a 'strong state'.[11]

The unique qualification of ordoliberalism for building a bridge from the authoritarian liberalism of interwar Germany, as conceived by Schmitt and analysed by Heller, to the neoliberalism that began to dismantle the post-war political economy in the 1980s can be seen when comparing it to the economic common sense of the 1950s and 1960s. The Frankfurt School of 'Critical Theory', for example, was convinced that the capitalist economy had become inseparably merged into the state, which in the process had turned into the dominant institutional complex in contemporary society.[12] After 'the end of laissez-faire', the place of liberal capitalism was supposed

---

9   Friedrich A. Hayek, 'The Economic Conditions of Interstate Federalism'. In: Hayek, Friedrich A., ed., *Individualism and Economic Order*, Chicago: Chicago University Press 1980 [1939], pp. 255–272.

10   Foucault, *The Birth of Biopolitics: Lectures at the College de France, 1978–1979*.

11   Andrew Gamble, *The Free Economy and the Strong State*, Basingstoke: Macmillan 1988.

12   On this see for example Friedrich Pollock, *Stadien des Kapitalismus*, München: Beck 1975; Friedrich Pollock, 'Staatskapitalismus'. In: Dubiel, Helmut and Alfons Söllner, eds, *Wirtschaft, Recht und Staat im Nationalsozialismus*, Frankfurt am Main: Europäische Verlagsanstalt 1981 [1941], pp. 81–109.

to have been taken by three competing economic systems, communism, fascism and New Deal democracy. All of them were seen as deeply politicized, democratically or not, with markets having given way to large, bureaucratically organized corporate monopolies closely affiliated with the bureaucracies of the state. In its own way, each of the three systems resembled Schmitt's total state, with the New Deal variant carrying the risk of a democratic subversion of market justice, under the influence of pluralist democracy. Schmitt and Heller would have recognized this, from their opposite points of view, and both might have seen the possibility, and indeed the probability, of capitalist pressures for a return to the market: that is, for a new politics carving out a space for free markets sustained and guarded by state authority while protected from egalitarian-democratic infringement. Such pressures for, as I have put it,[13] a Hayekian succession to the Keynesianism social welfare state – the replacement of growth through egalitarian redistribution by growth through stronger incentives for the winners and more severe punishment for the losers – were easily conceptualized in ordoliberal terms, informed as ordoliberalism was, all the way from Schmitt to Hayek, on the intricate dialectic of state strength and state weakness in a liberal order: strong in fending off democratic-political claims for market correction; weak in leaving the governance of the economy to the self-regulating clockwork of the market, as put in place and preserved by political authority.

So far on the general idea. Today's post-democratic, or better perhaps: a-democratic, Hayekian capitalism, after the victory, or almost-victory, of neoliberalism, may be regarded as a historically updated version of ordoliberalism. What it has in common with it is the insulation of a politically instituted market economy from democratic politics, an insulation on account of which both the neoliberal state and the neoliberal economic regime qualify as authoritarian in the sense of Schmitt and Heller. I said historically updated since the neoliberal configuration can do without a background memory of fascist totalitarianism and the catastrophes associated with it; its background are the *trente glorieuses* of the capitalist welfare state. Nor does it depend, as did the authoritarian state project of the early 1930s, on a von Papen pro-capitalist state-of-emergency would-be dictatorship.[14] Today the neutralization of democracy and the recalibration of state power in the service of a market economy with *politically constructed political autonomy* do not primarily take

---

13   Streeck, *Buying Time*.

14   As proclaimed by the von Papen sycophant, Walther Schotte (*Der Neue Staat*, Berlin: Neufeld & Henius 1932), to whom Heller refers.

place through repression but by moving the governance of the political economy to a level where democracy cannot follow, and to institutions constitutionally
designed to be exempt from political contestation, with legally enshrined
missions, whose authority does not come out of gun barrels but is derived
from 'scientific' economic theory. As democratic politics is in the process
emptied of political-economic content, the vacated public space is re-dedi-
cated to consumerist politainment.

Understanding how the politically engineered depoliticization of contemporary European capitalism works requires detailed attention to its institutional
framework. One aspect of it is the relocation of political-economic decisions
from the national to a new, specifically constructed international level, into the
hands of international organizations: to an institutional context, in other
words, that unlike the nation state was consciously designed not to be suitable
for democratization.[15] Ideologically the political-economic preemption of the
nation state – of democratic national institutions in favour of technocratic
supranational ones – makes use of certain positive normative connotations of
internationalism, especially on the Left, to fill the role that in Schmitt's authoritarian nation state was to be filled, presumably, by appeals to patriotic
discipline. Using left internationalism for left disempowerment is a particular
ironic method to de-democratize a capitalist political economy, especially if
deployed by the Left itself. It comes with a moral denunciation of borders and
protectionism *tout cours* in the name of a misunderstood cosmopolitanism,
identifying 'globalization' with liberation, not just of capital, but of life in
general. To dispel concerns about a possible hegemony of global markets over
democratic participation, and with it of the economic over the social, pipe
dreams of a future global or, at a minimum, continental democracy are offered
as baits for left idealists: promises of a better future in which international
democracy will have regained control over international capital, if not tomorrow then the day after tomorrow.

To repeat, the language of authority being out of fashion in today's
Europe, it must be replaced with a mixture of technocratic claims to superior expertise and resigned submission to the 'realities' of 'globalization'.
Since this may not always suffice, the architects of the neo-authoritarian
political-cum-economic regime find it necessary to offer the public a
preview of international democracy, a trailer of things to come, in the
shape of the so-called 'European Parliament' with its 'European elections'.
Of course that 'parliament' has no executive to control; its lacks the right of
legislative initiative; and it cannot change the constitution of 'Europe', if

---

15   Peter Mair, *Ruling the Void: The Hollowing of Western Democracy*, London: Verso 2013.

only because there is no such thing as the rules of the European game are written by the national executives in the form of unbelievably complex and, even for specialists, entirely unreadable international treaties.[16] Just as there is no governing majority in the Parliament, there is no opposition either: voters who are sceptical or do not care about the European construction abstain from voting, and indeed in rising numbers. To the extent that those who do vote elect what the Euro-establishment calls 'anti-Europeans', their representatives are mercilessly sidelined in the 'Parliament's' everyday operation, so much so that during the five years between elections one never hears of them. For decades now, the business of the 'European Parliament' was managed by a centrist Grand Coalition, which functions as a powerful lobby for the relocation of decision-power from national democracies to a 'Europe' immunized against democratic expectations and devoid of opportunities for, in Schmitt's terms, 'democratic-pluralist' interference with the free-market capitalist clockwork.

Europeanization today is by and large identical with a systematic emptying of national democracies of political-economic content, cutting off the remnants of potentially redistributive 'social' democracy, housed in nation states, from an economy that has long grown beyond national borders into a politically constructed and contracted 'Single Market'.[17] Where there are still democratic institutions in Europe, there is no economic governance any more, lest the management of the economy is invaded by market-correcting non-capitalist interests. And where there *is* economic governance, democracy is elsewhere. Since this might become a problem if it became all-too-obvious, the champions of the Brussels non-parliament took for last year's 'European election' – the first since the European ramifications of the global 'financial crisis' were felt – to some of the same devices that have long been used in national democracies to make voters believe they have a choice.[18] Rather than asking for a vote for or against 'Europe' or the euro, the leaders of the two centrist blocs, the centre-right and the centre-left, who had never been able to discover even the slightest difference in their interests and political persuasions, decided

---

16   The literature on the European 'democratic deficit' is unending. Contributing authors are divided between those who feel they should offer institutional remedies for it, and those who don't because they consider the absence of democracy in 'Europa' to be functionally necessary: either to make European unity possible or to promote neoliberal capitalism, or one in pursuit of the other.

17   On this and the following see also Fritz W. Scharpf ('Monetary Union, Fiscal Crisis and the Pre-Emption of Democracy', *Zeitschrift für Staats- und Europawissenschaaften*, vol. 9, no. 2, 2011, pp. 163–198; 'Monetary Union, Fiscal Crisis, and the Disabling of Democratic Accountability', *Politics in the Age of Austerity*, pp. 108–142).

18   On the European election of 2014 and its aftermath see Susan Watkins ('The Political State of the Union', *New Left Review*, no. 90, 2014, pp. 5–25).

to personalize the election and present themselves as *Spitzenkandidaten* competing for the presidency of the European Commission (which, of course, is filled *not* by the 'Parliament' but by member state governments) – an exercise in *Fassadendemokratie* (Habermas) if there ever was one. That they never managed to explain where they disagreed, even more so than their Social-Democratic and Christian-Democratic equivalents in national politics, obviously did not bother them, nor did the fact that in several countries their competition was not even noticed. In any case, voter turnout declined once again, to 43 per cent, and no less than 15 per cent of those who bothered to vote voted for parties classified as 'anti-European' by the 'true Europeans'. Regardless, the *Spitzenkandidat* whose party won 30 per cent of the seats (i.e., the backing of roughly 13 per cent of the electorate) claimed victory while his nominal opponent, commanding 25 per cent of the seats, rushed to support his demand for the office of Commission President, in the act claiming for himself, as it turned out: in vain, the vice presidency.

Next to the so-called 'European Parliament' there are four more political institutions that run, maintain and protect the politically depoliticized liberal-capitalist market of Europe united by a common currency. In discussing them briefly, I will pay particular attention to how they match the model of Schmitt's 'authoritarian state' in shielding the capitalist economy from the spectre of 'democratic pluralism'.

(1) The *European Council*. It consists of the heads of national governments and is supported by various councils of ministers, especially of finance and foreign affairs. Of particular importance here is the so-called Euro Group of the finance ministers of European Monetary Union (EMU) member states. The Council is legislative and executive of the multinational European non-state in one, a combination that is by itself a defining feature of an authoritarianism regime. The Council also serves to keep national democratic institutions, especially national parliaments, at bay in that it operates through negotiations, typically in secret, between the governments of sovereign states. Once a decision has been reached it is near impossible for national publics and their representatives to undo it, an effect that has been studied in various contexts under the heading of multi-level diplomacy.[19] Not only is it unlikely that all countries involved will feel equally concerned, but reopening what will typically be a complex package deal may entail unknown risks, with uncertain and asymmetric outcomes. Governments will bring this to bear in national ratification debates and find their power increased by it, also because

19   Peter B. Evans, Harold K. Jacobson and Robert D. Putnam, eds, *Double-Edged Diplomacy: International Bargaining and Domestic Politcs*, Berkeley: University of California Press 1993.

non-ratification would impair their standing with the other governments and thereby weaken the country's position in future negotiations.

Another consequence of the primacy of the Council in European economic governance is that it redefines class conflicts as international conflicts, turning distributional issues between classes into international issues.[20] This not only encourages cross-class coalitions at national level, but it also mitigates economic conflicts as it envelopes them into larger issue packages, hands them over to diplomats, and above all entangles them with issues of international peace. Diplomacy thus takes the place of class struggle, and international cooperation takes precedence over social justice as long as repressed class conflicts can be prevented from returning in the form of international hostilities. Even then, however, the capitalist market economy will likely remain shielded from egalitarian correction, for example by economically stronger nations defending their interest by drawing on the toolkit of national sovereignty.

Moreover, the more diverse a multinational regime in terms of national economic structures and interests, the less likely it is that its governing body will be able to take discretionary measures to correct the outcome of markets. That federations of states can best agree on liberating their economies from state intervention – i.e., on what contemporary political science has called 'negative integration'[21] – has been pointed out by Friedrich von Hayek as early as 1939.[22] International federation, so says Hayek, will be needed in the future to restore and preserve international peace; but a federation that fails to integrate its economy will not stand; and economic integration among countries both different and equal can proceed only in the form of market integration: the institutionalization of a single market free from state intervention, *because member states will not be able to agree anything other than that.* Hayek's 1939 article builds a bridge between Austrian economics, Schmitt's interwar 'authoritarian liberalism', German post-war ordoliberalism and the neoliberalism of European Monetary Union since the 1990s.

(2) The *European Commission*. From early on, the Commission has aspired to establishing itself as the executive branch of a supranational European superstate, similar to the 'European Parliament', claiming the status of a European legislature. Events since the 2008 crisis, however, have confirmed and indeed cemented the predominance of the Council, arresting the

---

20   Streeck, *Buying Time*, pp. 90ff.
21   Fritz W. Scharpf, 'Negative and Positive Integration in the Political Economy of European Welfare States.' In: Marks, Gary et al., eds, *Governance in the European Union*, London: Sage 1996, pp. 15–39.
22   Hayek, 'The Economic Conditions of Interstate Federalism'.

Commission in its role as a bureaucratic agency charged with implementing Council decisions and overseeing member countries' adherence to the treaties. While subservient to the Council,[23] however, the Commission can and does use its administrative powers to protect the Single Market by preventing member states from protecting their national economies, as well as national institutions like labour law that provide workers with collective political capacity. Basically, the institutional interest of the Commission in safeguarding and extending its powers and functions is best served by devoting its agency to liberating national economies from national political market distortion, democratic as it may be, thereby advancing the integration of the European economy in the form of a politically constructed and safeguarded common market cleansed of national and unimpeded by supranational pluralist democracy.

(3) The *European Court of Justice* (ECJ). A court is an authoritative institution, and a *de facto* constitutional court like the ECJ charged as a last instance with interpreting the law of the land may even be considered an authoritarian one. This should be all the more so in the absence of a true parliament by which it could be overruled. In fact, the real legislator facing the ECJ, the Council, typically requires unanimity to correct a Court decision, and sometimes even the unanimous revision of an international treaty. The ECJ's original normative capital, as is well known, was competition law of the kind developed by the German ordoliberal school. The Court has continuously extended that capital, by using its authority to institute competitive markets wherever an opportunity for this arose and identifying them with the so-called 'four freedoms': the free circulation of goods, services, capital and labour in the Union. Like the Council and the Commission, the Court operates on the general premise that it is the mission of 'Europe' to expand the institutional space for free markets and fend off whatever attempts may be made to contain or distort markets, nationally as well as internationally. The neoliberal, pro-market bias in ECJ jurisdiction has long been noted, and so has the tactical shrewdness with which the ECJ pursues its agenda.[24] Having established early on the principle of 'supremacy and direct effect' of European law, including of course its own rulings, the ECJ

---

23   Martin Höpner allows a more independent role for the Commission, in particular for the time before the crisis (see his *Wie der Europäische Gerichtshof und die Kommission Liberalisierung durchsetzen: Befunde aus der MPIfG-Forschungsgruppe zur Politischen Ökonomie der europäischen Integration*, MPIfG Discussion Paper 14/8, Cologne: Max Planck Institute for the Study of Societies 2014).

24   Benjamin Werner, *Der Streit um das VW-Gesetz: Wie Europäische Kommission und Europäischer Gerichtshof die Unternehmenskontrolle liberalisieren*, Frankfurt am Main: Campus 2013.

commands powerful tools to intervene into national political economies and impose on them what is essentially a liberal and indeed neoliberal economic constitution, protected from democratic politics partly by design and partly by default, in any case exactly as envisaged by both German ordoliberal doctrine and Schmitt's 'authoritarian liberalism'.

(4) The *European Central Bank* (ECB). The ECB is the kingpin of the European Monetary Union (EMU), and indeed its sovereign. While other central banks are embedded in a state with coextensive jurisdiction and have to face a government and a public at the same territorial and political level, the currency and the common market the ECB runs are stateless (as is, essentially, the legal system governed by the ECJ). This makes the ECB the most independent central bank in the world, and its monetary regime the most depoliticized. Unlike Keynesian money, the euro is nothing but a means of exchange and a store of value; it is in particular not suitable for democratic market correction, for example in pursuit of full employment. European money, as conceived in the treaties that created it, is Austrian, ordoliberal and neoliberal money.

Indeed, there is hardly an institution that corresponds more closely to the ideal of authoritarian liberalism than the ECB. EMU, with its 'Single Market' and minimalist institutional furniture, looks conspicuously like an ideal realization of Schmitt's 'authoritarian state' some eighty years after its conception. The legitimacy of its core institution, the ECB, rests exclusively on its supposed technical expertise with respect to what kind of public policy a free market economy requires if it is to remain one. In theory this is very little, while in practice it can easily become very much. On the surface the ECB's mandate is simply to provide for a desirable rate of inflation for the combined economy of its member states and ensure the health and viability of their financial and payment systems. Since the national political economies that are part of EMU are historically governed by diverse institutions, however, they tend to respond differently to the ECB's money regime and monetary policy. If this raises the possibility of the common currency failing, as it did in the succession of crises since 2008, the ECB, being the only institution in charge of EMU as a whole, is forced or feels free to do 'whatever it takes' to preserve it.[25] Who would not be reminded of Carl Schmitt's definition of the state of emergency, the *Ausnahmezustand*, being *die Stunde der Exekutive*, the hour of the executive when *Not kennt kein Gebot*, when the sovereign is entitled and proves himself

---

25   The now famous phrase used by the president of the ECB in a meeting with financial investors in London, on 27 July 2012, when asked what the ECB would do to keep the euro alive. He continued: 'And believe me, it will be enough.'

as such in being able to suspend the law and use whatever means available, legal or extralegal, to secure the survival of the community?[26]

For several years now the ECB has routinely been acting *extra legem* to fill the political vacuum created at the centre of the EMU by its founders, with the intention to build Euroland into the apolitical capitalist market economy of neoliberalism.[27] ECB intervention, on the surface limited to stabilizing the euro at a targeted inflation rate and keeping payment systems functional, and legitimate only with reference to this narrow mandate, has penetrated deeply into national institutional arrangements and political settlements to 'reform' them, so as to adjust them to the common neoliberal money regime – so as put an end, in the name of sound money, to previous national practices of adjusting the money regime to national political settlements, in particular to politically negotiated and nationally institutionalized ideas of market-correcting social justice.

Together with the Council, the Commission and the ECJ, but if need be also without them, the European Central Bank has developed into the *de facto* government of the biggest economy on earth, a government entirely shielded from 'pluralist democracy' that acts, and can only act, as the guardian and guarantor of a liberal market economy. Since the crisis of 2008, which is of course far from over if it ever will be, the Bank has acquired wide-ranging capacities to discipline the sovereign states and societies in and under its jurisdiction to make them pay proper respect to the rules of a neoliberal money-cum-market regime. Today the ECB can at its discretion withhold liquidity from the banking systems of states that refuse to follow its precepts as to their public finances, the size and composition of their public sectors, and even the structure of their wage-setting systems. States and governments that do not 'reform' themselves in line with capitalist rectitude, and thereby fail to earn the confidence of international *haute finance*, can be punished in a broad variety of ways – while states that carry out institutional reforms as promoted by the Bank can be rewarded, even by the ECB printing fresh money for them, in violation or circumvention of EMU treaties.[28] Given the jurisdictional

---

26   Carl Schmitt, *Politische Theologie. Vier Kapitel zur Lehre von der Souveränität*, Berlin: Duncker und Humblot 1922. On this also Christian Joerges, *Europe's Economic Constitution in Crisis and the Emergence of a New Constitutional Constellation*, ZenTra Working Papers in Transnational Studies No. 06/2012, Revised Edition Sept. 2013, Bremen: Center for Transnational Studies of the Universities of Bremen and Oldenburg 2013.

27   This precedes the crisis, and so does the insight of quite a few perceptive observers that the ECB, the way it is instituted, is a continuing drag on democracy in Europe. See for example Sheri Berman and Kathleen R. McNamara, 'Bank on Democracy', *Foreign Affairs*, vol. 78, no. 2, 1999, 2–8.

28   For example, by dressing up the support of national banking systems and the extension of credit to governments running deficits (with strict conditions as to neoliberal 'reforms' attached) as monetary policy.

asymmetry between the ECB and the EMU member countries, as well as the absence of an equally effective political counterpart at the level of the EMU as a whole, the ECB is the ideal dictator – the only agent capable of taking decisive action – when it comes to crisis management, for example in the case of a member state defaulting. The same holds for making member countries converge on the model of neoliberal financialized capitalism, in adaptation to the requirements of a common, one-size-fits-all monetary regime in good standing with 'financial markets'. The 'authoritarian state' as creator and protector of 'authoritarian liberalism' has arrived.

CHAPTER SEVEN

Why the Euro Divides Europe

To understand the conflicts that have erupted in and around the Eurozone over the past five years, it may be helpful to begin by revisiting the concept of money.[1] It is one that figures prominently in Chapter 2 of Max Weber's monumental *Economy and Society*, 'Sociological Categories of Economic Action'. Money becomes money by virtue of a 'regulated organization', a 'monetary system', Weber thought.[2] And following G. F. Knapp's *The State Theory of Money* [1905], he insisted that under modern conditions, this system would necessarily be monopolized by the state. Money is a politico-economic institution inserted into, and made effective by, a 'ruling organization' – another crucial Weberian concept; like all institutions, it privileges certain interests and disadvantages others. This makes it an object of social 'conflict' – or, better, a resource in what Weber refers to as a 'market struggle':

> Money is not a 'mere voucher for unspecified utilities', which could be altered at will without any fundamental effect on the character of the price system as a struggle of man against man. 'Money' is, rather, primarily a weapon in this struggle, and prices are expressions of the struggle; they are instruments of calculation only as estimated quantifications of relative chances in this struggle of interests.[3]

Weber's socio-political concept of money differs fundamentally from that of liberal economics.[4] The founding documents of that tradition are Chapters IV and V of Adam Smith's *Wealth of Nations*, in which money is explained as an increasingly universal medium of exchange, serving an (ultimately, unlimited) expansion of trade relations in 'advanced societies' – that is, societies based on a division of labour. Money replaces direct exchange by indirect exchange, through the interpolation of a universally available, easily transportable, infinitely divisible and durable intermediate commodity (a process described

1 This essay originated as the Distinguished Lecture in the Social Sciences, Wissenschaftszentrum Berlin, 21 April 2015. Published in: *New Left Review*, vol. 95, September/October 2015, pp. 5–26.
2 Max Weber, *Economy and Society*, Guenther Roth and Claus Wittich, eds, Berkeley: University of California Press 1968, pp. 48, 166.
3 Weber, *Economy and Society*, p. 108.
4 In what follows I am indebted to the important and stimulating discussion in Geoffrey Ingham's *The Nature of Money*, Cambridge: Polity 2004.

by Marx as 'simple circulation', C–M–C). According to Smith, monetary systems develop from below, from the desire of market participants to extend and simplify their trade relations, which increase their efficiency by continually reducing their transaction costs. For Smith, money is a neutral symbol for the value of objects to be exchanged; it should be made as fit as possible for purpose, even if it has an objective value of its own, arising in theory from its production costs. The state makes an appearance only to the extent that it can be invited by market participants to increase the efficiency of money by 'putting its stamp' on it, thus making it seem more trustworthy. Unlike Weber, who differentiated monetary systems according to their affinity to countervailing distributive interests, for Smith the only interest that money can serve is the universal interest in ensuring the smooth functioning of as extensive a market economy as possible.

Remarkably, the post-war sociological tradition chose to follow Smith rather than Weber. The demise of the Historical School of Economics – and the fact that structural functionalism, above all Talcott Parsons at Harvard, ceded the economy as an object of study to Economics faculties increasingly purified in a neo-classical spirit – enabled sociology, as it became established in the *post-histoire* decades after 1945, to dispense with a theory of money of its own. Instead it opted for a quiet life and chose to conceive of money, if at all, in the manner of Smith, as an interest-neutral medium of communication, rather than as a social institution shot through with power – as a numerical value, a *numéraire*, rather than a social relation.[5] This led to a rupture, both in sociology and economic theory, with the fierce debates of the interwar years about the nature of money and the political implications of monetary systems. These had been at the heart of Keynesian theory, in particular: see the battles around the social and political implications of the gold standard, driven notably by Keynes himself, or around Irving Fisher's full-reserve banking model.

Of paradigmatic importance here was Parsons and Smelser's 1956 work *Economy and Society*, subtitled 'A Study in the Integration of Economic and Social Theory'. In Parsonian systems theory, money appears as a representation of purchasing power, the capacity to control the exchange of goods. It also has the special social function of conferring prestige, and thus acts as a mediator between 'detailed symbols and a broader symbolization'.[6] Historically, money develops, as in Smith, through the growth of the division of labour,

---

5   Ingham, *The Nature of Money*.
6   Talcott Parsons and Neil Smelser, *Economy and Society: A Study in the Integration of Economic and Social Theory*, London: Routledge and Kegan Paul 1984 [1956], p. 71.

which demands an abstract representation of economic value so as to make the expansion of exchange possible. Money appears in this process as a 'cultural object' which, together with credit instruments and certificates of indebtedness, 'constitute rights or claims on objects of economic value' – and hence in Weber's terms as 'mere vouchers for unspecified utilities'.[7]

MONETARY WEAPONS

That money is far more than this is something for which Parsons, and American sociology in general, might have found ample evidence in his own country – not merely in the interwar years, which after 1945 were somehow declared an exceptional era, but in its earlier history. The discovery of that evidence, however, had to await the emergence in the 1990s of the 'new economic sociology', which undertook the rehabilitation of Weber's view of money as weaponry in the 'market struggle'. A contribution to this development, as important now as it was then, was furnished in 'The Color of Money and the Nature of Value', a study by Bruce Carruthers and Sarah Babb of the domestic political conflicts over a new U.S. monetary system after the Civil War.[8] The authors adopted an analytical distinction proposed by the political scientist Jack Knight: monetary systems, like institutions in general, could not be judged merely according to 'the coordination-for-collective-benefits conception of social institutions' – in other words, by whether they provided an inter-subjectively communicable symbolization of values and value claims. Just as legitimate and even requisite, according to Carruthers and Babb, was the conflict perspective – we might even call it the political

---

7   Parsons and Smelser, *Economy and Society*, pp. 106, 140ff. See also Parsons's 1964 essay, 'Evolutionary Universals', in which 'money and the market' appear as one of the four fundamental historic achievements of modern societies, alongside bureaucratic organization, a universalistic legal system and democratic forms of association. Parsons sees 'evolutionary universals' as structural features of social systems, without which major developmental steps would be blocked. As interconnected institutions, money and the market make 'a fundamental contribution to the adaptive capacity of societies' in which they have developed, because they facilitate the release of resources from their ascriptive bonds and make it possible to dedicate them to new ends. In this process, money is indispensable as a 'symbolic medium' that 'represents' in 'abstract', 'neutral' form the 'economic utility' of the concrete goods for which it is exchangeable, as opposed to the competing claims of other orders. Money develops differently in different societies since its functions can, to a greater or lesser degree, be assumed by bureaucratic organizations. But the question is always to what extent the institutional elements of a concrete monetary system fulfil the task of providing 'the operative units of society, including of course its government, with a pool of disposable resources that can be applied to any of a range of uses and within limits can be shifted from use to use': Parsons, 'Evolutionary Universals in Society', *American Sociological Review*, vol. 29, no. 3, June 1964, p. 350.

8   Bruce Carruthers and Sarah Babb, 'The Color of Money and the Nature of Value: Greenbacks and Gold in Postbellum America', *American Journal of Sociology*, vol. 101, no. 6, 1996, pp. 1558ff.

perspective – put forward by Knight, in which a monetary system comes into existence as the result of disagreements between actors with competing interests.[9] As such, it may possess more or less asymmetrical distributive effects and conflicting interests, which are often more important in social reality than their efficiency.[10]

'The Color of Money' reconstructs the political and economic divisions over the future monetary regime of the United States, and the nature of money in general, during the last third of the nineteenth century. At that time, the battlefront ran more or less centrally between the Smithian and Weberian conceptions of money. The first emphasized the dependability of money as a medium of symbolic communication, for efficient economic coordination and social integration; this was linked to a naturalist value theory and the call for a return to the gold standard. The alternative view, based on a remarkably well-developed social-constructivist theory of the value of money, espoused the introduction of freely created paper money. As was to be expected, the advocates of gold stressed the public interest in a value-symbolization that could inspire confidence, while the supporters of 'greenbacks' – printed dollar bills – emphasized the divergent distributive effects of the two concepts of money, representing different material interests. And indeed the rival approaches were rooted in different accumulation practices and ways of life: advocates of the gold standard represented East Coast 'old money' and were interested above all in stability; the paper-money contingent was based in the South and West and wanted free access to credit, either to help devalue the debts they had incurred or to boost expansion. Conflicting interests over which development path the fast-growing capitalist economy should take were linked to opposing structures of class power and privilege: the lifeworld of a patrician urban class, above all in New York, against that of the indebted farmers and 'cowboy operators' in the rest of the country.

---

9   Jack Knight, *Institutions and Social Conflict*, Cambridge: Cambridge University Press 1992.

10   In this sense, monetary systems can be regarded as analogous to political systems, which typically have a built-in tendency to distort decisions in favour of privileged interests. They have a dynamic of their own, which E. E. Schattschneider, referring to the pluralist democracy of the United States, has characterized as a 'mobilization of bias'; 'the flaw in the pluralist heaven is that the heavenly choir sings with a strong upper-class accent': *The Semisovereign People*, New York: Holt, Rinehart and Winston 1960, p. 35. I owe the reference to a recent essay by Jacob Hacker and Paul Pierson, 'After the "Master Theory": Downs, Schattschneider, and the Rebirth of Policy-Focused Analysis', *Perspectives on Politics*, vol. 12, no. 3, 2014. In *The Nature of Money*, Ingham describes money as a 'social relation', whose concrete shape is determined by the particular monetary system underlying it.

CASH AND COMMUNICATIVE ACTION

Coming of age in the 1980s, German sociology took its concept of money not from Weber but from Parsons – and, via Parsons, from the economic tradition going back to Smith. This is true not just of Niklas Luhmann, in his adaptation of systems theory, but equally of Jürgen Habermas, even though – or perhaps, precisely because – Habermas developed his 'Theory of Communicative Action' in large measure through an immanent critique of Luhmann's work. The problem, as I understand it, lies in the fact that Habermas's critique of the concept of a 'steering medium', which he took from Luhmann and Parsons, leaves its validity for 'the functional domains of material reproduction' untouched, since these domains can, uniquely, be 'differentiated out of the lifeworld'.[11] Although in Habermasian terms no one really 'speaks' in modern economic subsystems – that remains the prerogative of the lifeworld – the 'special "language" of money' suffices for that subsystem to perform its function.[12]

The assumption here, of course, is that 'the economy' *can* be thought of as a technical subsystem of modern societies, purified of lifeworld connections and able to function without them in an instrumentally rational, neutral manner. Within the sphere of competence of the economy so conceived there is no compulsion to act; it is possible instead simply to 'steer'. Thus 'the economy' can be seen as a predictable mechanism of means, entirely in the spirit of standard economic theory – although embedded in a more comprehensive context of communication and action, and capable in principle of being organized on a democratic basis. With the aid of money, a 'steering medium' that is not just adequate to the task but ideally suited to it, this mechanism confines itself, albeit with a reduced level of communication, to coordinating the actors involved and focusing their efforts on the efficient deployment of scarce resources.[13]

The theoretical consequences are far-reaching. Habermas's partial incorporation of systems theory – the recognition of a technocratic claim to dominance over certain sectors of society, analogous to relativity theory conceding a limited applicability to classical mechanics – depoliticizes the economic, narrowing it down to a unidimensional emphasis on efficiency, as the price for smuggling a space for politicization into a post-materialist theory

11   Jürgen Habermas, *The Theory of Communicative Action, vol. 2: Lifeworld and System*, trans. Thomas McCarthy, Boston: Beacon Press 1985, p. 261.
12   Habermas, *Theory of Communicative Action*, p. 259.
13   For the treatment of money in Habermas, see also Nigel Dodd, *The Sociology of Money: Economics, Reason and Contemporary Society*, New York: Continuum 1994.

of 'modernity'. The fundamental insight of political economy is forgotten: that the natural laws of the economy, which appear to exist by virtue of their own efficiency, are in reality nothing but projections of social-power relations which present themselves ideologically as technical necessities. The consequence is that it ceases to be understood as a capitalist economy and becomes 'the economy', pure and simple, while the social struggle against capitalism is replaced by a political and juridical struggle for democracy. The idea that money functions as a 'communication system' supersedes the notion of a monetary system, in Weber's sense; with it vanishes any idea of money's political role, as distinct from its technical function. The same holds true for the realization that monetary systems, as political and economic institutions, conform first to power and only secondarily to the market. As a rule, then, they have a bias towards one or other ruling interest. We may say with Schattschneider that, as with the 'heavenly choir' of a pluralist democracy, the language of money always speaks with an accent – and normally the same upper-class accent as the choir's.[14]

MARKET STRUGGLE IN THE EUROZONE

For if money were nothing but a neutral medium of communication – a symbolic language to facilitate the productive coordination of certain types of human action – then we should expect that, after more than a decade, the euro would have brought its users together in a shared identity. Just as the Deutschmark is said to have created a 'Deutschmark nationalism',[15] so the euro should have created a European patriotism, as its inventors expected. In 1999, Jean-Claude Juncker – who, as prime minister of Luxembourg, was a leading tax adviser to multinational firms – declared that, once citizens held the new notes and coins in their hands at the start of 2002, 'a new we-feeling would develop: we Europeans'.[16] The same year Helmut Kohl, by then already an

---

14 One could add that global money speaks with an American accent; while we are always told that, like the metre or the yard, 'money has no colour', the dollar is undeniably green, not gold, just as the euro is black, red and yellow.

15 Jürgen Habermas, 'Der DM Nationalismus', *Die Zeit*, 30 March 1990.

16 Dirk Koch, 'Die Brüsseler Republik', *Der Spiegel*, 27 December 1999. Juncker's theory of identity fits comfortably with a theory of cognition that informs the policy of social engineering he is pursuing. As an example of 'permissive consent', it is splendidly summed up in the following account of his practice: 'We decide something, put it out into the world and wait for a while to see what happens. If there is no great uproar and no rebellions *because most people don't really grasp what we have decided*, then we just move on to the next stage – step by step, until there is no going back' (ibid., my emphasis). As to the underlying practical ethics, we recollect the maxim Juncker proclaimed when he presided over the Eurozone bank rescue: 'When matters get serious, we have to tell lies'. In 2014, to the general acclaim of all right-thinking Europeans, Juncker was elected president of the European Commission;

ex-German Chancellor, predicted that the euro would create a 'European identity' and that it would take 'at most five years before Britain also joined the currency union, followed directly by Switzerland'.[17] At a slightly lower level, media advertisements solicited support for the single currency with photos of youthful travellers of both sexes gazing into each other's eyes, in a way that brings nations closer together. Their radiant smiles expressed their joy as they calculated how much money they had saved in commission payments and exchange-rate losses, travelling to their rendezvous – identity theory and efficiency theory in one!

The 'European idea' – or better: ideology – notwithstanding, the euro has split Europe in two. As the engine of an ever-closer union the currency's balance sheet has been disastrous. Norway and Switzerland will not be joining the EU any time soon; Britain is actively considering leaving it altogether. Sweden and Denmark were supposed to adopt the euro at some point; that is now off the table. The Eurozone itself is split between surplus and deficit countries, North and South, Germany and the rest. At no point since the end of the Second World War have its nation states confronted each other with so much hostility; the historic achievements of European unification have never been so threatened. No ruler today would dare to call a referendum in France, the Netherlands or Denmark on even the smallest steps towards further integration. Thanks to the single currency, hopes for a European Germany – for integration as a solution to the problems of both German identity and European hegemony – have been superseded by fears of a German Europe, not least in the FRG itself. In consequence, election campaigns in Southern Europe are being fought and won against Germany and its Chancellor; pictures of Merkel and Schäuble wearing swastikas have begun appearing, not just in Greece and Italy but even in France. That Germany finds itself increasingly faced by demands for reparations – not only from Greece but also Italy – shows how far its post-war policy of Europeanizing itself has foundered since its transition to the single currency.[18]

---

according to Jürgen Habermas, 'Any other decision would have been a blow to the heart of Europe': *Frankfurter Allgemeine Zeitung*, 29 May 2015.

17 Rainer Hank, 'Europa der Heuchler', *Frankfurter Allgemeine Zeitung*, 15 March 2015.

18 There have been some personal tragedies along the way. Schäuble, of all people – the long-standing champion of a 'core Europe', with Germany and France as its indissolubly united centre – stood accused in April 2015 of an 'intolerable and unacceptable hostility to France', based on his alleged wish to place its economy 'under supervision'. These attacks came in response to Schäuble's remarks in Washington to the effect that 'it would be better for France to be compelled to introduce reforms . . . but this is all difficult, such is the nature of democracy' – the common sense of every German finance minister, of whatever party. It was reported that the chairman of the French Socialists would be calling for 'confrontation with the European Right', and especially 'with the CDU–CSU'. The Parti de Gauche demanded that Schäuble 'apologize to the French people'; his statements were said to exemplify 'the

Anyone wishing to understand how an institution such as the single currency can wreak such havoc needs a concept of money that goes beyond that of the liberal economic tradition and the sociological theory informed by it. The conflicts in the Eurozone can only be decoded with the aid of an economic theory that can conceive of money not merely as a system of signs that symbolize claims and contractual obligations, but also, in tune with Weber's view, as the product of a ruling organization, and hence as a contentious and contested institution with distributive consequences full of potential for conflict.

REGIONAL PECULIARITIES

The 'varieties of capitalism' literature supplies some helpful preliminary indications as to why the single currency is dividing Europe, instead of uniting it – at least in so far as this work is historical-institutional in cast, rather than efficiency-theoretical.[19] Over their course of development, every country in the Eurozone has configured the critical interface between its society and its capitalist economy in its own way; the different monetary systems played a key role in the resulting national economies.[20] The single currency can be understood as the attempt, from whatever motive, to replace the national monetary systems, which were adapted to their institutional and political contexts, with a supranational monetary system that would be equally valid for all the participating societies. It was designed to inject a new, neoliberal form of money into the national economies that would enforce the development of an institutional context appropriate to its own needs.

Modern monetary systems and practices are embedded in nation states and can differ fundamentally from one country to the next.[21] In the case of the

---

new German arrogance', Germany was out to dominate Europe, etc. See 'Schäuble will Dividenden-Steverschlupfloch stopfen', *Frankfurter Allgemeine Zeitung*, 18 April 2015.

19   On this distinction, see my 'E Pluribus Unum? Varieties and Commonalities of Capitalism'. In: Granovetter, Mark and Richard Swedberg, eds, *The Sociology of Economic Life*, Boulder, CO: Westview Press 2011.

20   As Fritz Scharpf emphasizes in his critical discussion of Habermas's integration theory, the institutions of political economy – and not just the liberal guarantees of freedom and equality – belong among the historical achievements fought for through nation states; they cannot simply be standardized at a supranational level or abolished in favour of supranational nostrums. Anyone who has witnessed the interminable debates between European trade unions over the right forms of co-determination in large and small enterprises will be well aware of this. See Scharpf, 'Das Dilemma der Supranationalen Demokratie in Europa', *Leviathan*, vol. 43, no. 1, 2015, and Habermas, 'Warum der Ausbau der Europäischen Union zu einer supranationalen Demokratie nötig und wie er möglich ist', *Leviathan*, vol. 42, no. 4, 2014.

21   See Georg Friedrich Knapp, *Staatliche Theorie des Geldes*, Munich and Leipzig: Verlag von Dunder and Humblot 1905; published in English in an abridged edition as *The State Theory of Money*, trans. H. M. Lucas and J. Bonar, London: Macmillan 1924.

single currency, it will suffice to distinguish between the Ideal-Types of the Mediterranean countries and those of Northern Europe, Germany in particular.[22] The European South produced a type of capitalism in which growth was driven above all by domestic demand, supported where need be by inflation; demand was driven in turn by budget deficits, or by trade unions strengthened by high levels of job security and a large public sector. Moreover, inflation made it easier for governments to borrow, as it steadily devalued the public debt. The system was supported by a heavily regulated banking sector, partly or wholly state owned. All these things taken together made it possible to harmonize more or less satisfactorily the interests of workers and employers, who typically operated in the domestic market and on a small scale. The price for the social peace generated in this way was a loss of international competitiveness, in contrast to hard-currency countries; but with national currencies, that loss could be made good by periodic devaluations, at the expense of foreign imports.

The northern economies functioned differently. Their growth came from exports, so they were inflation-averse. This applied to workers and their unions, too, despite the occasional use of 'Keynesian' rhetoric – and all the more so in the era of globalization, when cost increases could so easily lead to production being relocated to cheaper zones. These countries do not necessarily need the option of devaluation. Despite the repeated revaluations of its currency, due in part to the revaluation of its products, the German economy has thrived since the 1970s, not least by migrating from markets that compete on price to those that compete on quality. Unlike the Mediterranean states, the hard-currency countries are wary of both inflation and debt, even though their interest rates are relatively low. Their ability to survive without a loose monetary policy benefits their numerous savers, whose votes carry significant political weight; it also means they don't need to take on the risk of market bubbles.[23]

---

22   On what follows, see among others, Armingeon and Baccaro, 'Political Economy of the Sovereign Debt Crisis'; Lucio Baccaro and Chiara Benassi, 'Softening Industrial Relations Institutions, Hardening Growth Model: The Transformation of the German Political Economy', *Stato e mercato* 102, 2014; Blankart, 'Oil and Vinegar'; Hall, 'The Economics and Politics of the Euro Crisis'; Bob Hancke, *Unions, Central Banks, and EMU: Labour Market Institutions and Monetary Integration in Europe*, Oxford: Oxford University Press 2013; Martin Höpner and Mark Lutter, *One Currency and Many Modes of Wage Formation: Why the Eurozone is too Heterogeneous for the Euro*, MPIfG Discussion Paper 14/14, Cologne 2014; Johnston and Regan, *European Integration and the Incompatibility of Different Varieties of Capitalism*; Torben Iverson and David Soskice, 'A structural-institutional explanation of the Eurozone crisis', paper given at LSE, 3 June 2013.

23   'First save, then buy' is the motto of traditional German cultural and economic behaviour, supported by a complex bundle of mutually complementary political and economic institutions. See recently Daniel Mertens, *Privatverschuldung in Deutschland*.

INEQUALITY FROM DIVERSITY

It is important to stress that no one version of the interface between capitalism and society is intrinsically morally superior to the others. Every embedding of capitalism in society, every attempt to fit its logic into that of a social order will be 'rough and ready', improvised, compromised and never entirely satisfactory for any party. This does not stop the partisans of the various national models from decrying the alternatives and promoting their own as the most correct and rational. The reason for this is that what is at stake in the conflict of economic models is not just people's standard of living but also the moral economy that has become established in each case.

In Northern Europe such cultural chauvinism produces the cliché of the 'lazy Greeks', while in the South it results in the notion of the 'cold-blooded Germans' who 'live to work instead of working to live', with calls for each side to acknowledge its errors and mend its ways. Thanks to such distortions, it seldom occurs to the Germans who call on the Greeks to 'reform' their economy and their society to put an end to extravagance and corruption, that they are really asking the Greeks to replace their out-of-date, local forms of corruption with modern, global forms, à la Goldman Sachs.[24]

Monetary systems designed for different social dispensations can coexist, as long as states retain sovereignty and can adjust their currencies to compensate for fluctuations in competitiveness. By contrast, an integrated monetary regime for such disparate economies as Europe's supply-based North and demand-based South cannot work equally well for both. The consequence is that qualitative horizontal diversity is transformed into a quantitative vertical inequality. When politically differentiated national economies are forced together in a currency union, those disadvantaged by it come under pressure to 'reform' their mode of production and the social contract adapted to it along the lines of the countries privileged by the currency. Only if they can and wish to do so – in other words, only if the integrated monetary system creates an integrated capitalist order – can a currency union function free of friction.

---

24 I leave open the question of how desirable it would be for societies like Greece or Spain to 'modernize' in the sense of casting off their 'feudal shackles' (see Hirschman, 'Rival Interpretations of Market Society') for two reasons: first, intervening in another country in this way is not an option; second, there is more than one way of (temporarily) harmonizing capitalism and society. Even more than individual American states, European nation states can and should be treated as 'laboratories of democracy' (see Lewis Brandeis in *New State Ice Co. vs Liebman*, 1932), where 'democracy' may be deemed to include, not just the institutional formalities of collective debate and policy development, but the always-provisional configuring of the conflict zone between society and the capitalist economy.

ORIGINATING BATTLES

The strategic goals and compromises of European Monetary Union were shaped from the start by these inevitably uneven outcomes; the national economies were thereby forced into selective adaptation. The euro was always a contradictory and conflict-ridden construct. By the late 1980s France and Italy, in particular, were fed up with the hard-currency interest policy of the Bundesbank – which, given the premise of the free movement of capital in a financializing common market, had become the *de facto* central bank of Europe. They were also irked, the French above all, by the periodic necessity of devaluing their currency vis-à-vis the Deutschmark to maintain their competitiveness; this was felt to be a national humiliation. By replacing the Bundesbank with a European Central Bank, they hoped to regain some of the monetary sovereignty they had ceded to Germany, while also making monetary policy in Europe a little less focused on stability and directed rather more towards political goals, such as full employment. To be sure, Mitterrand and his then Finance Minister Jacques Delors also hoped to use a currency union – which would exclude the devaluation option and impose a harder currency – to force the French Communist Party and trade unions to give up their political and economic goals. The Banca d'Italia had similar ideas.

The Bundesbank and the overwhelming majority of German economists, predominantly ordoliberal and monetarist in outlook, opposed the single currency because they feared it would undermine Germany's 'stability culture'. Kohl would have preferred to see the currency union preceded by a political union – ideally with a German economic policy, of course. His European partners were not calling for a common currency in order to sacrifice even more of their sovereignty, however. Kohl gave way, for fear of losing their support for German reunification; but he probably expected the currency union to be followed, somehow or other, by political union – an expectation still cherished today by Germany's Europhile centre left, the last supporters of neo-functionalist integration theory. When major allies in Kohl's political camp threatened to rebel, he overcame their resistance by ensuring that the common monetary regime would follow the German model, with the European Central Bank as a copy of the Bundesbank writ large.

This set the scene for the conflicts of the years to come. The slogan used by the German government to win over sceptical voters was 'The Euro: Stable as the Mark'. Despite this, the other member states ratified the Maastricht Treaty, presumably relying on their ability to rewrite it under the pressure of economic 'realities' – in practice, if not on paper. It helped that the 1990s was a time in which the Western economies, with the United States in the lead, were all pursuing a policy of fiscal consolidation in the transition to neoliberal, finan-cialized economies.[25] Committing one's country to a debt ratio no greater than 60 per cent of GDP, and budget deficits of not more than 3 per cent, corre-sponded to the spirit of the age; in addition, 'the markets' would have ways and means of punishing countries that refused to abide by these rules.

The unequal effects of the currency union soon made themselves felt. Today it is Germany, the Netherlands, Austria and Finland that profit above all from the single currency, but this has only been the case since 2008. In the early phase of the euro, uniform monetary policy turned Germany into the 'sick man of Europe'. The ECB interest rate was higher than the German inflation rate, though lower than that of the Mediterranean countries, which therefore enjoyed the luxury of negative real interest rates.[26] The cost of government credit also sank dramatically in the South, largely because of the capital markets' assumption – inspired in part by the European Commission – that, regardless of the treaties, the single currency contained a shared or even a specifically German guarantee of the solvency of the member states. The outcome was a boom in the South and stagna-tion in Germany, with high unemployment and rising government indebtedness.

LINE STRUGGLES

All this changed in 2008, with the arrival of the credit crunch – or in other words, with the collapse of the financial markets' illusions about German or European willingness to act as lenders of last resort for the debts of the South, combined with the fall of interest rates to near zero. The reason why the single currency now favoured Germany lay in the so-called over-industrialization of its economy, a fact lamented as recently as the 1990s. This made it less sensitive to the fiscal crisis and the collapse of credit than states that were more depend-ent on their domestic markets. For one thing it enabled Germany to focus more strongly than ever on supplying global markets with higher-quality industrial goods. A further factor was the undervaluation of the euro as a currency for Germany, in contrast to the Eurozone more generally.[27] In this way, without wanting or planning it, Germany controversially became the European hegemon, until further notice.

---

25   On this see chapter four.

26   Fritz Scharpf, *Political Legitimacy in a Non-Optimal Currency Area*, MPIfG Discussion Paper 13/15, Cologne: Max Planck Institute for the Study of Societies 2013.

27   According to Morgan Stanley in 2013, at an exchange rate of 1.36 to the dollar, the euro was undervalued by 13 per cent for Germany and overvalued by 12–24 per cent for Italy and Greece.

At the same time, the differing compatibilities of the member states' econ-omies unleashed an increasingly vicious tug-of-war between North and South. The struggle raised, and still raises, three distinct questions: first, the interpre-tation – and, perhaps, the revision – of the monetary system agreed in the Maastricht Treaty; second, the duty of member states to undertake institu-tional 'reforms', so as to align the South with the North, or vice versa; and third, assuming a persistent disparity of incomes and living standards, the question of balancing payments from North to South.

It should be stressed that none of these problems can be remedied by the methods currently being tried, however fruitful those may be.[28] All three are manifestations of a deep-seated division in the single currency as a political system. And this split, far from being eliminated by any financial 'rescue', will only then be felt in its full force. As far as the first problem is concerned – the disagreement over the practical operation of the Treaty – attempts by Southern states to soften up the euro, with the help of the ECB, and thus return to inflation, debt-financing and currency devaluation, have been indignantly countered by the Northern nations, which no longer want to be dragged by majority resolutions into acting as substitute lenders and guarantors for those pre-emptive injections of funds, without which their Southern partners as they stand cannot function. To this extent the internal politics of the single currency already plays a part in the alliances of member states, which are trying to pull the common monetary regime in opposite directions, one group to the South, the other (back) to the North. In their current political and economic configurations, each bloc can only function by gaining control of the interpretation of the monetary regime. But neither wishes to manage *without* the other. While the Northerners value fixed exchange rates for their export industries, the Southerners want low interest rates; they are prepared to accept treaty restrictions on debt ceilings and deficit limits in the hope that, in an emergency, their fellow members will be more susceptible than the financial markets to diplomatic pressure or appeasement.

In the debates about the 'correct' interpretation of the single currency, the current German government and its allies still have the upper hand, at least as long as the South remains dependent on their multi-billion-euro bailouts. If this continues, the Southerners will have no choice but to adapt their political and economic institutions to the neoliberal version of the European monetary

---

28   A striking failure of the present political debate, especially in Germany, is that the problems of the Eurozone are being treated as a single, albeit serious crisis, which can be overcome by means of what may be costly payments to rescue banks or states, or both, but which – it is assumed – will only have to be made once.

regime as authoritatively interpreted by the North.[29] The outcome of such an adjustment process would be unknown; even if all went well, it would entail a lengthy transition period, full of political unrest and economic uncertainty. It would mean, for example, that the South would have to accept fully 'flexible' labour markets, à la the North; while in the opposite eventuality the Germans would be forced to abandon their 'destructive' saving habits and give up their 'selfish' export-based economy.

The market struggle is thus displaced onto the second question: the institutional 'reforms' required of member states. In addition to its economic predominance, the North can appeal to the wording of the Treaties and the reform-and-consolidation packages emanating from the ECB; the South for its part might assert its majority on the boards of the Eurozone institutions and the ECB, as well as leveraging the German political class's need for harmony in Europe. To be sure, both sides would have to reckon with fierce, democratically legitimated resistance to reforms that strike at the heart of their nations' political-economic settlements. The outcome might be the permanent parallel existence of incompatible institutions, beneath the common monetary regime. In this scenario, the Southerners would defend public-sector job security and protection against dismissal, while employees of Northern export firms would be unwilling to abandon their 'factory-floor alliances' or enter into wage agreements that might jeopardize their competitiveness and with it, jobs; the South would not be able to raise its productivity, nor the North its costs, to the point where the two could converge.[30] The struggle between the two approaches would continue, the share of exports and trade surpluses of the North rising, while the pressure on the South for deflation and rationalization would persist.

The result – and this brings us to the third level of conflict – would be a state of permanent friction over the Eurozone's financial constitution. The struggle might be analogous to the endless disputes in Germany about the financial settlement between central government and the Länder, except that

---

29 In that event, the current ECB programme of quantitative easing would not imply a shift to the 'Southern' view but merely a temporary fix, in exchange for which the South will have to impose Northern 'reforms'. In as much as political convictions can be discerned in someone like Draghi, they tend more in this direction than towards a regime change in favour of the South.

30 Some time ago, in recognition of this, the German Left (Lafontaine, Flassbeck) withdrew their long-standing demand that German trade unions should adopt an aggressive wage policy in order to dismantle Germany's competitive advantage in the single currency and thus, by adjusting to the economies of the South, help to bring about the necessary convergence. Their current demand, for the abolition of the single currency in its present form, is the logical consequence of this. See Heiner Flassbeck and Costas Lapavitsas, *Nur Deutschland kann den Euro retten: Der letzte Akt beginnt*, Frankfurt am Main: Westend Verlag 2015.

in the EMU this would be a conflict between sovereign states, without the overarching framework of a shared democratic constitution, or anything like the close network of common institutions in a nation state. Nor would it be fought out inside a single, more or less unified economy, but rather between differently constituted national variants of capitalism, and through the medium of volatile and emotive international relations. The sums involved would be considerable, and they would constantly fall due – even if the 'structural reforms' demanded of the South were actually implemented and the countries affected were able to start recovering, after a deflation of 20–30 per cent. The idea that, after all this, they would be able to grow their economies faster than the Northern countries, without any assistance at all, is something only economists could imagine.[31]

How huge the fiscal transfers from the North would have to be cannot be specified with any certainty, but we can be sure they would not suffice to bridge the gulf between North and South. Recognizing that this would involve not only Greece but also Spain and Portugal, and possibly the entire Mediterranean region, the payments required of the North would be proportionally at least as great as the annual transfer of resources made by the FRG to its new Länder after 1990, or by Italy to the Mezzogiorno since the end of the Second World War: roughly 4 per cent of GDP in both cases, with the modest result of merely preventing the income gap between the affluent and the poor regions from growing any larger.[32] As for the EU's budget, this would have to increase by at least 300 per cent, from 1 to 4 per cent of its GDP. At a conservative estimate, member states might have to transfer some 7 per cent of their public expenditure to Brussels. In Germany, where the Federal budget amounts to about half of public expenditure, the increase would have to be around 15 per cent – during a period of low growth and general fiscal constraint.[33]

These are the principal fault lines inherent in all future Eurozone domestic politics. Over and above one-off 'rescue payments' that might be justified on humanitarian grounds, transfers will be politically feasible only if they do not

---

31 Comparable to economists' belief in convergence through reform is the belief of the Europhile centre left in convergence through debt relief; both are equally unrealistic and comprehensible only as rhetorical devices to immunize a utopian ideology against empirically based doubts.

32 See my paper with Lea Elsasser, *Monetary Disunion*, p. 14. To put the transfer policy in perspective, it should be considered in relation to the geostrategic orientation of the EU, whose accession policy is the more strongly inspired by the United States, the further east it goes. Transfers would then be necessary to the whole of the Balkans, from Serbia to Albania – all states that are potential, self-defined recipients of subsidies. It is noteworthy how little discussion there has been of the problems and costs of an expansion to the south-east, with or without a resolution of the Mediterranean crisis. The relevant keyword here might be 'overextension'.

33 The idea that Germany will make good Europe's economic asymmetries off its own bat – whether out of fear of Europe or love for it – raises wishful thinking to a whole new level.

dramatically exceed the EUs long-standing Regional Development Funds and can credibly be presented as helping a state to help itself. Regular redistributive injections of cash, as an expression of solidarity with less competitive econo-mies in a hard-currency environment, could not be sustained in the Northern meritocracies, with their constant exhortations to work harder; nor in the long run would they be compatible with the self-esteem of the recipient countries. In the case of subsidies that are supposed to render themselves superfluous – as with regional policies at national level, or development aid in the international domain – there are bound to be questions about the payments' end date, as well as charges that the aid is being used for consumption rather than investment. To prevent transfers legitimated as temporary emergency aid being transformed into *de facto* long-term assistance, the donors will grant them only under strict conditions, with the power to monitor their use. This inevitably leads to tensions between sovereign states, with accusations that donor nations are behaving like imperialists, interfering in the internal affairs of others and undermining their democracies. Recipient countries will complain about inadequate payments and unwarranted abrogation of sover-eign rights, while donors will regard the requested sums as excessive and the accompanying conditions as inadequate. In future, then, the domestic policy of the Eurozone will revolve round the axis of money in exchange for control – thereby offering immeasurable opportunities for nationalist demagogic mobilizations, on every side.

A NEW SYSTEM?

It has been a long time since we last heard positive arguments for the single currency, whether political or economic. The only grounds adduced by the defenders of the status quo against the abandonment of what Polanyi would doubtless have called a 'frivolous experiment' is that the consequences of a breakup, though not foreseeable, would be worse than a continuation of what has become a permanent institutional crisis. Underlying this is probably the fear of the European political class that voters might present them with the bill for having casually placed the prosperity and peaceful coexistence of the conti-nent at risk.

Yet the costs of dismantling the single currency cannot survive much longer as an argument in favour of its continuation. The Northern hope of escaping from the current predicament with a one-off payment – or even a one-off deflation to bring about structural reform in the South – will evapo-rate, as surely as Southern hopes for long-term support for social structures ill-suited to a hard-currency regime. Meanwhile, the notion that a pan-European democracy might spring up out of the European Parliament and somehow ride to the rescue will turn out to be an illusion – and the longer the wait, the greater the disillusionment.[34] Less feasible still is the dream of achieving such a democracy by dint of letting the Eurozone crisis drag on until 'the pain' becomes too great – not so much the economic pain in the South as the moral and political anguish in the North, above all in Germany.

More likely than a headlong rush into pan-European democracy is that the national polities will fall prey to aggressively nationalist parties. The only remaining supporters of euro-led integration, apart from politicians fearful of losing their seats, will be the middle classes of the South, who dream of achieving a social-democratic consumer paradise on the coat-tails of Northern capitalism, even as this implodes; and the Northern export industries, which want to preserve the credit-financed consumption of the Southerners as long as possible, together with the competitive advantages of an undervalued pan-European currency. However, if convergence in any real sense is definitively ruled out, and the full extent of the need for regular redistributive cash injections becomes evident, the current situation will no longer be sustainable in electoral terms, even in Germany.

For this reason it is essential to stop sanctifying the single-currency regime and supercharging it – in 'typical German' fashion – with the expectations and attributes of a post-national salvation.[35] It would then be possible to dispense with the usual horror scenarios – Angela Merkel's 'If the euro fails, then Europe fails' was a particularly crass example – and start seeing the single currency for what it is: an economic expedient that will have lost its *raison d'être* if it fails to serve its purpose.[36] In *Buying Time*, I tentatively proposed recasting the single currency along the lines of Keynes' original Bretton Woods model: the euro as an anchor for national or multinational individual currencies, with agreed mechanisms to cancel out economic imbalances, including the possibility of resetting exchange rates. This would in practice do away with the 'gold

---

34   See chapter eight, my comment on Wolfgang Merkel, 'Is Capitalism Compatible with Democracy?', *Zeitschrift für Vergleichende Politikwissenschaft*, 7 February 2015.

35   Such as the claim that the single currency is the guarantee of peace and therefore indispensable. The long European peace began in 1945, while the single currency was not launched until 1999. Together with the Common Market (with its national currencies), it was above all NATO and the Cold War that pushed the countries of Europe to maintain the peace, in contrast to the interwar period. The single currency, by contrast, became the cause of discord in Europe rather than peace. And as for the EU's contribution to the maintenance of peace in general, the official story hardly stands up if we consider the case of Ukraine, where 'Western' plans for a further expansion of the EU to the East have persistently exacerbated the current state of war.

36   Merkel's ineffably demagogic dictum (19 May 2010) is widely treated as dogma even today in the ranks of the centre left. Europhiles like Merkel confuse Europe's cultural tradition with the bad policy decisions for which they are responsible.

standard' implicit in the single currency, which drains the democracies dry without helping to establish a supranational democracy. Broadly speaking, this would be a return to the situation of 1999–2001, when the euro and the national currencies of the member states existed in parallel, admittedly with fixed, non-variable parities. The difference would be that now the parities could be revised by a process regulated by treaty – not by foreign-exchange markets or unilateral government intervention. Since I understood even less about the technical details than I do today, I did not elaborate on this proposal. Moreover, I was quite sure that the elites governing Europe would cling stubbornly to their unification project, however divisive it might prove to be – which is exactly what happened.

Yet since 2013, an astonishing number of voices have been heard in favour of a flexible currency regime, one that could enable democratic politics to even out imbalances through less destructive means than internal devaluations. The suggestions made range from a return to national currencies, via the temporary or permanent introduction of parallel currencies, together with capital controls, right through to a Keynesian two-tier currency system.[37] No 'nostalgia for the Deutschmark' is required to see the urgent need for joint reflection on the reconstruction of the European single currency, in a way that might be beneficial for Europe, democracy and society. In principle, this theme might also emerge from the no less urgent search for a better *global* monetary system than exists at present – one that has become increasingly dysfunctional since the definitive dismantling of the Bretton Woods regime in the early 1970s, and almost brought the world economy to the point of collapse in 2008.

The failure of the euro is just one development among many to dispel the illusion that arose from the anomalously peaceful conditions of the post-war period – the conviction that what money is and how it should be managed is a question that has been settled once and for all. Debates about a new global monetary and financial regime are now well overdue. Their task will be to devise a system flexible enough to do justice to the conditions and constraints

---

37   The relevant literature here is too extensive to refer to it in detail. It should be noted that it hails from both 'right' and 'left', and includes reflections on how the costs of leaving a currency union can be loaded at least in part onto countries whose unrealistic promises, both explicit and implicit, had lured soft-currency countries into the currency union to begin with. See especially Heiner Flassbeck and Costas Lapavitsas, *Against the Troika: Crisis and Austerity in the Eurozone*, New York: Verso Books 2015, with an introduction by Oskar Lafontaine; as well as ongoing contributions by the American economist Allan Meltzer ('Die Südländer brauchen ihren eigenen Euro', *Frankfurter Allgemeine Sonntagszeitung*, 16 November 2014), the Dutch economists and journalists around André ten Dam ('The Matheo Solution'), the French economists Jacques Maizier and Pascal Petit ('In Search of Sustainable Paths for the Eurozone in the Troubled post-2008 World', *Cambridge Journal of Economics*, vol. 37, no. 3, 2013, pp. 513–532) and, among many others, Wolfgang Münchau ('Why Smoke and Mirrors are Safer than Cold Turkey', *Financial Times*, 16 March 2015).

governing the development of all societies participating in the world economy, without encouraging rival devaluations, or the competitive production of money or debt, together with the geostrategic contests they foster. Agenda items would include the successor to the dollar as a reserve currency, the empowerment of states and international organizations to set limits to the free movement of capital, regulation of the havoc caused by the shadow banks and the global creation of money and credit, as well as the introduction of fixed but adjustable exchange rates. Such debates could take their cue from the astonishing wealth of ideas about alternative national and supranational monetary regimes produced in the interwar years by such writers as Fisher or Keynes. They would teach us at the very least that money is a constantly developing historical institution that requires continual reshaping, and must be judged as efficient not just in theory but also in its political function. The future of the European single currency could in that way become a subordinate theme of a worldwide debate about a monetary and credit system for capitalism – perhaps even for a post-capitalist order of the twenty-first century.

Or not, as the case may be. Now more than ever there is a grotesque gap between capitalism's intensifying reproduction problems and the collective energy needed to resolve them – affecting not just the necessary repairs to the monetary system, but also regulation of the exploitation of labour-power and the environment. This may mean that there is no guarantee that the people who have been so kind as to present us with the euro will be able to protect us from its consequences, or will even make a serious attempt to do so. The sorcerer's apprentices will be unable to let go of the broom with which they aimed to cleanse Europe of its pre-modern social and anti-capitalist foibles, for the sake of a neoliberal transformation of its capitalism. The most plausible scenario for the Europe of the near and not-so-near future is one of growing economic disparities – and of increasing political and cultural hostility between its peoples, as they find themselves flanked by technocratic attempts to undermine democracy on the one side, and the rise of new nationalist parties on the other. These will seize the opportunity to declare themselves the authentic champions of the growing number of so-called losers of modernization, who feel they have been abandoned by a social democracy that has embraced the market and globalization. Furthermore, this world, which lives under the constant threat of possible repetitions of 2008, will be especially uncomfortable for the Germans, who for the sake of the euro will find themselves having to survive without the 'Europe' to which they had once looked to provide them with a safe dwelling place, surrounded by well-disposed neighbours.

CHAPTER EIGHT

Comment on Wolfgang Merkel, 'Is Capitalism Compatible with Democracy?'

There is good news and bad news – and as sometimes, good news inside the bad.[1] The bad news is that the crisis of Western-liberal democracy has apparently grown to a point where it can no longer be ignored by mainstream political science – while the good news is that it is now actually being noticed there. What is more, it is beginning to make its leading representatives to leave behind institutionalism pure and simple and move forward (or in fact back?) to a political economy perspective on democracy that deserves its name. Democracy and capitalism is now the subject, if not of choice then of necessity. Gone are the good times, or so it seems, when *Glasperlen* issues as harmless and comfortable as first-past-the-post vs. proportional representation, Westminster vs. veto point, consociational vs. majoritarian democracy, parliamentary vs. presidential rule, unitary vs. federal government, monocameralism vs. bicameralism etc., etc. could rule supreme in the discipline's official journals. Back to the basics! – so I read the message of Merkel's remarkable essay[2] in which he challenges nothing less than the foundational assumption of post-war political science that capitalism and democracy are birds of a feather: that just as capitalism needs as well as supports democracy, democracy needs as well as supports capitalism, the two flocking together in everlasting pre-established harmony.

Is capitalism compatible with democracy? Responding to the problem posed in the title of his paper, Merkel offers an impressive catalogue of historical developments during the past three or four decades that, according to him, have deeply diminished the efficacy of democracy in the capitalist world – in a way that suggests that the answer to his question must be: increasingly not. Rightly, I believe, Merkel designates capitalism as 'the challenger, the independent variable, while democracy functions (in his model – WS) as the dependent variable'[3] – although I would have preferred a simpler language of ultimate cause and proximate effect, reminiscent of the

1   This chapter first appeared in: *Zeitschrift für Vergleichende Politikwissenschaft*, vol. 9, 2015, pp. 49–60.

2   Wolfgang Merkel, 'Is Capitalism Compatible with Democracy?', *Zeitschrift für Vergleichende Politikwissenschaft*, vol. 8, no. 2, 2014, pp. 109–128.

3   Merkel, 'Is Capitalism Compatible with Democracy?', p. 111.

materialist image of social relations that unmistakably and quite rightly underlies Merkel's reasoning. In particular, Merkel focuses on the transformation of the post-war 'social market economy' – of what he calls 'embedded' capitalism – in the course of its financialization, a process that began in the 1980s and reached its climax, for the time being, in the financial crisis of 2008. Among other things, Merkel mentions deregulation and privatization, the retrenchment of the welfare state, the ideational swing towards neoliberalism, the growth of a global financial sector, international competition undermining national regulation while failing to give rise to regulation at the global level, the victory of shareholders over workers and the associated tipping of the balance of class forces. Among the consequences for democracy, Merkel emphasizes four: asymmetric political participation – the exclusion of the lower classes from the political process – caused by rising inequality and poverty; the impossibility in open polities for democratic politics to stem the rise in economic inequality; the pressures in financialized national economies on governments to turn their countries into 'market-conforming democracies' (Angela Merkel); and the transfer of decision-making powers under globalization towards the executives, at the expense of parliaments.

There is nothing in Merkel's list that I feel should not be there. I might have added a few points and slightly changed the emphasis on some. For example, one might have mentioned declining overall growth rates intensifying distributional conflicts and sharply paring down the willingness of the rich to make concessions to the poor. One could also have spent more time on what I believe is a particularly important aspect of the weakening of states and governments, which is the immense capacity today of rich citizens and corporations to escape taxation by moving income to low-tax jurisdictions, or capital to tax havens. The results include a weakening ability of states to redistribute to the bottom of their societies, together with increasingly degressive taxation and rising indebtedness of underfunded states unable to discharge their obligations to their citizens with their stagnant or shrinking tax revenue. An upshot is the growing dependence of citizens on private borrowing to compensate for declining public services and supports. Moreover, rising public debt means a growing share in public spending of interest payments to creditors, putting pressure on social expenditure and public investment. Oligarchic redistribution thus comes with a neoliberal rebuilding of the state, manifested among other things in a shrinking public sector.[4] Public poverty opens a space for oligarchic

---

4   See 'The Rise of the European Consolidation State', chapter 4, this volume.

philanthropy, in an emerging neo-feudal relationship between private wealth and the public sphere.

In terms of political power, the transition currently under way in Europe from a debt state towards a consolidation state shows the meanwhile well-established primacy of what I have identified as the second constituency of contemporary capitalist democracy – the financial markets – over its first and original constituency, its citizens.[5] In this context, and that of the rise of executive power mentioned by Merkel, I would have more explicitly emphasized the ascendancy of the leading central banks to the status of quasi-sovereign economic governments, free from any sort of democratic control. Furthermore, that their desperate efforts to revive inflation have up to now failed testifies to the effective destruction of trade unions in the course of the neoliberal revolution – another channel of political participation through which the asymmetry of power in a capitalist political economy has sometimes been redressed. We also observe an emerging new political configuration pitting Grand Coalitions of centre-left and centre-right TINA parties – parties that subscribe to the *There Is No Alternative* rhetoric of the age of globalization – against so-called 'populist' movements cut off from official policymaking: an opposition excluded from ever becoming the government, and easy to discredit as insufficiently *responsible* due to being improperly or unrealistically *responsive* to those that feel railroaded by developments that established democratic parties tell them they can do nothing about.[6]

Why is it so difficult, in spite of a veritable plethora of alarming symptoms, for people to understand the crisis of contemporary democracy and take it as seriously as it deserves? Too many, I believe, still cling to the traditional, putsch-like view of democracy being abolished: elections cancelled, opposition leaders and dissenters in prison or forced into exile or murdered, TV stations taken over by storm troopers – the Argentinian or Chilean model. There are also the strong voluntaristic illusions associated with democratic institutions, as imprinted on people in civics lessons: that as long as 'we' can speak up and throw out the rascals at the ballot box, 'we the people' are responsible for the condition of our community: if we really wanted it to be different, we would only need to get up and rectify things, provided we can convince a sufficiently large number of fellow citizens of the validity of our

---

5   Streeck, *Buying Time.*

6   Typically, it is political leaders or organizations that promise voters that they will resist the demands of international financial and other investors that are most likely to be branded 'populist' – 'left' or 'right', often interchangeably – by the TINA parties of the centre, who define themselves as 'responsible' on account of their willingness faithfully to comply with the rules of the market.

grievances. As long as there are still elections, our world is what we have willed, or what 'the people' have willed. Wolfgang Merkel importantly departs from this to suggest that at the heart of the matter is the relationship between democracy and social structure, and indeed the specific dynamic of the social structure of capitalism and how it affects, among other things, the status and effective reach of democracy in society. It is with respect to this relationship that I have argued that we have come a long way already on the road to a 'Hayekian dictatorship of the market', a vision that Merkel finds 'apocalyptic' but with which he nevertheless seems reluctantly to concur. What I meant when I characterized the emerging political economy of neoliberalism as 'Hayekian' was a condition of acquired inconsequence, of inflicted as well as self-inflicted irrelevance, of contracted insignificance of democratic politics in relation to the capitalist economy, a condition in which democracy has lost its egalitarian-redistributive capacity, so that it makes no difference any more who is voted into office in what may or may not continue to be more or less competitive elections.

Putting, that is, Merkel's question slightly differently to ask whether democracy *can be made* compatible with *contemporary* capitalism, my answer is: only by building a Chinese Wall between the two – by sterilizing the redistributive potential of democratic politics while continuing to rely on electoral competition to produce legitimacy for the outcomes of free markets shielded from egalitarian distortion. Hayekian democracy serves the function of making a capitalist market society appear to be 'the people's choice' even though it has long been removed from democratic control. What I refer to as a technocratic-authoritarian market dictatorship is a political-economic regime that delegates decisions on the distribution of people's life chances to the 'free play' of market forces or, which is the same, concentrates them in the hands of executive agencies that supposedly command the technical knowledge necessary to organize such markets so that they perform best. Emptied of distributional politics, Hayekian democracy is free to busy itself with national interests and international conflicts, especially on the exotic margins of the capitalist world, or with the public spectacles offered by the personal rivalries and private lives of competing leaders. Culture wars, 'family values', lifestyle choices, 'political correctness', the age and sex of politicians, and the way they dress and look and speak deliver an unending supply of opportunities for pseudo-participation in pseudo-debates, never allowing for boredom to arise: whether the foreign minister should or should not have his male companion accompany him on a state visit to the Middle East; if there are enough women cabinet members, and in sufficiently powerful positions; how female ministers attend to their small children, too little or too much; whether the president of

COMMENT ON WOLFGANG MERKEL   189

the Republic should use a motor cycle when visiting his lover; and how often a week the minister of economic affairs takes his daughter to *Kindergarten* in the morning. With exciting issues like these filling the public space, who will want to hear about the entirely predictable failure of international financial diplomacy to agree on meaningful regulation of offshore banking and the shadow banking system?

While I fully concur with Merkel's diagnosis of the current demise of democracy in the course of capitalist development, I am a little concerned about the way Merkel sets up his argument conceptually, in particular about the 'model' language he uses to structure his exposition. To determine if and under what conditions democracy and capitalism are compatible, Merkel distinguishes three 'types' of capitalism – 'market-liberal', 'organized and embedded' and 'neoliberal' – and three types of democracy – 'minimalist', 'embedded' or 'middle-ground', and 'maximizing'.[7] Having laid out his menu, he then picks the two models, one of capitalism and one of democracy, that he thinks best match each other. Not surprisingly, it turns out that these are the two 'embedded' ones – although their superior fit has obviously failed to protect their union from breaking up as capitalism extracted itself from the joint embedding and morphed into its neoliberal, financialized, or Anglo-American version (defining the political problem of our age as making capitalism morph back into embedded capitalism and rejoin embedded democracy, so they might live 'happily ever after' [*glücklich und zufrieden bis an ihr Lebensende*]).

What worries me about this conceptual *spiel* is that it may all too easily evoke the image of an intelligent designer picking from a collection of prefabricated parts those that work optimally together in producing a desired outcome. Alternatively, in a less technocratic reading, it may give rise to a voluntaristic conception of politics in which an all-powerful *ideeller Gesamtbürger* – an ideal collective citizen, to paraphrase Karl Marx – reflects, assisted by knowledgeable political scientists, on how to build an optimal political economy out of the institutional material furnished by history, and then puts in place what he thinks is best, or repairs what has got out of control when nobody was paying attention. What I am missing here (more precisely: what I am afraid other readers may not recognize is missing, thereby being seduced into a technocratic-voluntaristic doability worldview that is more likely to contribute to the problem rather than help resolve it) are the fundamental political categories of *class* and *power* – and the insight that both capitalism and democracy are shorthand summary concepts that in order to

---

7   Merkel, 'Is Capitalism Compatible with Democracy?', pp. 112–13.

make sense need to be broken down, unpacked and repackaged, de-and reconstructed in terms of underlying conflicts between social classes and their different and historically changing capacities to impose their interests on society as a whole.

Capitalism and democracy, in short, are not two modules, like an engine and a steering system, to be combined or not depending on their technical compatibility. They are both, individually as well as in their respective combination, the outcome of specific configurations of classes and class interests as evolved in a historical process driven, not by intelligent design, but by the distribution of class political capacities. Thus post-war democratic capitalism was not a selection by skillful social engineers or concerned citizens from a range of less optimal alternatives, but a historical compromise between a then uniquely powerful working class and an equally uniquely weakened capitalist class that was as never before on the political and economic defensive – which was true in all capitalist countries at the time, among the winners of the war as well as the losers. For the capitalist hunting licence to be restored after the Great Depression, with its international repercussions and the subsequent global devastation, a high price had to be paid by the capitalist class, including a promise of politically guaranteed full and stable employment, steadily rising prosperity, redistribution of income, wealth and life chances in favour of ordinary people, social protection in the workplace through strong trade unions and free collective bargaining, and beyond the workplace through a comprehensive welfare state – all negotiated, as it were, with a pistol pointed to the head of liberal capitalism, forcing it into a shotgun marriage with social democracy. Subtle distinctions of the 'varieties of capitalism' sort do not apply here: post-war Japan had a trade union membership density of 80 to 90 per cent and a socialist government until it was removed by the American occupation; in Germany the country's leading capitalists were in prison until they were freed by the Americans to be of help in the Korean War, and in the 1947 party manifesto of the Christian Democratic Union (CDU) capitalism was declared a threat to the 'vital political and social interests of the German people';[8] in the United Kingdom a Labour government was voted in, which nationalized some 40 per cent of the country's industrial capacity; and the United States was still the land of the New Deal, with

---

8 'The capitalist economic system has served neither the state's not the German people's vital interests. After the terrible political, economic, and social collapse that resulted from criminal power politics, a new order is required, and it must be built from the ground up. The content and goal of this new social and economic order can no longer be the capitalistic pursuit of power and profit; it must lie in the welfare of our people.'

extensive capital controls, a highly regulated financial sector, strong industrial trade unions, and ambitious social programmes to compensate its
soldier-citizens for the sacrifices they had made for their country on the
global battlefield.[9]

I cannot possibly discuss here in detail how this settlement – Wolfgang
Merkel's twice-embedded capitalist-democratic compound – broke up after it
had held together, by and large, for roughly three decades. What Merkel refers
to as a transformation of European embedded capitalism in an Anglo-
American, financialized direction – the stepwise progress of the neoliberal
revolution – goes back to a secular shift in the relative power of capital and
labour, or of the owners and governors of increasingly mobile capital on the
one hand and ordinary people on the other. It was this shift which pulled the
floor out from under the social-democratic post-war compromise in which
the latter had agreed to the restoration of markets and private property in
exchange for a promise of the former to provide for steady economic improvement and social security for all ('*Wohlstand für alle!*'). Underlying the
neoliberal turn one finds a long trajectory of change in the structure of classes
and wealth, in the mode of production, and in political constraints and
opportunities, with an important role played by both contingent circumstances and the differential endowment of classes and their political
organizations with strategic skills and capacities.[10] What matters here is that
for decades now, it was the development of capitalism that has driven the
development of democracy rather than vice versa, with advancing capitalism
breaking through its post-war democratic-institutional containment to
enthrone a new political-economic paradigm: the Hayekian formula of
economic progress by redistribution from the bottom to the top – greater
incentives for the winners, more severe punishments for the losers – taking
the place of the Keynesian recipe of bolstering aggregate demand by taking
from the rich to give to the poor.

Looking at the sequence of crises in the course of which the post-war
settlement of democratic capitalism unravelled, one cannot escape the impression that the relationship between capitalism and democracy is a good deal
less mechanical or additive, and much more dialectical and dilemmatic, than
is suggested by Merkel's modelling exercise. Taking class and power into
consideration, one can see the state, government and politics in democratic-capitalist societies being fundamentally exposed to continuous pressures to

---

9   Ironically, it was in the aftermath of the two great wars of the twentieth century, in 1918 and
1945, respectively, that the working classes under capitalism made their most effective advances in the
capitalist political economy (Piketty, *Capital in the Twenty-First Century*).

10   I have sketched out this dynamic in *Buying Time*.

accommodate contradictory needs and demands – pressures that per
produce new constraints and opportunities for revision of the in
governing the political economy. On the one hand, it is only by polit
vention into the free play of market forces that the collective bene
democratic society expects from a capitalist economy can be extra
it – that, in other words, the private vice of profit maximizatio
converted into the public benefit of social progress, to sustain a po
librium helping the sitting government to build political legitima
other hand, except in special situations of very high economic
would appear that the social corrections of the market that ar
achieve political equilibrium in a democracy tend to undermin
dence of capital owners and investors, thereby upsetting th
equilibrium that is equally essential for capitalist-democratic stability.
Capitalism and democracy thus seem to *simultaneously support and undermine* one another: while an economic equilibrium is necessary for a democratic
society to reap the collective benefits of private capital accumulation, it is put
at risk by the very same policies that are needed to make private capital accumulation socially acceptable; and while a political equilibrium is needed to
generate consent also with capitalism, it is threatened by the policies that are
required for economic equilibrium. Democratic governments under capitalism, this implies, are faced with a dilemma between two systemic crises, one
political, the other economic, where managing one of them is possible only at
the price of rekindling the other, forcing politics to move back and forth
between them, in the hope that the crisis cycle will allow them enough time to
regroup for addressing the inevitably emerging new problem caused by the
most recent solution.

Wolfgang Merkel ends his essay on a less than completely pessimistic
note, by urging 'democratic and economic reforms' to put an end to 'the present form of financialized disembedded capitalism' and restore a
not-just-minimalist concept of democracy that 'takes the imperative of political equality . . . seriously' and allows for the setting of 'autonomous norms'[11]
by the *pouvoir publique*. But while nobody could disagree with this, one feels
obliged to ask where those reforms are to come from, reversing a now decades-
old mainstream of economic and political-institutional development that went
in the exact opposite direction – with capitalism building itself a new democracy ('minimalist', in Merkel's term), rather than the old 'embedded democracy'
stabilizing its complementary 'embedded capitalism'? Can a democratic
renewal – a re-establishment of the primacy of democratic politics over the

---

11   Merkel, 'Is Capitalism Compatible with Democracy?', p. 126.

inherent dynamics of capitalist development – really be expected from a public no longer used to taking politics seriously, after decades of re-education in the spirit of what Merkel calls the 'cultural turn of progressive democratic politics' – like the struggle for gay marriage, the symbolic 'gendering' of everything, and the promotion of high-class women to high-class management positions on the boards of large firms as a signal policy objective of, one would not believe it, social-democratic parties and trade unions, at a time when the greatest risk of poverty is associated with being a single mother? How much serious politics are the democratic masses, politically expropriated by their 'responsible' cartel parties,[12] willing and able to concern themselves with? Under the spell of post-Fordist consumerism and post-democratic politainment, how many people still believe that there can be collective goods worth fighting for? In a world where the culturally most highly esteemed skill seems to have become the competitive coping with adversity in good spirits, as opposed to establishing common interests with others and organizing for them – where democracy has been emptied of serious content and politics trivialized beyond recognition – democratic participation, as Merkel reminds us, is all too easily mistaken for the saving of whales and similar local improvements, replacing political conflict with the public expression of private moral convictions: a depoliticized pluralistic *laissez-faire* under which political participation is turned into something like a morally correct form of advanced consumption.

Again, who is to be the driving force – the 'revolutionary subject', as one used to say – in the historical turnaround envisaged by Wolfgang Merkel, and how much time do we have left before the path towards, at best, authoritarian neoliberal technocracy becomes entrenched beyond redemption? Who is to demand and force through the democratic reforms that will, for example, end and reverse the growth of precarious employment; stop privatization and restore equitable public services; tax Google and its ilk; increase public social investment, to make for more equal starting positions and opportunities in the marketplace; control working time; make the production and regulation of money more transparent, less oligarchic and less dangerous? In Europe we are being told that this can only be done at the supranational level, by democratizing the European Union and, in particular, its Monetary Union. Of course, at present European institutions are ruled by a camarilla of national governments conspiring to hide from their citizens what they are doing in their name – to ensure that the loans the international money industry has pushed into their economies get properly serviced – all

12   Mair, *Representative versus Responsible Government*.

of this presided over by a power-grabbing central bank insulated from popu-
lar-democratic pressures and therefore free to align itself at will with its
comrades in global finance. Fittingly the majority of the European electorate
refused to take part in the 2014 European Parliament election charade, in
spite of several years of economic crisis and institutional turmoil.
Nevertheless, the travesty of the two old 'European' soul mates, Juncker and
Schulz, running against each other as self-appointed *Spitzenkandidaten* for
the job of president of the European Commission – a performance celebrated by their respective claques as an epoch-making step towards European
democracy – resulted in the promotion of the master architect of 'Europe' as
a tax haven for global corporations, and from 2005 to 2013 chairman, of all
things, of the command centre of the European bank rescue effort, the 'Euro
Group', to the position of chief administrator of the 'European project', as
publicly demanded on the day after the 'election' by none other than Jürgen
Habermas himself.[13]

If appointing a notorious bank lobbyist and privy tax councilor to
global corporations to the highest office of 'Europe' exemplifies the kind of
democratic reform currently in reach at the European level – and it must
appear that this is what Habermas wanted to let us know – then clearly
there is little hope if any for 'Europe' being of help with Merkel's project to
re-establish egalitarian-democratic control over financialized capitalism.
Merkel says nothing specific about the 'democratic and economic reforms'
that he deems necessary for us not to end up in 'an oligarchy formally legit-
imized by general elections',[14] excusing him from having to take a stand on
the European Union – although it arguably was the first post-war political
structure in Western Europe that was purposely designed *not* to be subject
to democratic control,[15] making it an early forerunner of what was to come
in train with the neoliberal transformation of post-war capitalism. Actually
it would appear that after decades of 'widening' and 'deepening', and with
its adoption in the 1980s and 1990s of a 'supply-side' economic policy,
culminating in EMU, the European Union is now the foremost institution
that would need to be 'reformed' if there is to be any restoration of democracy of the sort Merkel has in mind. Indeed, it is in this context that the

---

13   See 'Jürgen Habermas im Gespräch: Europa wird direkt ins Herz getroffen', *Frankfurter
Allgemeine Zeitung*, 29 May 2014. One interesting irony is that Juncker ascended to the presidency
shortly after the publication of Thomas Piketty's now famous book in which he demands a general
wealth tax to correct the long-term and inherent increase in inequality under capitalism (Piketty,
Capital in the Twenty-First Century). On the farce of last year's 'European election' see Susan Watkins,
'The Political State of the Union'.

14   Merkel, 'Is Capitalism Compatible with Democracy?', p. 126.

15   Mair, *Ruling the Void*.

idea of resolving Europe's 'democratic deficit' by providing the European Union with a new constitution, hoping to reunite democracy with capitalism by having the former follow the latter from the national to the supranational level, is being traded on the centre left especially of the German public.

If Juncker won't solve the problem, would a European constitution, in spite of the complete disaster of the first attempt to create one?[16] I believe a major reason why there can still be talk of a democratizing constitution for 'Europa' is that the recent history of the project has been utterly forgotten. Moreover, its promoters have been unbelievably successful evading all questions on even the most essential specifics, like who is to draft, discuss and pass the new constitution, what it is to deal with and what not, and when it is to begin working its miracles, at a time when Juncker and associated European governments are busy securing punctual repayment of the loans pressed by global finance into European economies. How is the constitutional assembly to be convened? By the governments, like last time, when consequently it became composed of national notables like the Giscards and Herzogs of the European world? Or is it to consist of insurgent citizens, elected like the *Arbeiter- und Bauernräte* of the past, bypassing nation states and their artists of the possible that have not so long ago sold democracy to neoliberalism? Or something in between? And which countries are to be invited – only EMU members, all EU members, or a coalition of the willing including Serbia, Turkey, Ukraine, Georgia? What about Catalonia, Scotland, Corsica, Flanders, Padania – will they be represented by the delegations of the nation states to which they (still) belong, or will they get delegations of their own? And how to deal with the growing nationalist opposition to 'Europe' – will they be admitted, excluded or tactically sidelined by the *juste milieu* as in the 'European Parliament'?

While this alone should take time to work out, except in a revolutionary situation which, however, would take at least as much time to arise, the next issue would be what is to get on the agenda. Immigration and asylum? Abortion and 'marriage for all'? The constitutional status of churches and of religion? Perhaps agreement could be reached, improbably, to set aside the culture

---

16 The project to give the European Union a constitution began in 2001 with a resolution to this effect by the then member states of the EU. Two years later a Convention appointed by the national governments went to work, and in 2004 the member states signed the document it had produced. What was billed as a 'European Constitution' was essentially a compilation of the existing treaties and consisted of a book of 160,000 words. It was to take effect in 2006, five years after its inception – and this in a period when the famous 'permissive consensus' on European integration was still around. When it failed to be approved in two national referenda it was replaced by the Treaty of Lisbon (effective 2010).

wars[17] and focus on political-economic matters first, like guarantees or not of private property; tax systems and the division of tax revenues between 'Europe' and its local, regional or national constituents; the extent and the limits of fiscal solidarity of the rich with the poor states and regions; balanced budgets or debt limits; rights for the federation to intervene in the fiscal behaviour of member states; an industrial and regional policy regime; the regulation of financial and labour markets; the extent of the responsibility of the central government for equalizing living conditions across the Union; the unification (or not) of social insurance systems; a uniform pension age (or not); how to make tax collection in different parts of the union equally effective; and perhaps most importantly, how to conduct monetary policy in the triangle between Europe's central and regional governments and its 'independent' central bank.

A democracy may or may not need a *demos* – perhaps it can include several *demoi*, together constituting what some of those eager to transfer 'European democracy' to the supranational level now call *demoicracy*. But this does not mean that a common democratic constitution does not presuppose a stock of common experiences, practices and perspectives – of shared understandings of how things are and should be done on which to build a shared edifice of rights and obligations. A democratic constitution cannot be produced out of thin air – even the German *Grundgesetz* of 1949 was not, nor was the Weimar *Reichsverfassung* or, for that matter, the constitution of the United States as written by the planter aristocracies of the British colonies in North America. A constitution must represent a settlement of issues and interests that is recognizable for citizens as reflecting their histories, values, aspirations and compromises, and what they have learned about themselves, their world and how things and people work in it. Such a settlement takes time to evolve: it requires extended contemplation on and collective sifting of the complex and diverse materials constituting a community's collective memory. Even in the best of cases, to be acceptable to its *demos,* or *demoi,* a constitution may have to bracket a range of issues where experiences and expectations and capacities differ too much, or it may have to place under special protection and exempt from collective interference values and practices that, for whatever reason, cannot be generalized across the political community as a whole.

There is to my knowledge not a single example of two or more

---

17   Improbably, because the culture wars tend to be incited precisely in order to divert attention from the political economy – fanning the passions of popular majorities kept in the dark on the real issues to make them forget their interests.

democratically constituted *demoi* voluntarily merging to form a multi-*demoi* democracy – apart from the nascent states, hardly comparable to modern European nations and highly homogeneous in comparison, of eighteenth-century North America. By the end of the twentieth century, not even the joint experience of Russian rule was sufficient to make the three Baltic States, Lithuania, Latvia and Estonia, enter a federated *demoi-cracy* – although they are all extremely small.[18] There are, however, examples of federated *demoi* parting company to set up their own democracies, like Czechia and Slovakia – not to mention the *demoi* of the former Yugoslavia after the end of Communism that never even thought of *'demoi-cratizing'* their federation. (In the United States, incidentally, the supply of interstate commonalities ran out soon after federation and had to be replenished in the Civil War, which formally removed what had become an unbridgeable political-economic cleavage: slavery. True federation under a truly shared constitution began, if at all, only a hundred years later when Presidents Eisenhower, Kennedy and Johnson deployed the National Guard to end official racial separation in Southern states' educational systems.)

The idea of a constitutional convention entering the European stage at the last minute as a democratizing *and thereby crisis-resolving deus ex machina* is a pipe dream, and a dangerous one to boot – dangerous because it diverts attention and energy from much more urgent work to be done.[19] Europe, the really existing Europe after two hundred years of nation-building, is far too heterogeneous for a meaningful common constitution; not only does it lack a *demos* but its *demoi* are too different to fit into one encompassing democratic polity. Abraham Lincoln's famous dictum on the United States before the Civil War, 'A house divided cannot stand', would apply also and *a fortiori* to a European *demoicracy*, given the wide variety of labour market practices, corporate governance regimes and state traditions, not least with respect to monetary and fiscal policies, that have evolved in centuries of *Klassenkämpfe* in European

---

18   Which was why they were eager to join the European Union and NATO, on the premise and indeed the condition that neither of them will contest their claim to democratic legitimacy and national sovereignty. As to the European Union in particular, the Baltic States, like most other small member states, from Malta to Luxembourg to Ireland, consider it the most effective guarantee available of their continued sovereign independence. This is the exact opposite of the way the European Union is sometimes seen by German Europhiles: as a vehicle for trading in national identity for a 'European' one. Economically, sovereignty is regarded especially by small nations as an indispensable capacity for them to carve out a niche for themselves in the global economy – or, alternatively, like in EMU, as a power tool for extracting 'solidarity' from larger countries.

19   Work that Europe's 'responsible' intellectuals have today delegated to the likes of Occupy!, ATTAC or SYRIZA.

nation states – the manifold settlements that have been fought for and negotiated and subsequently became engrained in a wide variety of nationally specific
interfaces between modern capitalism and modern society.[20]

The disaster of the first attempt to produce a 'European Constitution' was
far from an accident. Another try would and could only result in another
hugely complex technocratic document bracketing more than what it resolves,
replete with exceptions, reservation rights, open issues to be dealt with by the
powers of the day (and we know who these will be) – a document that will not
prevent and indeed promote continued chipping away at national democracies
in the same way as the Maastricht and Lisbon Treaties. Both the politics of the
culture wars and political-economic diversity would effectively block progress
towards a Merkelian 'embedded democracy' and instead help fortify the emerging Hayekian economic order of Europe. The heavy bleeding of democracy at
the national level would not be stopped, quite to the contrary. Supranational,
non-parochial, *verfassungspatriotische* democracy emerging on the coat-tails
of international capitalism is a dangerous chimera: far from the Habermas
project of European democracy being promoted by the Goldman Sachs project
of global plutocracy, the former would unintentionally provide legitimacy to
the latter until it would lose its usefulness for it and be discarded by it.

What is to be done to restore a democracy capable of serving as a meaningful corrective of capitalism? If there is nothing in supranational 'Europe'
that could provide for the sort of social cohesion and solidarity and governability that would be required, of the kind that was over two centuries more or
less successfully established in European nation states – if all there is at supranational level are the Junckers and Draghis and their fellow financial
functionaries – then the general answer is that rather than, like latter-day Don
Quixotes, trying to extend the scale of democracy to that of capitalist markets,
to do what you can to reduce the scale of the latter to fit the former. Bringing
capitalism back into the ambit of democratic government, and thereby saving
the latter from extinction, means *de-globalizing capitalism*; it is as simple and

---

20   As Fritz Scharpf has recently pointed out in a reply to Habermas's Sorbonne lecture (Jürgen
Habermas, 'Warum der Ausbau der Europäischen Union zu einer supranationalen Demokratie nötig
und wie er möglich ist', *Leviathan*, vol. 42, no. 4, 2014, pp. 524–538; Fritz W. Scharpf, 'Das Dilemma der
supranationalen Demokratie in Europa', *Leviathan*, vol. 43, 2015), what I would suggest to call the
acquises démocratiques of the national *demoi* in Europe include much more than liberal guarantees of
freedom and equal treatment before the law (roughly what Merkel calls the minimalist version of
democracy). It also and importantly comprises a wide range of political-economic institutions that
provide for democratic correction of market outcomes – for democracy as *social* democracy. We
should have learned, at the latest after the neoliberal turn of European integration in the 1980s, that
these cannot instantly be absorbed into a pan-European *acquis communautaire* – and that, if this is
tried against the interests and, sometimes at least, the resistance of those who depend on them, they are
at an overwhelming risk of being watered down into a neoliberal one-size-fits-all market regime.

as difficult as that. There is no denying that this would be a huge agenda, and in certain respects, perhaps, also a costly one, with no guarantee of success. But it would at least be a goal worth fighting for. *Restoring embedded democracy means re-embedding capitalism.* In this context, thinking about a monetary regime less destructive of democracy than the pitiful monstrosity that is EMU would be a task that would justify the sweat of the best and brightest.

CHAPTER NINE

How to Study Contemporary Capitalism?

Once upon a time sociologists knew that *modern* society is *capitalist* society: that capitalism is not one thing – a particular kind of economy – and modern society another.[1] The crisis of 2008, which is still unfolding, should have reminded us of how deeply intertwined economy and society are under capitalism. Two implications stand out: that the capitalist economy is too important to be left to economists to study; and that contemporary society cannot really be understood by a sociology that makes no reference to its capitalist economy.

To study contemporary capitalism, I argue, sociology must go back before the disciplinary division of labour with economics negotiated on its behalf by its twentieth century founding figure, Talcott Parsons.[2] For this it will be helpful to rediscover the sociology in classical economists from Smith to Pareto, Marshall, Keynes and Schumpeter, and the economics in classical sociologists like Weber, Sombart, Mauss and Veblen, to name only a few. Particular interest might usefully be paid to the institutional economics of the *Historische Schule* and to Marx the social theorist, as opposed to the deterministic economist. The lesson to be learned from all of them is *that capitalism denotes both an economy and a society,* and that studying it requires a conceptual framework that does not separate the one from the other.

How to study contemporary capitalism, then? My first answer is: not as an economy but as a society – as a system of social action and a set of social institutions falling in the domain of sociological rather than today's standard economic theory.[3] This is in fact the tradition of political economy in the nineteenth century. Political-economic theory was to identify the actors and interests underlying, or hiding behind, the 'laws of movement' of 'the economy', translating economic relations into social relations and showing the former to

---

1 This chapter originated as a presentation at a plenary session on 'Studying Contemporary Capitalism', 10th Conference of the European Sociological Association, 'Social Relations in Turbulent Times', Geneva, 7–10 September, 2011. Published in: *European Journal of Sociology*, vol. 53, no. 1, 2012, pp. 1–28.

2 Charles Camic, ed., *Talcott Parsons: The Early Essays*, Chicago: University of Chicago Press 1991.

3 Not to be confused with economic theory as defined by Alfred Marshall in his *Principles of Economics*: 'Political economy or economics is a study of mankind in the ordinary business of life; it examines that part of individual and social action which is most closely connected with the attainment and with the use of the material requisites of wellbeing. Thus it is on the one side a study of wealth; and on the other, and more important side, a part of the study of man' (Alfred Marshall, *Principles of Economics*, Amherst, NY: Prometheus Books 1997 [1890], Introduction). I owe this reference to a benevolent reader of an early version of this manuscript.

be a special case of the latter. Treating the economy as a society, or as socially and politically constructed or 'constituted',[4] is the obverse of treating the society as an economy, which is the approach of 'rational choice' economic imperialism. Indeed, ultimately the approach I suggest amounts to a sort of imperialism as well, only in the opposite direction: from sociology to economics.

To begin with a definition, a capitalist society is a society that has instituted its economy in a capitalist manner, in that it has coupled its material provision to the private accumulation of capital, measured in units of money, through free contractual exchange in markets driven by individual calculations of utility.[5] Such a society may be said to be capitalist, or one under capitalism, due to its dependence for its sustenance on the successful accumulation of privately appropriated capital. Calling a society capitalist also implies that it is as a society at risk of the social relations governing its economy penetrating into and taking possession of previously non-capitalist social relations. Unlike in what I believe are simplistic readings of Marxian political economy, or 'historical materialism', noting the hegemonic tendencies of the capitalist economy in a capitalist society does not imply that 'the economy' is always the predominant 'subsystem' of a society, in the way of a 'substructure' governing a 'superstructure'. It does imply, however, that this could contingently be the case and that, as will be seen, a progressive subsumption of social life under the organizing principles of a capitalist economy is an inherent ever-present danger of life under capitalism that needs to be politically counteracted.

Today's political-economic theory is typically one of two sorts. In the first, capitalism is reduced to a reified 'economy' conceived as a wealth creation machine – one that functions according to distinctive laws of nature esoteric enough to require a specialized natural science, economics. Politics operates on the economy from the outside, as if it were a black box, making it produce desired outputs by providing it with the right inputs. In the second, rather than an inert object of more or less adept technical manipulation, 'the economy' appears as producing inputs for politics, in the form of competing group interests, preferably presenting themselves as functional imperatives of efficient economic management, that need to be politically adjudicated.

---

4   Jens Beckert and Wolfgang Streeck, *Economic Sociology and Political Economy: A Programmatic Perspective*, MPIfG Working Paper 08/4, Cologne: Max Planck Institute for the Study of Societies 2008.

5   A broader concept would emphasize the historical connection in modern capitalism between the civilizational impulse of modernity towards methodical improvement of life, individual freedom and technological mastery of nature on the one hand, and the possessive individualism of market exchange on the other.

Neither of these approaches, I claim, does justice to the nature of contemporary capitalism, if only because the borderline between capitalist society and capitalist economy is not as fixed as they assume, and indeed is subject to continuous contestation. A capitalist society, or a society that is inhabited by a capitalist economy, is one that has on a current basis to work out how its *economic social relations,* its specific relations of production and exchange, are to connect to and interact with its *non-economic social relations.* This is so in particular because, as suggested, the former happen to have an inherent tendency to expand into and become dominant relative to their social context. For this reason alone, capitalism must be studied, not as a static and timeless ideal type of an economic system that exists outside of or apart from society, but as a *historical social order* that is precisely about the relationship between the social and the economic – a social order that came into its own in Western Europe in the early nineteenth century and has been continuously evolving since. Seen this way, what is represented by economic theory as a technical arrangement for economic convenience, or as a causal structure of variable properties more or less suitable for expert control, can be recognized as a socially and historically constructed dynamic complex of institutional constraints and opportunities, expectations, rights, resources and powers, with far-reaching ramifications into the surrounding society: its distribution of power, status and life chances, its action dispositions and capacities, and its social identities and ways of life.

No general theory of modern capitalism is in sight today, which is why I limit myself to four illustrations of the interaction, or *Wechselwirkung,* between economic and non-economic social relations under contemporary capitalism. Each of my four sketches, or vignettes, deals with a different facet of the relationship between economy and society under capitalism, with economic relations conceived as a particular kind of social relations nested, in a way that is supportive and subversive at the same time, into more encompassing social relations. In each case,[6] I will show how economic relations upon closer inspection turn out to be social ones, while social-political-cultural relations are found to be fully intelligible only with recourse to their interaction with the underlying capitalist economic order.

I will begin by arguing for treating capitalism as an *endogenously dynamic* and *dynamically unstable* social system, one driven to expand and dependent on expansion, and on this account more often than not, and in particular today, in critical condition (*capitalism as history*). Secondly, I will show that conceiving of the capitalist economy, as is frequently done, as of a regime of

---

6   More cases could be added, and my selection does not follow any systematic order.

rational action in response to material scarcity underestimates the role in modern capitalist society of socially generated and sustained *imaginaries, expectations, dreams* and *promises*. Not only is *capitalism* a culture, but the capitalist *economy* is one as well. Thirdly, with reference to the conflicts that arise when capitalism is combined with democracy, I will discuss capitalism as a political system, or as a *polity*, driven by a fundamental tension between a *moral economy* vested in capitalist *society*, and an *economic economy* vested in its *economy* – the latter, I argue, being ultimately a moral economy as well, namely that of the owners of capital. I suggest that it is that tension, rather than political mismanagement, that accounts for the successive economic imbalances that have been in evidence since the end of the post-war growth period. Fourthly and finally, I will argue for conceiving of capitalism as a *way of life* shaped by multiple interactions between market expansion, the structure and collective values of the social lifeworld, and government social policy, by drawing on the case of the relationship between female labour market participation, family life, fertility and the changing role of market and state in the raising of children.

CAPITALISM AS HISTORY

Much current work in political economy describes capitalism, or its 'varieties,' as a self-equilibrating system of complementary institutions stabilizing each other, in the pursuit of efficiency and economic performance or of different variants thereof. Politics comes in as the collective design and maintenance of institutions that provide for the optimal functioning of the respective type of capitalism conceived as 'market economy'.[7] This is in sharp contrast to traditional accounts of capitalism and capitalist society, from Smith and Marx to Schumpeter[8] and Keynes, that emphasize its endogenous dynamism, critical instability and continuous change – accounts that, I claim, are today more pertinent than at any other time in the post-war period.[9]

Capitalism is and always was about capital accumulation, or in a more modern expression: economic growth. Growth takes place in the form of an

---

7   Peter A. Hall and David Soskice, 'An Introduction to Varieties of Capitalism'. In: Hall, Peter A. and David Soskice, eds, *Varieties of Capitalism: The Institutional Foundations of Comparative Advantage*, Oxford: Oxford University Press 2001, pp. 1–68.

8   See in particular his essay, Joseph A. Schumpeter, 'The Instability of Capitalism', *The Economic Journal*, vol. 38, no. 151, 1928, pp. 361–386.

9   Wolfgang Streeck, *Re-Forming Capitalism: Institutional Change in the German Political Economy*, Oxford: Oxford University Press 2009; Wolfgang Streeck, 'Institutions in History: Bringing Capitalism Back In'. In: Campbell, John et al., eds, *Handbook of Comparative Institutional Analysis*, Oxford: Oxford University Press 2010, pp. 659–686; Streeck, 'E Pluribus Unum?'

expansion of markets, subsuming traditional relations of social exchange under the money economy and replacing relations of reciprocity with catallactic relations.[10] This is a process which Rosa Luxemburg, in her work on imperialism, called 'land-grabbing' in a more than just literal sense.[11] Capitalist land-grabbing through market expansion is accompanied by a deep transformation of social structures and social life; it is in this sense that the Marxist founding document, *The Communist Manifesto*, refers to the bourgeoisie as the most revolutionary class in human history.[12] Importantly, there is no need for capitalist expansion to be caused from the outside once a capitalist economy has been put in place, as the tendency to expand is a fundamental property of capitalism. Any capitalism that is worth its name, or its money, is necessarily on the move, and always from within.[13]

That capitalism permanently revolutionizes the society that it inhabits is anchored in its institutional fabric, in particular in the legitimacy it affords to competition – to depriving one's peers of their livelihood by outbidding them – and in the absence of a ceiling on legitimate economic gain.[14] While competition makes for *fear*, unlimited gain encourages *greed*; together the two produce the characteristic restlessness of a capitalist political economy and society.[15] Greed and fear also contribute to the superior innovativeness of capitalist economies, as innovation both protects from competition and is highly profitable.[16] It also is unpredictable, and so are its social and economic consequences. Continuous innovation therefore creates continuous *uncertainty* in social relations, given that capitalist economies are governed by self-regulating markets with freely fluctuating relative prices. As relative prices

---

10   Karl Polanyi, 'The Economy as Instituted Process'. In: Granovetter, Mark and Richard Swedberg, eds, *The Sociology of Economic Life*, Boulder, CO: Westview Press 1992 [1957], pp. 29–51.

11   Rosa Luxemburg, *Die Akkumulation des Kapitals: Ein Beitrag zur ökonomischen Erklärung des Imperialismus*, Berlin: Buchhandlung Vorwärts Paul Singer GmbH 1913.

12   Karl Marx and Friedrich Engels, 'The Communist Manifesto'. In: McLellan, David, ed., *Karl Marx: Selected Writings*, Oxford: Oxford University Press 1977 [1848], pp. 221–247.

13   This is, among other things, why 'globalization' is not a force external to capitalist political economies. It originates inside them, pushing out, rather than outside trying to get in (Streeck, *Re-Forming Capitalism*).

14   Wolfgang Streeck, 'Taking Capitalism Seriously: Towards an Institutional Approach to Contemporary Political Economy', *Socio-Economic Review*, vol. 9, no. 1, 2011, pp. 137–167. On the microfoundations of a theory of capitalism as a dynamic social order see a recent paper by Jens Beckert on the 'four C's' of capitalism: credit, commodity, competition and creativity (Jens Beckert, *Capitalism as a System of Contingent Expectations: On the Microfoundations of Economic Dynamics*, Cologne: Max Planck Institute for the Study of Societies, Unpublished Manuscript 2012).

15   Dorothee Bohle and Bela Greskovits, 'Varieties of Capitalism and Capitalism "tout court"', *Archives Européennes de Sociologie*, vol. 50, no. 3, 2009, pp. 355–368.

16   Joseph A. Schumpeter, *Theorie der wirtschaftlichen Entwicklung*, Berlin: Duncker & Humblot 2006 [1912].

decide about the social status and the life chances of owners of different types of economic resources, innovation and the changing terms of trade it produces permanently put established ways of life at risk to the extent that they are tied to specific modes of production and relations of exchange.

Another mechanism in capitalism that drives its expansion is *credit*. A capitalist economy works by making it possible to pay for resources to be used in current production with entitlements to the fruits of future production, as its banking system converts promises of future payment into present purchasing power. Financial institutions, from banking systems to courts of law, must ensure that such promises are kept and the not-yet-existing virtual resources that are pulled forward from the future are in fact produced and so can be returned. Promises of repayment can, however, only be kept if there is growth; credit is nothing else than anticipated growth. If for whatever reason promises to repay generally lose credibility, for example when debtors default in higher than usual numbers, lending recedes, as does growth.

A metaphor for the dynamics of capitalist growth related to land-grabbing is *border-crossing*. Capitalist expansion, or development, consists of the establishment of market relations where hitherto there were none. Social institutions that demarcate areas of trade against areas of non-trade, from national borders to laws prohibiting, say, the sale of organs, children or cocaine, will find themselves under pressure from profit-pursuing actors seeking to extend economic exchange across demarcation lines. Capitalist expansion, in this perspective, amounts to an extension of private, voluntary-horizontal, contractual social relations of exchange from markets where they are already legitimate, to not-yet marketized social fields still governed by reciprocity or authority.[17] Current concepts for border-crossing in this sense are commercialization, commodification or liberalization. I maintain that studying contemporary capitalism requires that processes of this sort are recognized as fundamental rather than contingent, and as principal driving forces of institutional change and historical development. This implies that where they happen not to be in evidence or ineffectual in a capitalist political economy, this can only be because they have temporarily been suspended by identifiable countervailing forces.

Endemic pressures for liberalization and the efforts of capitalist innovators pursuing unlimited gain by revolutionizing economic and social relations give rise to perpetual tension in the capitalist social order and continuing conflicts over it. Again, the study of contemporary capitalism must expect

---

17   Streeck, *Re-Forming Capitalism*; Streeck, 'Taking Capitalism Seriously'.

such tension and conflicts to be normal, rather than occasional and periph-
eral and in principle easily manageable in self-stabilizing 'market economies'.
I will briefly mention two examples, the unequal battle between market forces
and the *social regulation* of markets, and the struggle over *social protection*. As
to the former, markets need all sorts of rules against potentially rampant
opportunism in extended chains of production and exchange, which is why
regulatory law has grown and continues to grow alongside capitalism. After
all, the logic of market capitalism is one that licenses the pursuit of self-interest and, given unlimited potential rewards, must expect traders to be
aggressively advantage-seeking.[18] Nevertheless, the status of regulation in the
system is precarious as the foundational ideology of free markets presumes
that freedom of contract and *caveat emptor* are basically sufficient to keep
competitors honest.

More importantly, although rules and regulations are vital for the functioning of markets as they establish trust by protecting market participants
from asymmetric information, it is in the nature of capitalist competition that
profit-seekers will try to evade or circumvent them. Illegal or sublegal just as
innovative trading – the two often being the same – tend to be more profitable,
due to being riskier, than trading in the usual paths. This is why regulations
that limit freedom of trade are typically attacked by enterprising traders, calling forth considerable intelligence and inventiveness in efforts to render them
ineffectual. Since self-interested businesses know their trade better than
anybody else, and often also command substantial economic resources and
political power, they typically move faster than the public agencies charged
with regulating them, in particular where trading crosses the boundaries of
existing jurisdictions, like national states. This is why regulatory policies in
contemporary capitalism fundamentally remain confined to following the lead
of the market and trying to catch up with highly agile, creative and unpredictable actors endowed with superior knowledge and resources that enjoy a
permanent first mover advantage and are usually one or more steps ahead.[19]

Concerning social protection, relative prices in a capitalist economy tend
to move faster than people are able and willing to adapt their lives to them.
Social relations, expectations and status orders are typically inert in

---

18   Streeck, 'Taking Capitalism Seriously'.

19   The principal example for this, of course, is the 'globalization' of economic relations, which
is typically followed by often desperate efforts to replace national regulation, having become
increasingly ineffectual, with what is called 'global governance'. That the building of authoritative
regulatory institutions under capitalism tends to lag behind the dynamic growth of voluntary trading
relations should not come as a surprise to students of contemporary capitalism or regulatory policy and
should in fact be assumed to be in the nature of the beast.

comparison to free markets, leading people as citizens to demand political intervention to stabilize their social existence against market pressures for permanent adjustment. It is this conflict between the dynamism of capitalist development and the inertia of established ways of life that is the very substance of politics in contemporary capitalism. Politics has many facets, some highly complex and even paradoxical, but this must not detract from the fact that under capitalism, it is essentially driven and shaped by what Karl Polanyi has characterized as an almost Manichaean battle between a 'movement' towards liberalization and 'counter-movements' for social stabilization, or for collective political control over markets and the direction of social change.[20] One upshot of this is that politics under capitalism is fundamentally *not* a consensual pursuit of economic efficiency (as it is in Hall and Soskice),[21] given that a central issue of political conflict is precisely how far efficiency may be allowed to govern social life and where the zone of protection begins in which social relations are to be governed by obligations rather than by contract, by responsibilities to others rather than to self, by collective duty rather than individual voluntarism, or by respect for the sacred as opposed to the maximization of individual utility.

Finally, by considering capitalism as an endogenously dynamic economy-cum-society bent on growth through continuous expansion of market relations, we are able to introduce in macro-sociological theory a *qualified notion of directionality* of social change. Qualified that notion is, not just in the sense of being specific of capitalism, but also in that the direction of change is regarded as contested between, with Polanyi, capitalist movement and protective or even anti-capitalist counter-movement. Conceptually, the perspective I propose makes it possible to take leave of the Newtonian vision of a universe of changeless motion and allows for historical periodicity and irreversibility ('capitalism as history').

Moreover, focusing on capitalism's logic of continuous expansion directs attention to a number of *critical problems* of contemporary society and relates them to each other and to the social structure. A social system with a capitalist market economy that must perpetually extend the scale and scope of commercialized trading relations in order to survive is likely at some point to encounter obstacles to its progress, and the more so the longer its land-grabbing has already gone on. Again Polanyi's basic concepts serve as, today, all three of his 'fictitious commodities' – labour, land and nature[22] – seem to be in critical

---

20   Polanyi, *The Great Transformation*.
21   Hall and Soskice, 'An Introduction to Varieties of Capitalism'.
22   Polanyi, *The Great Transformation*, pp. 68–77.

condition as a result of their dynamically advancing commodification. Whereas the commodification of money in the course of 'financialization' has undermined its collective status as a reliable means of exchange and measure of value, the wasting of nature for commercial purposes is about to destroy the foundations of life as we know it, while the marketization of human labour power has reached a point where the physical reproduction of rich societies has had to become a public concern (more on this below). In all three respects, the logic of *growth by individual aggrandizement* that is constitutive of capitalism as a social system has come under suspicion as potentially dangerous for human society and the human species.

CAPITALISM AS CULTURE

Much of contemporary political economy clings to *a reified notion of scarcity* as an objective condition with respect to objectively needed material requirements of life. This reflects the treatment of needs in economic theory as both exogenously given and endless, thereby removing them from critical inquiry. Sociology, by comparison, has long known that needs are dynamic, and especially in capitalism; that what is 'necessary' for life is to a large extent socially defined, i.e., necessary only for social life in a given society; and that outside of the limiting case of complete deprivation, scarcity is neither absolute nor open-ended but socially contingent and constructed. Still, sociologists have by and large abstained from taking economists to task for disregarding the social and historical nature of economic needs and aspirations.[23]

If human needs are not fixed but fluid and socially and historically contingent, it must follow that scarcity is, to a considerable extent, a matter of collective *imagination*, and the more so the richer a society 'objectively' is. The insight that it is importantly imaginations that drive economic behaviour – imaginations that, other than material necessities, are inherently dynamic – points to a *cultural-symbolic dimension of economic life.*[24] That dimension is, of course, a fundamentally social one. Realizing this, we blur the border between 'hard' economics and 'soft' sociology, opening up the economy to sociological inquiry from a 'constructivist' perspective.

---

23 This was different before sociology and economics parted company. See, for example, Thorstein Veblen (*The Theory of the Leisure Class*, New York: Penguin 1994 [1899]) and his theory of conspicuous consumption.

24 The present section is inspired by a number of recent papers by Jens Beckert. See Jens Beckert, *Imagined Futures: Fictionality in Economic Action*, MPIfG Discussion Paper 11/8, Cologne: Max Planck Institute for the Study of Societies 2011; Jens Beckert, 'The Transcending Power of Goods: Imaginative Value in the Economy'. In: Beckert, Jens and Patrick Aspers, eds, *The Worth of Goods: Valuation and Pricing in the Economy*, Oxford: Oxford University Press 2011, pp. 106–130.

There are a wide range of cultural constructions supplanting or complementing objective conditions in motivating and controlling economic action, like 'trust' in a debtor's willingness and ability to live up to his or her obligations (see above); investor 'confidence', being an important requirement for economic growth (see below); or 'credible commitments' by governments to respect the interests of strategically important groups in the political economy. Standard economic theory does recognize the importance of such factors, but only grudgingly in the form of 'irrational' residual influences that all-too-often distort the effects of 'hard' and solid, 'really-economic' incentives. It also typically conceives them as 'psychological' rather than social, in a conceptually fuzzy language that attributes to what is called 'the markets' mental conditions like 'panic' or 'confidence'.

A highly promising approach to the study of contemporary capitalism that is, however, only rarely taken, focuses on *consumption* and the evolution of consumer 'needs', or better: desires. Here in particular, dreams, promises and imagined satisfaction are not at all marginal but, on the contrary, central. While standard economics and, in its trail, standard political economy, recognize the importance of confidence and consumer spending for economic growth, they do not do justice to the dynamically evolving nature of the desires that make consumers consume. A permanent underlying concern in advanced capitalist societies is that markets may at some point become saturated, resulting in stagnant or declining spending and, worse still, in diminished effectiveness of monetized work incentives. It is only if consumers, almost all of whom live far above the level of material subsistence, can be convinced to discover new needs, and thereby render themselves 'psychologically' poor, that the economy of rich capitalist societies can continue to grow. That the propensity to consume may become the Achilles heel of contemporary capitalism is hidden by a realist-rationalist-materialistic concept of economic action that represents historical social norms and imaginaries with ahistorical, pre-social, exogenously fixed 'necessaries'.[25]

It is not that post-war sociology had not been aware of consumption and the epochal significance of the rise of consumerism; an outstanding example is David Riesman's powerful analysis of the *Lonely Crowd* (1950).[26] There also was in the 1960s in the United States a broad popular literature on the advance of advertising (for example, Vance Packard's *The Hidden*

---

25   Smith, *An Inquiry into the Nature and Causes of the Wealth of Nations*, p. 22.
26   David Riesman with Nathan Glazer and Reuel Denney, *The Lonely Crowd: A Study of the Changing American Character*, New Haven, CT: Yale University Press 1950.

Persuaders).[27] Critique of consumer society culminated in the revolutionary era of the late 1960s and the 1970s, when concepts like 'consumption terror' fed into diagnoses of a 'false consciousness' among the masses, combined with calls for a more modest and less materialistic way of life. Later, however, these themes disappeared for decades, perhaps out of resignation in the face of a veritable explosion of consumption-driven growth in the years of globalization and new information technology. Also, it seems that sociology, in its desire for scientific recognition and professionalization, and for dissociating itself from the failed anti-capitalism of the 1970s, tried to avoid any appearance of moralizing, of telling people what to do as opposed to analysing 'value-free' what they do do.[28] Where cultural sociology still studied consumption, it did so without questioning standard economics' reification of economic needs and without relating its subject to capitalism and its need for economic expansion.

Today, debates on economic necessities, objective or imagined, and their limits are forcefully back, although they originate more in ecology and among heterodox economists than in sociology. A growing literature discusses the possibilities of less consumerist pathways to happiness, the nature of immaterial sources of satisfaction, and new, more comprehensive and less market-dependent measures of economic performance and growth. Sociologists, even economic sociologists, as far as I can see, are largely absent from these debates, and they seem in particular not to have grasped the explosiveness of the issue for contemporary capitalism. While the discipline's journals flow over with articles on wage differentials between men and women, on the household division of labour, the hours people work etc., the question why people today, being much richer than thirty years ago, work much more and much harder, seems almost taboo. The same applies to why people seem to find the increase in living standards since the 1970s worth the enormous effort that was necessary to produce it – not to mention the question of how advanced capitalist economies can hope in the future to generate the work motivation that will be needed to keep them growing.

One potential answer seems to be the increasingly immaterial nature of consumption in rich societies.[29] With physical needs largely covered, more

---

27   Vance Packard, *The Hidden Persuaders*, New York: D. McKay Co 1957.

28   This is an interesting contrast to economics which, thanks to its rational choice framework, can be prescriptive and analytical at the same time – or can dress up prescription as analysis.

29   Note in this context also the inflationary use in American public speech of the word, 'dream', as in 'American dream', in a culture that is both the most consumerist on earth and, allegedly, steeped in Yankee rationalism and utilitarianism. No politician can get elected in the United States without

and more goods seem to be purchased because of their *dream value,* as distinguished from their *use value:* for example, fashionable garments, branded accessories, sporting goods, cars, wine, lottery tickets, trips to far-away countries, antiques and the like. Many of these goods, which account for a growing share of rich countries' domestic product, also have a high status value – as does, incidentally, being able to sell one's labour power, especially for women. Moreover, participation in the consumption of symbolic goods and the commodification of social relations seem to have become vital for social integration; see the rapidly growing role of the computer-based 'social networks' in the structuring of modern life. More money than ever is today being spent by firms on advertisement and on building and sustaining the popular images and auras on which the success of a product seems to depend in saturated markets. In particular, the new channels of communication made available by the interactive internet seem to be absorbing a growing share of what firms spend on the socialization and cultivation of their customers. A rising share of the goods that make today's capitalist economies grow would not sell if people dreamed other dreams than they do – which makes understanding, developing and controlling their dreams a fundamental concern of political economy in advanced-capitalist society.

Sociologists have hardly begun to revive the subject, explored already in the early years of consumer capitalism[30] but then abandoned, of the social mechanisms by which a materially saturated capitalist economy may maintain its capacity to grow. Today, in the face of tightening ecological constraints, unprecedented risks associated with an overblown credit system, and growing stress on the social fabric, the *politics of immaterial economic needs* may be emerging as a crucial political-economic battlefield. The long-known fact that capitalism flourishes, not by covering existing needs but by eliciting new ones – that capitalist growth requires permanent demand-management not just in a *quantitative* but also in a *qualitative* sense – should be recognized as increasingly critical. It seems high time for sociology to rediscover a perspective that no other discipline would be better positioned to contribute to the study of contemporary capitalism.

---

confessing again and again to having 'dreams' for himself, his fellow Americans, and the world at large. The closeness of this to religious experiences is easy to recognize. Today, unlimited consumption seems to have replaced the Promised Land in the dreams dreamed by Americans almost as a matter of social obligation.

30 A social formation whose novelty at the time is beautifully reflected in the two volumes of the Lynds' study of 'Middletown' (Robert S. Lynd and Helen Merrell Lynd, *Middletown: A Study in Contemporary American Culture,* London: Constable 1929; Robert S. Lynd and Helen Merrell Lynd, *Middletown in Transition: A Study in Cultural Conflicts,* New York: Harcourt 1937).

CAPITALISM AS A POLITY

Capitalism, a non-violent, civilized mode of material self-enrichment through market exchange, had to extricate itself from feudalism in an alliance with liberal anti-authoritarianism and with popular movements for democracy. Still, the historical association between capitalism and democracy was always an uneasy one, marred, especially in earlier periods, by strong mutual suspicion.[31] Whereas capitalists were afraid of democracy going too far, with the dispossessed majority abolishing private property, the working classes worried about capitalists protecting themselves against expropriation by suppressing free elections and freedom of association. It was only after 1945 that democratic capitalism, or capitalist democracy, became a half-way stable political-economic regime in the Western part of the industrialized world, at least for the two or three decades immediately after the war when Keynesian full employment policies, an expanding welfare state and independent trade unions sustained, and were sustained by, high and steady economic growth.

This did not mean, however, that democratic capitalism was free of tensions. As a social system, capitalist democracy is ruled by two diverging sets of normative principles, *social justice* on the one hand and *market justice* on the other, the former vested in the society's *moral economy* and the latter residing in what may be called its *economic economy*. While the moral economy of democratic capitalism reflects what people believe is right and fair, the economic economy, or market economy, allocates resources on the basis of marginal productivity, and in this sense of maximized efficiency. Whereas democracy answers to the moral economy of democratic capitalism, the market is in equilibrium only if it can function according to the principles of economic economy.

By the end of the 1960s, it began to become clear that capitalism and democracy cannot operate side by side without more or less effectively undermining each other. Increasingly, social justice and market justice turned out to be difficult to reconcile, in spite of continuous efforts by governments, the media and standard economic theory to convince citizens that market justice is in fact the highest form of social justice. It is true that, if ordinary people could be re-educated to organize their communal life according to differences in marginal productivity, capitalism could be democratic *without* being internally contradictory and precarious. Up to now, however, most human societies continue to adhere to traditional principles of social justice that can all-too-easily come in conflict with market justice. Examples include the idea that

---

31 This section follows closely the argument in Wolfgang Streeck, 'A Crisis of Democratic Capitalism', *New Left Review*, no. 71, 2011, pp. 1–25.

someone who puts in a 'good day's work' should receive 'a good day's wage'; that people should not be poor because of old age; that nobody should starve, remained unattended when ill, or have to live on the streets; that workers in employment should have recourse to some sort of due process against arbitrary exercise of managerial authority; or that employers should give workers notice before they dismiss them.[32]

As long as capitalism has not yet managed to dissolve popular concepts of social justice into efficiency-theoretical notions of market justice, capitalism and democracy, or markets and politics, will not cease interfering with each other. As the moral economy invades economic policy, it extracts an efficiency fee from the economy, noted in the form of a profit squeeze, just as 'economic laws' and 'sound economic management' stand in the way of the satisfaction of democratic moral claims. As a result, governments are continuously at risk of having to face a forced choice between two equally unpalatable options: sacrificing economic stability and performance to defend democratic legitimacy, and overruling popular claims for social justice in the name of sound economic policy. Typically, that problem tends to be solved by addressing the two horns of the dilemma in turn, switching back and forth as a successful response to a crisis of democratic legitimacy results in economic imbalances, and successful measures for economic stabilization in social discontent.

The tensions inherent in democratic capitalism, and the limits of public policy trying to manage them, are illustrated by the sequence of crises that constitutes the economic history of rich capitalist democracies since the 1970s. After the end of post-war growth, governments in the 'free world' avoided conflicts with strong trade unions over wage increases and unemployment by allowing for high rates of inflation. Inflation, much like credit, served to pull forward in time as yet non-existing resources, enabling employers and workers to realize in nominal money terms claims whose sum total was in excess of what was in fact available for distribution. While workers believed they were achieving what they perceived to be their moral-economic right to a steadily rising living standard combined with secure employment in their present jobs, employers were able to reap profits in line with expectations of a proper return as established in the decades of post-war reconstruction. As inflation continued, however, it devalued accumulated savings and increasingly distorted price relations. Its conquest in the early 1980s, in the course of the 'Volcker revolution', did not bring stability, however. Instead it ushered in a period of rising government debt as electoral politics substituted for collective

---

32   The principles of justice that constitute a society's moral economy are subject to change under the influence of, among other things, changing economic conditions and social discourses.

bargaining as the political-economic mechanism of the time for mobilizing surplus resources to pacify otherwise disruptive distributional conflict. When this, too, became unsustainable in the 1990s, consolidation of public finances could be undertaken only by giving households access to deregulated private credit, allowing them to compensate for stagnant incomes and rising inequality by borrowing on their own account.[33]

The latest twist in the story of capitalism and democracy took place after 2008 when the debt pyramid finally collapsed and private debt that had lost its value had to be socialized to keep the money economy liquid. The result was another dramatic increase in public debt. This gave rise to a new era of fiscal consolidation that is still shaping up, one in which states are put under unprecedented pressure by 'financial markets' to cut spending on social protection and investment, so as to secure their capacity to repay their creditors. As the site for the mobilization of future resources for present purposes of political pacification has moved from collective bargaining to electoral politics and from there to markets for consumer credit and, finally, public debt, the ability of democracy to distort the economic on behalf of the moral economy has progressively diminished. Today, owners of financial capital are working with international organizations and debt-ridden nation states to insulate once and for all the economic economy from the moral economy of traditional social obligations and modern citizenship rights – and with greater prospect of success than ever in the four decades since the 1970s. As democratic states are being turned into collection agencies on behalf of a new global *haute finance*, market justice is about to prevail over social justice, for a long if not an indefinite period of time. In the process those who have placed their confidence as citizens in capitalist democracy must concede precedence to those who have as investors placed their money on it.

Studying contemporary capitalism in terms of a clash between moral economy and market economy invites more detailed investigation of the nature of distributional claims based on marginal productivity. According to standard economics, they differ from social entitlements in that they are technical and objective rather than moral and subjective. A sociological approach, however, should be able to recognize behind the veil of efficiency theory the moral economy of the owners and investors of capital or, more generally, of essential productive resources. A key concept here is that of investor 'confidence', as analysed in Kalecki's political theory of the business cycle.[34] Rather

---

33   Crouch, 'Privatised Keynesianism'.
34   Kalecki, 'Political Aspects of Full Employment', pp. 322–331.

than reacting mechanically to fixed rates of expected return, capital owners use pronouncements on their self-diagnosed 'psychological' condition, from pessimism to optimism, from panic to euphoria, to signal whether what they are offered in return for investing their resources conforms to what they feel they are entitled to. Expressions of low 'investor confidence' are strategically used in an interactive process of joint determination of what investors must be allowed to extract from the rest of the economy under given conditions of scarcity and distribution of political power. Currently one can observe investors in global financial markets using variations in the rate of interest they require from states for refinancing public debt to bolster demands for a more firmly institutionalized politics of austerity. Political economy based on social action rather than efficiency theory should be able to de-reify the market mechanism of standard economics and expose price and profit formation for what it is: the outcome of a struggle between conflicting concepts of and claims to justice – 'live and let live' vs. 'just return' – rather than between *subjective ideas* of what is *morally right* on the one hand and *objective laws* of what is *technically possible* or *required* on the other.

CAPITALISM AS A WAY OF LIFE

Finally, studying contemporary capitalism means studying a *way of life* as well as a historical social order, a culture and a polity. Market expansion, the driving force of capitalist development, has ramifications into the remotest corners of society as it continuously revolutionizes social relations and the institutions governing them. Capitalist development is deeply interwoven with how people organize even their most personal and intimate social life, in line with changing cultural assumptions, themselves affected by the expansion of markets, as to what is and is not 'natural', 'normal', and to be taken for granted. This includes family life and the way society provides for its physical reproduction.[35]

The last three decades have witnessed a fundamental restructuring of the family and child-rearing in rich Western societies, in close interaction with new constraints and opportunities created by the progress of markets, of labour markets as well as markets for consumer goods. To analyse capitalism as a way of life, rather than just an economy, one might conveniently start by remembering the post-war era of the 'Fordist' mode of production

---

35   On the following see Wolfgang Streeck, 'Flexible Employment, Flexible Families, and the Socialization of Reproduction'. In: Coulmas, Florian and Ralph Lützeler, eds, *Imploding Populations in Japan and Germany: A Comparison*, Leiden: Brill 2011, pp. 63–95.

complemented by the 'Fordist' family. Then it was a matter of pride for families and a sign of economic success if women were relieved from paid work,
so they could fully devote themselves to unpaid work for their family.
Nothing has more completely disappeared than this. Beginning in the 1970s,
growing numbers of women went into paid employment as working for a
wage became the path of choice for them to personal independence, as well
as a condition of social respect and full membership in the community.
Simultaneously, marriage rates dropped, divorce rates increased, family relations became less tight and obligatory, and birth rates declined, with children
increasingly born both outside marriage and in disproportionate numbers to
women lacking opportunity in the labour market. Morally, entering into
paid employment became not just a choice for women but a *de facto* obligation, taking the place of marriage and child-bearing in the 1950s and 1960s.
'Work' became identical with paid work, while not being in paid work –
being a *Hausfrau* or a housewife – became associated with not working at all
and increasingly turned into a personal disgrace.

There are two alternative and, to a certain extent, competing accounts of
what started the exodus of women from the subsistence economy of the family
into the money economy of the market. One is about push and economic need,
the other about pull and personal liberation. When real wages began to stagnate after the end of post-war growth, American families continued their
pursuit of the American dream of ever-rising prosperity by selling ever more
hours to employers in the labour market. Moreover, post-war educational
expansion had prepared a new generation of women for the growing number
of positions in the emerging 'service economy'. To them earning 'their own
money' amounted to a successful escape from what came soon to be generally
perceived as personal servitude in traditionally male-dominated families. The
rise of consumerism did its part to reinforce both the push out of the household and the pull into the market. So did a more individualistic way of life,
partly facilitated by market expansion and partly facilitating it, with more
people remaining single; a higher probability of personal relations and families
breaking up; and changes in family law that emphasized the responsibility of
divorced women to find a job and take care of themselves.

The movement of women into the labour market vastly added to the
labour supply of capitalist economies at a time when labour and the demands
of workers for higher wages and better employment conditions had become a
bottleneck for continued capital accumulation. As female participation
increased, trade union density declined, unemployment become endemic,
strikes 'withered away' and wage pressure on profits were relieved. More often
than not employers managed to enlist women as allies in a fight for

deregulation of employment, as both had reasons to push for 'flexible' labour markets allowing 'outsiders', typically female, to compete effectively with, typically male, 'insiders'.[36] In the course of the liberalization of both markets and social life, the abolition of the family wage coincided with increasingly precarious family relations to make paid employment, even at deteriorating conditions, an economic necessity for women, including the rising number of single women with children. The result was and is further pressure on wages and working conditions. Nonetheless, as waged employment became an essential condition of personal autonomy and social esteem, women's move out of the family and into the market provided employers with a wave of eager new arrivals in the labour force and an ample supply of compliant workers happy to be employed at all. Culturally the result was an astonishing rehabilitation of waged employment as compared to the 1960s, turning it from despised industrial servitude ('dependent labour') into a desired social privilege. Step by step, workplaces began to replace the family and the local community as focal sites of social integration, turning among other things into society's most important marriage markets.

The commodification of female labour gave rise to new patterns of child-rearing that reflect the advance of capitalist development. As couples spend more time in employment, they have less time for children. This means they must externalize childcare, either to the market or to the state. Of course many have no children at all, devoting their time entirely to the exigencies and attractions, as the case may be, of work and consumption. Typically, children are most numerous among the less educated and the poor, who have few prospects of success outside of the family. While precarious employment postpones childbirth among the middle classes, it has little effect if any on the lower classes. Precarious families, for their part, produce comparatively many children as the number of couples of reproductive age that are married is declining in an era of individualization and growing flexibility of social relations. Contemporary capitalist societies that want more children must therefore prepare for a growing share of them being born to unwed mothers. Unwed mothers, of course, are at high risk of poverty. Especially in Europe, public assistance has in this way become the *de facto* leading family policy, as it in

---

36   In the media and in the government propaganda of most if not all rich capitalist countries today, the 'battle of the sexes' has nearly completely eclipsed all other distributional conflicts. A bizarre case in point is the European Union and most of its member states planning to introduce a quota for women on the executive boards of large publicly held companies, with the support of all political forces, including the Left, and under enthusiastic media applause. This happens at a time when social policy 'reforms' have effectively pulled the bottom out from under the labour market, resulting in a rapidly growing low-wage sector populated overwhelmingly by women, with single motherhood having everywhere become the most frequent cause of poverty.

effect pays mothers to devote themselves fulltime to child-rearing. This outcome is considered unfortunate by labour market policymakers bent on raising the level of fulltime labour market participation of women to that of men. It is also seen as disastrous by those concerned about the supply of the sort of 'human capital' that is believed to be required to make national economies productive and competitive. In response, to reduce the share of economically undesirable children, governments have taken measures to shift fertility from the lower to the middle classes, in an effort at what could be called social eugenics. But to compensate for the attractions of career and consumption in dual-earner middle-class families, financial incentives must be strong, and spending on them not only runs up against fiscal austerity but also has to be so blatantly degressive that it may at some point become hard to defend politically.

In all countries of advanced capitalism, governments and employers have joined in efforts to further increase the female labour supply. For both, too many women still hesitate to work fulltime in the labour market, especially mothers who are generally suspected of being excessively devoted to their children (or using them as an excuse for 'not working'). Whereas employers cannot have enough competition on the supply side of the labour market, governments need to convert unpaid into paid labour so it can be taxed and thereby help fund the social welfare system. Moving people from welfare to 'work' also promises much-needed fiscal relief. A special target group for this is, again, single mothers. Getting them to take up paid employment, however, in particular if it is to be fulltime, is in itself costly as it requires provisions for childcare, typically public, since private childcare is unaffordable for low-income earners.

While seeking to increase female employment, governments must also be concerned about low fertility, if only because a sufficiently large next generation is needed to pay off the debt incurred by the present one. Pressure on women to get employed may be harmful to fertility unless accompanied by expensive provisions for childcare, which are increasingly difficult to finance under tightening fiscal constraints. The alternative would be increased immigration making it possible to adopt the American solution, where high economic inequality makes private nannies cheap and immigrants, being poor, contribute more than their share to society's offspring.[37] The alternative approach, enabling mothers and fathers to combine employment and family obligations through improved employment protection and, importantly, shorter working hours, is not normally on the agenda, as it is not welcomed by

---

37 Although, of course, their children are less desirable from a human capital point of view.

220 HOW WILL CAPITALISM END?

employers, certainly outside the public sector. Paying mothers for staying at home, as demanded by social conservatives, would save money since it would be less expensive than public childcare, but it would not please employers either; nor would it yield revenue for the social security system or fit in with now predominant cultural views on the relative value of domestic-informal and marketized labour. Today, the instruments of choice in many countries, cheap but of questionable effectiveness, are public campaigns to re-educate men to become 'new fathers' and share equally in housework and childcare duties, to enable their female 'partners' in human capital production to deliver more hours to the labour market.

Meanwhile an astonishing number of parents, single or coupled, have cheer-fully adjusted to a high-pressure way of life somehow combining child-rearing with ever longer hours of ever more demanding and insecure employment.[38] Rather than complaining or rebelling, many seem to take the stress as a test of their personal capacity for permanent improvement, much like high-perfor-mance athletes. Living the contemporary capitalist way of life, parents comply with social expectations that they subject themselves in good spirit to the strict regimentation of a self-enforced rigid time regime and take pride in enduring the hardships of a new sort of 'inner-worldly asceticism'[39] in the service of career, income, consumption and human capital formation. In fact, looking at the ideal-ized middle-class family of today, one is tempted to speak of the rise of a new protestant ethic leading to ever more detailed rationalization of everyday life. Contributing to it are rising demands on the education of children that respond to a need perceived by parents for the next generation to acquire as early as possible the human capital that the even more competitive labour markets of the future will presumably ask of them. While quality children learn Chinese at age three in Kindergarten, their quality parents work long hours to be able to pay for the quality childcare they do not have the time to provide themselves, and for the SUV they need for the quality time to spend with their offspring during their – rare – free weekends. That the high-pressure family life of today is not free of tensions is indicated, among other things, by the often-reported bad conscience of women, either for 'working' and neglecting their children, or for 'not working' and failing to prove their worth by earning money in the market. Of course governments and employers, and the culturally hegemonic public discourse of contemporary capitalist society, do what they can to talk women out of the former and, where still necessary, into the latter.

---

38   Recently this has come to be referred to as the 'yes we can family'.
39   Max Weber, *The Protestant Ethic and the Spirit of Capitalism*, trans. Talcott Parsons, Introduction by Anthony Giddens, London: Unwin Paperbacks 1984 [1904/1905].

FROM STABLE VARIETIES TO PRECARIOUS COMMONALITIES

What is distinctive about the approach I suggest for the study of contemporary capitalism? All four of my vignettes, on capitalism as history, as a culture, a polity and a way of life, emphasize differences *in capitalism over time* rather than *between capitalisms in space*.[40] This is in opposition to much of comparative political economy today, for which it is cross-sectional variations between, typically, national 'capitalisms' that matter most. Where comparative political economy sees essentially frozen 'varieties'[41] of capitalism, my perspective highlights the commonalities of its varying institutional embodiments, or more precisely: the common dynamics that are responsible for the parallel trajectories on which national capitalisms historically move.[42]

Obviously, differences and commonalities come hand in hand, which raises the issue of whether giving precedence to one over the other is more than a matter of personal taste, or of regarding a glass as half full or half empty. I believe that it *is* more than that, and that the inherent generic dynamism of all capitalist political economies is much more instructive for the study of contemporary society than are the differences between them. Rather than focusing on differences, I believe I have made a case for the generic tensions and conflicts driving the development of social structures under capitalism; the culture of consumerism; the political-economic frictions and imbalances endemic to democratic capitalism; and the deep impact of capitalist markets on social life in contemporary rich societies. While the responses offered by politics to the questions posed by the restlessness of markets and their relentless endogenous pressures for expansion may differ, it is the dynamism of capitalist development that dictates the agenda of political choices, instead of the other way around. Comparative political economy, I claim, attributes too much autonomy to collective decisions and overlooks the fact that they can only be made under socio-economic conditions that are fundamentally not at the disposition of politics as instituted under democratic capitalism.

Add to this that the national capitalisms that are the units of comparison in the 'varieties of capitalism' literature are in fact much more interdependent than allowed for by the theory, as a result of their ever closer interaction in capitalist world markets.[43] Importantly, such interaction may give rise to both *convergence* by institutional transfer and emulation and *divergence* by specialization. Specialization, rather than ending commonalities, is premised upon

---

40   Streeck, 'E Pluribus Unum?'.
41   Hall and Soskice, *Varieties of Capitalism*.
42   Streeck, *Re-Forming Capitalism*.
43   Streeck, 'E Pluribus Unum?'.

them: it results from niche seeking under an encompassing logic of capitalist progress, within a range of possibilities defined by it. Moreover, mutual inter-action between national capitalisms and the states they sustain, as well as the available space of possibilities for differentiation and specialization, are governed by differences in economic, political and ideational power. For example, if the United States adopts financialization as its preferred strategy of wealth creation, this redefines the constraints and opportunities for the rest of the world to such an extent that it becomes hard if not impossible for others not to adapt to it, one way or another.

A further reason to give priority to *longitudinal commonalities* as identi-fied by a *political economy of capitalism* over *cross-sectional differences* as emphasized by a *comparative political economy of 'varieties of capitalism'* is the central role played in the former of internal contradictions and conflicts, as opposed to the dominance in the latter of functionalist concepts such as complementarity and competitiveness. In this important respect, comparative political economy resembles standard economic theory, in particular the so-called 'new institutional economics'.[44] The guiding idea the two share is that it is stability of institutions over time that matters, to be explained in terms of equilibrium in the service of economic performance. In contrast, I suggest to conceive of capitalism, past as well as present, 'liberal' just as 'coordinated', as of a political economy in *permanent disequilibrium* caused by continuous innovation and pervasive political conflict over the relationship between social and economic justice; over frictions between collective obligations to protect individuals from the fallout of 'creative destruction', and individual obligations to adjust to economic change; and over the moral limits, if any, to the individ-ual pursuit of economic advantage. As the current crisis forcefully reminds us, it is both theoretically and empirically far more instructive for the study of contemporary capitalism to focus, not on stability, but on uncertainty, risk, fragility, precariousness and the generally transitory and never quite pacified nature of social and political settlements in capitalist societies.

Only by abandoning an efficiency-theoretical perspective, then, will one be able to conceive of capitalism as of a society with an open future, a society that is both historical and political. Capitalist entrepreneurial land-grabbing and the omnipresence of self-undermining institutional change make *a priori* assumptions of an always-imminent return to a stable and efficient equilib-rium unrealistic and indeed render them wishful thinking. Catastrophic outcomes can, as we are currently reminded, never be precluded; mistakes of calculation may have profound and lasting consequences; and systemic

---

44   Streeck, 'E Pluribus Unum?'.

uncertainty makes mistakes possible and even likely. A theory of contemporary capitalism must rid itself of any implication, as deeply hidden as it might
be in its logical fabric, of an assured recovery from critical disturbances,
considered temporary and exceptional, to lasting normality, either by political
planning or by market-driven self-organization. There also is no guarantee
that the structure, the culture, the politics and the life-world of modern capitalism will always evolve in parallel, supporting and reinforcing each other's
progress towards ever higher levels of commodification. While obviously the
different strands of capitalist development that we have sketched out are
related and in fact intertwined, there is enough 'play' between them to produce
frictions, tensions, retardation, modifications of direction, and potentially at
least effective resistance to their continued progress.

Where does economic sociology fit in the picture? I believe economic
sociologists have to decide if what they aim for is a sociology of the economy,
in the same sense in which there is a sociology of education, of sports, of the
family – what is called a *Bindestrichsoziologie* (a 'hyphenated sociology') in
German, a language where hyphens are more often used than in English. In
this version economic sociology would compete with standard economics on
its turf and terms, by offering to add a 'social factor' to the economists' account
of economic affairs while accepting their definition of what is and is not
'economic'. What this must amount to is, in essence, an *extended efficiency
theory* with strong prescriptive implications: to make markets really work, you
need to factor in networks and trust and the like as indispensable devices for
reducing transaction costs, and generally to recognize the hidden efficiencies
of particularistic as distinguished from universalistic social relations even in
presumably impersonal and in this sense 'rational' markets and organizations.
In a more ethnographic mode, this sort of economic sociology undertakes to
produce thick descriptions of how the economy is 'being done on the ground':
with intuition and tacit knowledge, following half-conscious rules of thumb,
and of course deviating widely from the rationalistic *homo economicus* model
of standard economic theory. The ironic point the theory makes is that it is
only because of such deviation that 'the economy' can function as efficiently as
economists assume it functions only if actors behave according to their ideal
rather than empirical model of rational individualism.

Behind this – I believe all-too-modest – self-definition of economic sociology seems to be a particular reading of the work of that towering figure of
twentieth-century social science, Karl Polanyi, and especially of his concept of
the 'embeddedness' of economic in social action. In this reading, even the
most capitalist economy must and will always be founded on an infrastructure
of con-capitalist social relations by which it needs to be and is socially

sustained.[45] A fully liberal political economy, as imagined by neoliberal doctrine, is no more than a utopian dream: a figment of sociologically unin-formed wishful thinking. Capitalism is 'always embedded', for factual as well as political reasons: factual, since it is impossible for economic action to be disso-ciated from social action, and political, because profit-seeking capitalists, unlike neoliberal ideologues, know that their profit-making depends on the presence of supportive social relations they are therefore, out of self-interest if nothing else, willing to respect.

This, however, may be doubted, and with good reasons.[46] A less compla-cent view of the capitalist political economy need not deny that profitable capitalist action requires a supportive non-economic social infrastructure. Where it differs is that it allows for the possibility, and indeed stipulates the inherent tendency, of expanding capitalist markets subverting their non-cap-italist foundations through the powerful pressures emanating from markets for liberation from social constraints. Although it is true, in this version of Polanyi as in any other, that capitalism cannot exist without a non-capitalist 'embedding', it cannot create or preserve it either, and in fact tends to erode and consume it – which makes capitalism, if unchecked, a self-destructive social formation. Capitalists, at least some of them, may well recognize this; *as capitalists*, however, they typically face a fundamental collective action problem that prevents them from acting on their preferences, in particular their longer-term, enlightened ones. This is why politics and political power are essential under capitalism, and indeed a politics that supports capitalist markets, not by *supporting* but by *counterbalancing and constraining* them, so as to *protect them from themselves*.[47]

Unlike the 'always embedded' interpretation of Polanyi, the 'always precar-ious' or 'always contested' one that I suggest takes neoliberalism seriously: not, or not just, as an ideological pipedream but as an imminent danger to modern society and, ultimately, capitalism itself. Rather than the *straightforward* func-tionalism of much of the 'new economic sociology', the approach I propose features a *dialectical* version of it, one under which the functioning of

45   Fred Block, 'Rethinking Capitalism'. In: Biggart, Nicole Woolsey, ed., *Readings in Economic Sociology*, Oxford: Blackwell 2002, pp. 219–230; Fred Block, 'Understanding the Diverging Trajectories of the United States and Western Europe: A Neo-Polanyian Analysis', *Politics and Society*, vol. 35, no. 3, 2007, pp. 3–33; Fred Block, 'Varieties of What? Should We Still Be Using the Concept of Capitalism?', *Political Power and Social Theory*, vol. 23, 2012, pp. 269–291.

46   Jens Beckert, 'The Great Transformation of Embeddedness: Karl Polanyi and the New Economic Sociology'. In: Hann, Chris and Keith Hart, eds, *Market and Society: The Great Transformation*, New York: Cambridge University Press 2009, pp. 38–55.

47   For a first elaboration of this dialectical figure of thought, see the chapter on the 'Working Day' in the first volume of *Capital* (Marx, *Capital*, Vol. 1).

capitalism depends vitally on the presence, essential but never guaranteed, of effective opposition to it. Whether such opposition can arise and do its work depends, in turn, on the existence of political resources that allow for the mobilization of countervailing power, a condition that cannot fundamentally be entrusted to the self-interest of capitalist profit maximizers. Capitalism entails, in addition to whatever else it may entail, an ever-present possibility of *self-destructive destruction of its social containment*, in the course of a politics of liberalization conceived as progressive removal of boundaries of all sorts, towards a final triumph of collectively irresponsible individual interests. Preventing this requires a *non-capitalist politics* capable of defining and enforcing general interests in the sustainability of human society, bringing capitalist actors to their senses and forcing them to act in line with their better insights, whether they already have them or not. Here, in the analysis of the ongoing battle over the limits to be drawn and continuously redrawn by modern society for its capitalist economy, is where economic sociology and political economy blend into each other – and as I have tried to show, it is here that the study of contemporary capitalism can and must make the most progress.

CHAPTER TEN

On Fred Block, 'Varieties of What? Should We Still Be Using the Concept of Capitalism?'

Capitalism – the thing, not the name – was anything but popular in the years following the Second World War, and this was so everywhere in the industrialized world, including the U.S. Outside of the Communist bloc, free markets and private property had to be made palatable again to a politically empowered working class, by wrapping them into a collection of containing and constraining policies and institutions that were to protect societies from a repetition of the disasters of the 1930s.[1] As we now know, however, the political provisions that were to turn capitalism into something else – called a 'mixed economy' or a 'social market economy', to make the new appear sufficiently different from the old[2] – lasted only a quarter century. With the end of post-war reconstruction in the 1960s, a grinding process of gradual institutional change set in that insensibly undermined and eventually removed most of the safeguards once devised to make capitalism compatible with then powerful collective demands for security, stability, equal opportunity, shared prosperity and the like.

Forty years later, we are beholding the results of an extraordinary historical development: a newly liberated capitalism having successfully extricated itself, Houdini-like, from the social fetters it had temporarily had to pretend to be willing and able to live with. Among the collective safety provisions that have fallen victim to capitalism's remarkable escape act are politically

1 This chapter was first published in: Julian Go, ed., *Political Power and Social Theory*, Bingley: Emerald Group Publishing Limited, Vol. 23, 2012, 311–321.

2 In post-war Germany capitalism simply was a no-no word. In Frankfurt where I studied sociology in the late 1960s, Adorno preferred to speak of *Tauschgesellschaft* (catallactic society), perhaps because the notion of capitalism was then too much associated with Communist orthodoxy. On the other hand, the neo-socialist young generation, to which I was proud to belong, spoke of 'social market economy' only tongue-in-cheek; to us the term was all-too-obvious capitalist propaganda. If, as Block claims, capitalism has recently become a positive concept in the U.S., the same is not true in Europe. Here the word came again in use after the end of Communism when Michel Albert's book, *Capitalism Against Capitalism* (Michel Albert, *Capitalism Against Capitalism: How America's Obsession With Individual Achievement and Short-term Profit Has Led It to the Brink of Collapse*, New York: Four Walls Eight Windows 1993 [1991]), became a bestseller. The book distinguishes between good and bad capitalisms, the former associated with a widely defined Rhineland and the latter with Anglo-America. It prefigured current dichotomies between 'coordinated' and 'liberal' capitalisms or indeed 'market economies'. Since the crisis doubts have been growing whether good capitalism is really so much better than bad capitalism.

228 HOW WILL CAPITALISM END?

228   HOW WILL CAPITALISM END?

guaranteed full employment, economy-wide free collective bargaining, industrial democracy at the workplace, a broad public sector offering secure employment in good jobs, extensive public services, economic planning to prevent the return of business cycles and crises, a social welfare state guaranteeing a general floor of social rights for every citizen and protecting people's lives from the commodifying pressures of market competition, and so on. It is important to note that these developments, and the pressures emanating from them for a deep reorganization of life and society in response to market pressures for competitiveness, flexibility and profitability, were not at all limited to the U.S. but appeared in locally diversified forms in all industrial societies, some leading in the breaking of the promises of the post-war era and others lagging, but all of them essentially moving in the same direction.[3]

How is what we have seen in the past four decades to be interpreted? In terms of Fred Block's essay, have we seen the rise of one out of a range of other, equally possible variants of 'market society', brought about by wrong-headed theories and bad political decisions, mysteriously synchronized across countries and sectors but in principle open to reversal by better theories and decisions in the future? Or are we witnessing an inherent dynamic of a politically hard-to-govern, self-driven social process – in the words of traditional theories of capitalism: the functioning of an anarchic regime of economic action that is a *problem* for government and politics rather than its *product*? While Block opts for the first answer, inspection of the historical sequence during which capitalism became 'unleashed'[4] from its post-war chains makes me tend towards the second. It is under this impression that I advocate that we stick to the concept of capitalism and some of the theoretical tenets that come with it, rather than abandoning it and instead calling the beast, as Block suggests, 'market society'.

Why capitalism? *Name ist Schall und Rauch*, as Goethe has it.[5] Still, it may be useful to be reminded that it is certainly not *labourism* that we have in mind when referring to contemporary political economy as it is capital, measured in units of money, and not human capacity, that is being accumulated in it – or human capacity only to the extent that it is conducive to capital accumulation. Markets are, as we learn in Economics 101, 'where

---

3   For the case of Germany, presumably the paragon of a 'coordinated', i.e., socially domesticated 'market economy' (Hall and Soskice, 'An Introduction to Varieties of Capitalism'), see Streeck, *Re-Forming Capitalism*.

4   Andrew Glyn, *Capitalism Unleashed: Finance Globalization and Welfare*, Oxford: Oxford University Press 2006.

5   In English, approximately: 'Names are smoke and mirrors'. Faust, Part I, Marthens Garten.

supply and demand meet'. But what makes the difference is that under capitalism, supply and demand meet *as commodities* in order to turn money into more money, according to Marx's venerable formula, M→C→M'.[6] It is here that the peculiar dynamism, the *Eigendynamik*, of the capitalist socio-economic formation is rooted.[7] When speaking of capitalism we have in mind, or at least could and should have, the specific restlessness[8] of an economic regime that is bent on permanently revolutionizing, not just itself but also the society in which it is located, as a condition of its prosperity and indeed survival.[9] A capitalist economy, technically speaking, is one that depends on the relentless commercialization-through-monetarization of ever more social relations. The result is disequilibrium as the normal condition of a society placed under continuous pressures by its 'economy' for ongoing reorganization in line with a need for continued, maximally efficient capital accumulation. One could also say that the concept of capitalism refers to a society that has enlisted the possessive individualism of its members as its main vehicle of social progress, measured again as an increase in wealth-as-money – a society that has made the amelioration of its collective living conditions and the realization of its core value of personal freedom both dependent on and subservient to successful activation of the profit motive and the maximization of the rate of increase of its capital. With this in mind and in this sense, I do think that, *pace* Block, capitalism as a system *does* have 'a fundamental unity',[10] due to its 'economy' extending far into its society and profoundly shaping and conditioning social life.[11]

Practising Polanyian that I have become, not least under the influence of Fred Block,[12] I still hesitate to discard the Marxian heritage as light-heartedly as he does. Marx, of course, needs no defence; he is easily recognized as the by far most sophisticated among the nineteenth century founding figures of sociology. While he does not depend on us paying tribute to him, if only because he is no longer alive, exchanging him wholesale even for someone like Karl Polanyi might cut us off from important sources of inspiration, not to mention

6   Financialization, of course, has cut the sequence short, to M→M' (John McMurtry, *The Cancer Stage of Capitalism*, London: Pluto 1999).

7   Ingham, *The Nature of Money*; Geoffrey Ingham, *Capitalism*, Oxford: Polity 2008.

8   Sewell, 'The Temporalities of Capitalism'.

9   Schumpeter, *Theorie der wirtschaftlichen Entwicklung*.

10   Which, of course, unlike what Block seems to suggest, does not necessarily imply coherence. In fact an important lesson we can learn from Marx is that unity can be internally contradictory, or dialectical. More on this below.

11   For an elegant 'microfoundation' of a theory of capitalism as a social action system see a recent paper by Jens Beckert, on capitalism's 'four C's': credit, commodity, competition, creativity.

12   For proof see my *Re-Forming Capitalism*, in particular Ch. 17, pp. 230ff.

hiding from us the roots and deeper meanings of core concepts of political economy and economic sociology that we use every day. Examples where we, thanks to Marx, do not have to reinvent the wheel include dialectical figures of thought like the self-undermining of institutions;[13] the notion of historical tipping-points where quantity turns into quality; the memory of the violent roots of modern society including modern capitalism ('primitive accumulation'),[14] and of the coercive foundations of apparently voluntary exchange relations;[15] the analysis of the employment relationship as one of domination based on free but asymmetrical contract; the inverse shape of the labour supply curve especially at its lower end etc. Of course it has become commonplace to distance oneself from Marxian, or Marxist, 'determinism' and, even worse, 'historical materialism'. But concerning the former it must be allowed to remember that 'determinism' was the hallmark of nineteenth century science, and that it was in any case much more pronounced in, say, Spencer and the young Durkheim because they were ignorant of dialectics and had no concept of 'countervailing forces', as offered by Marx in his discussion of the declining rate of profit under the impact of an increasing 'organic composition' of capital.[16] As to historical materialism, one can still be impressed with the caution with which someone like Max Weber avoided challenging the Marxian account of the origin of capitalism directly,[17] just as one must not forget that Marx himself spent much of his time trying to organize a revolutionary political movement, instead of sitting back and waiting until the presumably iron laws of history delivered to mankind a socialist society.[18]

However that may be, it does not seem a good idea to replace Marxian

13   Avner Greif, *Institutions and the Path to the Modern Economy*, Cambridge: Cambridge University Press 2006; Avner Greif and David A. Laitin, 'A Theory of Endogenous Institutional Change', *American Political Science Review*, vol. 98, no. 4, 2004, pp. 633–652.

14   Marx, *Capital*, Vol. 1, pp. 873ff.

15   David Graeber, *Debt: The First 5,000 Years*, Brooklyn, New York: Melville House 2011.

16   Karl Marx, *Capital: A Critique of Political Economy*, Vol. 3, London: Penguin 1981 [1894], Chs. 2 and 13.

17   For example: 'We have no intention whatever of maintaining such a foolish and doctrinaire thesis as . . . that capitalism as an economic system is a creation of the Reformation . . ', in view of 'the tremendous confusion of interdependent influences between the material basis, the forms of social and political organization, and the ideas current in the time . . ' (Weber, *The Protestant Ethic and the Spirit of Capitalism*, p. 91). Or: 'It is, of course, not my aim to substitute for a one-sided materialistic an equally one-sided spiritualistic causal interpretation of culture and of history. Each is equally possible, but each, if it does not serve as the preparation, but as the conclusion of an investigation, accomplishes equally little in the interest of historical truth' (ibid., p. 183).

18   With the necessary good will, one may read the deterministic language in Marx as rhetorical in nature: as a strategic expression of optimism deployed to encourage readers to join the political counter-movement against capitalism and make the theoretical prophecy self-fulfilling in practice.

'determinism' with political voluntarism,[19] and be it in the form of a conceptual move to a Polanyian 'always embedded' 'market society'. There simply is
no 'primacy of politics' under capitalism, and cannot be. Nowhere is this
clearer than in the version of the 'varieties of capitalism' literature that Block
calls upon for support, which attributes the alleged differences between 'liberal'
and 'coordinated' political economies, *not* to the volitions of a democratically
organized citizenry, but to different strategies of firms in competitive markets
('firm-centered approach').[20] Block, unfortunately, explicitly subscribes to the
functionalist economism of that literature when, invoking Wallerstein, he
declares it to be an 'undisputable' fact that in the global economy, nations
compete against nations, and governments exist to improve the 'competitiveness' of their national economies.[21] It is interesting to note that in its empirical
analyses, the economistic-functionalist strand of what advertises itself as a
theory of the 'varieties of capitalism' speaks, like Block, not of capitalism but of
'market economies'.[22] In both cases, abandoning the concept of capitalism not
only hides its commonalities but falls in the trap of a functionalist concept of
the economy as a politically designed and controlled technical arrangement
for consensual wealth creation.

Clearly there *is* politics under capitalism, and indeed democratic rather
than just technocratic politics, but there is also the *Eigenleben* of the capitalist
system of action.[23] While highly politically consequential, and in this sense
fundamentally political indeed, capitalism is powerfully capable of protecting
and extracting itself from political control. In Polanyian terms, while politics
may operate as a counter-movement to the capitalist market, and sometimes
even as a successful one, the market moves on its own, generating the movement to which the counter-movement must try to respond. The concept of
capitalism, outdated as some may have thought it was, has the important
advantage that it reminds us of the fact that the political regulation of economic
life in contemporary modern societies is always precarious as it is typically
condemned to limping behind the dynamic expansion of commercialized

---

19   For an example see Fred Block ('Crisis and Renewal: The Outlines of a Twentieth-Century
New Deal', *Socio-Economic Review*, vol. 9, no. 1, 2011, pp. 31–57) on the possible 'construction of a new
regime of accumulation' by none other than – the Obama administration.

20   Hall and Soskice, 'An Introduction to Varieties of Capitalism'; cf. Wolfgang Streeck, 'Taking
Capitalism Seriously.'

21   On why this is mistaken even at the empirical, not to mention the conceptual level, see
Streeck (*Re-Forming Capitalism*, Ch. 13).

22   Hall and Soskice, 'An Introduction to Varieties of Capitalism'.

23   On the proper dynamic of capitalism as an institutional regime see my essay, 'Taking
Capitalism Seriously'. On how to study modern capitalism, see chapter nine of the present volume and
Beckert, *Capitalism as a System of Contingent Expectations*.

market relations. Speaking of capitalism, that is to say, protects us from forgetting that capitalist land-grabbing permanently imparts Schumpeterian creative destruction, not just on established 'economic' practice, but also on social structures and institutions, in particular by replacing the conservatism of social obligations with the voluntarism of free contractual exchange, regardless of the collective consequences.[24]

As I have shown empirically for the German case,[25] the decline of post-war pacified capitalism must primarily be attributed to endogenous subversion and erosion of an institutional framework that had become suboptimal for capital accumulation, rather than, as Block suggests, to the frivolous fancies of neoliberal economists and misled politicians. Post-war democratic capitalism was fragile from its beginning – it only looked stable due to extraordinary political circumstances and the studied optimism of political leaders after the end of the war. In fact it could never hope to last longer than, in historical terms, a very short period. When it began to decay in the 1970s, it was because of the helplessness of democratic politics, organized at and confined to the level of nation states, against capitalism's new international opportunities for evading the social constraints that had by the 1970s landed it in an increasingly uncomfortable profit squeeze. For a time, the dependence of politics and political success under democratic capitalism on uninterrupted capital accumulation – or in the technocratic language of standard economics: on economic growth – led inevitably optimistic politicians to place their hopes on riding the tiger and jump on the historical bandwagon towards liberalization and deregulation until the re-formed capitalist economic regime almost crashed as a result of its unfettered progress.

It may seem like hairsplitting if I now ask, in Block's terms as he reconstructs the Polanyian conceptual framework, whether the current crisis was due to the capitalist 'economy' having become *mis*embedded or *dis*embedded. Block declares the latter to be impossible, due to economic action always and inevitably being social action. But while one can fully and indeed emphatically agree with this, as I do,[26] there is no logical need to conclude from it that a capitalist political economy is governed by a primacy of politics. Instead I believe that a realistic theory of political economy must provide for the possibility that social institutions built to protect society and humanity from the

24 Streeck, 'Taking Capitalism Seriously'.
25 Streeck, *Re-Forming Capitalism*.
26 For why and how see Jens Beckert and Wolfgang Streeck, *Economic Sociology and Political Economy: A Programmatic Perspective*, MPIfG Working Paper 08/4, Cologne: Max Planck Institute for the Study of Societies 2008.

'vagaries of the market' *may be overrun by these* – and that capitalist action may break through its social containment unless that containment is continuously reinforced and vigilantly kept current.

Capitalism, that is to say, is indeed 'always embedded'[27] in that it takes place in a society, subject to social constraints and opportunities. Also, capitalism in an important sense depends on remaining so embedded as it thrives on the rule of law, mutual trust, normative coordination and institutionalized cooperation, creative intelligence and the like. Nevertheless, and at the same time, capitalist actors always struggle to escape from their social containment and free themselves from obligations and controls.[28] Ideas of solidarity and institutions of social regulation are as a result at a permanent risk of erosion, with capitalist patterns of action spreading like cancer[29] in the body social even though capitalism as such, pure and simple and liberated from social constraints, cannot exist. In this sense capitalism feeds parasitically on the society that it inhabits or befalls, with its expansion ultimately amounting to its self-destruction unless checked by social and political opposition. Sometimes, as in the neoliberal era, the capitalist advance may capture the very politics that should contain it for its own good, and turn it into a vehicle of its own self-destructive progress; this, I believe, is what Polanyi meant when he described the expansion of 'market society' as a 'frivolous experiment' of states and governments.[30]

Is the state, then, the executive committee of the capitalist class? The answer that does justice to the dialectical, i.e., inherently contradictory nature of capitalism as a social formation is that it *is*, but only to the extent that it is *not*. If government was entirely captured by capitalist interests it would be unable to protect them from destroying themselves – as none other than Marx himself has indicated in the famous chapter on the working day in Vol. 1 of *Capital* (340ff.). But while capitalism does depend on being saved from itself by a politics that is at least in part responsive to social counter-movements, capitalists cannot act on such dependence, if only because they are always irresistibly tempted to gamble on making a last killing before the casino will go bankrupt. So the social counter-movement on whose success the survival of capitalism – its sustained 'embeddedness' – depends must assert itself against the powerful resistance of its beneficiaries-cum-adversaries, a resistance that is not at all perfunctory or doomed to fail, but in fact dead serious. There is no

---

27 Block, 'Understanding the Diverging Trajectories of the United States and Western Europe'.
28 Streeck, 'Taking Capitalism Seriously'.
29 McMurtry, *The Cancer Stage of Capitalism*.
30 For a conclusive critique of the 'always embedded' concept of capitalism see Beckert, 'The Great Transformation of Embeddedness'.

functionalism here, and the stabilization of the capitalist system of action is a highly uncertain undertaking whose success is not guaranteed even though it would be in the interest of those working to prevent it. Capitalists can be taught that interest, but whether they will condescend to learn the lesson is up to them.[31] Power, after all, is the ability to refuse to learn.[32] As we have seen in the current crisis, such ability may require no more than being big enough for one's demise to be a threat to the community at large.

Coming to the end of my comment, I would also like to put in a word for not entirely abandoning concepts like socialism or even communism.[33] As to the latter, David Graeber in his book on the anthropology of debt (*Debt: The First 5,000 Years*) has succinctly pointed out the generically communist foundations of economic life, even in advanced capitalism. Concerning socialism, to me the concept is indispensable for connoting the counterpart of – posses-sive-consumerist – individualism, reminding us against the grain of today's 'cult of the individual' that, once again citing Marx, man is the only animal that can individualize only in a society.[34] What other concept is there in any case for the more communal, more other-regarding and more collectively responsible way of life that we today seem to need more urgently than ever, a life with much less licence to externalize the costs of private pleasure-seeking to the rest of the world? And how are we to name a social organization with much more shared control over the collective fate and with a strong collective capacity to avoid the unanticipated consequences of freely expanding market relations – conse-quences that unendingly mystify us today when as individuals we cause effects that we cannot possibly want, not just as a society but also as individuals?

Fred Block's notion of an 'always embedded' capitalism subject to a 'primacy of politics' radiates an optimism that conspicuously resembles what European social democrats have for a long time made themselves believe: that socialism, as defined above, could be had, preserved and surreptitiously expanded on top of a capitalist economy-cum-society, by serving its

---

31   Wolfgang Streeck, 'Educating Capitalists: A Rejoinder to Wright and Tsakalatos', *Socio-Economic Review*, vol. 2, no. 3, 2004, pp. 425–483.

32   Karl W. Deutsch, *The Nerves of Government: Models of Political Communication and Control*, New York: The Free Press 1963.

33   Needless to say that I am not here concerned with the technicalities of political salesmanship. My concern is that, if we abandon the terms in order to remain politically inoffensive, we may lose sight of what they signify.

34   'But the epoch which produces this standpoint, that of the isolated individual, is also precisely that of the hitherto most developed social (from this standpoint, general) relations. The human being is in the most literal sense a ζῷον πολιτικόν [a political animal], not merely a gregarious animal, but an animal which can individuate itself only in the midst of society.' Karl Marx, *Grundrisse: Foundations of the Critique of Political Economy*, trans. Martin Nicolaus, London: Penguin Books 1973 [*1857–1858*], p. 6.

inexorably growing functional need for collective governance. Looking back at the past four decades, however, we see a sustained process of institutional transformation, slow but irresistible and driven, not by democratic politics but by the dynamic logic of capitalist development, that has effectively destroyed most if not all of the political safeguards whose establishment had been the very condition for capitalism being allowed to return after the disasters of the first half of the twentieth century. That logic, and the reorganization – or disor-ganization – of social life that it dictated, culminates today in the dual crisis of the global financial as well as the national democratic state system. Decades of 'reform' aimed at meeting the ever more aggressive demands of capitalist markets have only exacerbated the capitalist wear and tear on the social fabric, often with the connivance of blackmailed states and governments, including social-democratic ones. Is this experience really compatible with a theory that considers 'market society' to be at the disposition of politics? Or does it not rather speak for attributing to capitalism as a social action system a life, a logic, a power and a dynamism of its own, on which social-democratic post-war *politics as usual* has more and more lost its grip? If one comes to conclude, as I have, that it is the latter that is the more realistic perspective, is it then still responsible to invest one's time and energy in developing responsible ideas as to how responsible governments may repair 'the system' or turn one 'variety of capitalism' into another? Or would it not be much more constructive to be less constructive – to cease looking for better *varieties* of capitalism and instead begin seriously to think about *alternatives* to it?

CHAPTER ELEVEN

The Public Mission of Sociology

A few years ago, at some international social science conference around the time when Michael Burawoy issued his call for 'public sociology', I was struck by the thought that never before in the history of mankind had there been so many people as today so well trained in analysing and explaining social life.[1] Still, the most powerful political leaders produced by that sociologically most sophisticated generation – *my* generation – were George W. Bush and Dick Cheney, reelected around the time of the conference and entrusted by popular will with governing the most democratic democracy in the world. In subsequent years I continued to be fascinated with the contrast between the progressive decay of the politics and economy of the United States and the star-studded social science departments from Harvard to Stanford. What was all this obvious brilliance good for? Sometimes I asked some of my American colleagues, privately and after work over dinner, how they had made themselves heard on, say, the nation-building projects in Iraq and Afghanistan – whether this was not something on which to bring social science to bear? The answer was always a resigned silence: why bother, nobody ever listens.

SOCIOLOGY AND ITS PUBLIC: A PROBLEM OF DEMAND?

Does sociology have a public audience this side of the Atlantic, on less dramatic subjects? I have not done empirical research on the issue, but from what I have seen as a participant observer over the years my impression is: a very limited one if at all. Regularly skimming the science sections of our quality newspapers, for reasons unrelated to this lecture, I find psychology, brain research and evolutionary biology far ahead of sociology in coverage. Economics also figures, especially its latest descendants: behavioural and neuro-economics. Its real turf, of course, are the economics and politics sections, which are undoubtedly much more influential than the science sections, and here sociology is entirely absent, with very rare exceptions.

Why should this be so? Among the many reasons that come to mind is that sociology corresponds less than other disciplines to what is popularly

---

1   An earlier version of this chapter was presented at a conference organized by the SSRC and the Wissenschaftszentrum Berlin, The Public Mission of the Social Sciences and Humanities: Transformation and Renewal, 16–17 September 2011.

considered science and what is found interesting about it. What fascinates a lay audience about psychology, behavioural economics, evolutionary biology and the like seems to be that they purport to identify *latent causes* of actions that we normally believe to be motivated by *manifest reasons* – causes that secretly control what we do without us knowing about them. Representative for the sort of research that has recently made waves in German science journalism are T-shirt sniffing experiments showing that women prefer the smell of men who best fit their genetic make-up, in the sense of promising more healthy offspring. Another subject that comes back again and again is, I apologize to our American colleagues, adultery among monogamous birds; it turns out to be much more frequent than expected, with females secretly mating with males other than their lifelong partner, in particular if their own fathers had been more than others unfaithful to their mothers, for whatever complicated reasons to do with, what else, the 'fitness' of their offspring.

Not that there was no interest at all in sociological research. A survey on sexual practices would, I am sure, be widely received; but sociologists don't seem to do sex any more. Instead they do gender, and news items on research findings having to do with the battle of the sexes in whatever of its many versions – unequal pay, the division of housework, the lives of unwed mothers – are eagerly printed and, I presume, as eagerly read by mass audiences. Something similar seems to apply to research on schools and educational success, on social mobility and elite formation, or on immigration and its discontents. Almost always, however, it is just the facts that are reported, not the theories explaining them.

Although theory as such is not always spurned. The bestselling German non-fiction book of the past decade, if not of post-war Germany, is *Deutschland schafft sich ab* (Germany Finishes Itself), by one Thilo Sarrazin. The book appeared in 2010 and it may be useful to spend a few words on it. Sarrazin was an SPD politician, from 2002 to 2009 Finance Minister of the *Land* of Berlin, after which he became a member of the Executive Board of the Bundesbank, until he was fired as an international liability to the Federal Republic of Germany. Sarrazin is known as a prominent so-called '*Islamkritiker*'. The book claims, in short, that immigration from Islamic countries together with low birth rates among educated middle-class women of German descent weakens the country's genetic base, especially by lowering the average IQ, and because of this will in the long run damage the competitiveness of the German economy. While Sarrazin is an academically trained economist, the book draws extensively on psychological and demographic research and frequently ventures onto sociological terrain, for example when discussing the relationship between intelligence and religion on the one hand and economic and social achievement on the other. It is probably no exaggeration to characterize the book as a neo-eugenic manifesto based on a biologistic worldview with strong racist connotations (incest among Arab extended families lowers the intelligence of their children), embedded in an efficiency theory of politics and society in a global economy. While the SPD originally considered expelling Sarrazin from membership, it later changed its mind in light of the enormous public resonance of his book and allowed him to remain a Social Democrat in good standing.

The episode is telling in several respects. One is that there is in fact a public audience in Germany, and not at all a small one, for scholarly books on social issues, even if peppered with statistics and with long, tedious discussions of articles in research journals. Academic sociologists, however, refrain from plying this field, perhaps because they expect that the conclusions *they* draw from *their* material will leave people unexcited. It could also be that they are not interested in talking to the Sarrazin readers, although these clearly constitute an important segment of the German middle class. Serious public debate on Sarrazin was carried almost exclusively by journalists working for quality newspapers, like *Frankfurter Allgemeine Zeitung* and *Süddeutsche Zeitung*. A few developmental psychologists came forward to state that intelligence may not entirely be a matter of inheritance, and scholars working on religion in general and Islam in particular pointed out that there are actually many different Islams inside Islam. Little if anything was contributed by sociologists, and as was to be expected nothing by economists to whom the book's rampant economism would naturally appeal.

Why is sociology absent in public debates of this kind? One could also ask: why do sociologists have so little confidence in their work that they talk about it only to each other, rather than to the world at large? One answer is: they know they have bad cards. Economists, the social gurus of our time, with their machine models of economy and society, still have the boldness to offer exact predictions, with one digit behind the decimal point, and continue to pretend to be in possession of a technology of wealth creation that tells us which levers must be pulled to make everybody better off. Who could afford not to pay attention? Moreover, economics as a discipline ideally conforms to the dominant scientistic understanding, or misunderstanding, of science. To most people, science is the discovery of general laws that yield parsimonious causal explanations translatable into technical know-how or moral justifications or both, as in the *homo economicus* model, in evolutionary biology (even the birds do it, and for good reason), or neurological discussions of the 'free will'. Sociology, by comparison, deals with historically unique situations in which more causal factors than one are at work, and if sociologists dare making predictions at all, these are typically highly hedged. Unlike psychology or the natural sciences, sociology can hardly promise to reveal secret material forces underlying and controlling the movements of the visible world. Typically, its findings come with extensive warnings against generalization, pointing to contextual conditions, social, economic or cultural, that interfere with and modify causal relations. Some of us consider this to be due to sociology being a young discipline that still has to become really 'scientific', whereas others regard it as reflecting the peculiar ontology of the social world. Be this as it may, what matters is that the sociology that is on offer generally fails to measure up to the *scientistic standard model of science* and is therefore bound to be found disappointing by a public that believes in that model and that sociologists have failed to educate about its deficiencies.

Another problem faced by sociology, at least in this country, is a public image that very much dates back to the 1970s. In short, sociology is still widely seen as 'soft', not just as a science, but also politically, and such softness is out of fashion in hard times. Sociologists are suspect in the eyes of many of excessive empathy with their subjects, who frequently are marginal groups like the long-term unemployed, the criminals, and the 'parallel societies' of immigrants and of the surplus population sorted out by an ever more demanding *Leistungsgesellschaft* (achievement society). Sociology often 'explains' their way of life by explicating the meanings, the *Sinn,* they attribute to themselves and the world. In German we speak, with Max Weber, of '*verstehende Soziologie*' (interpretive sociology). But *verstehen* (understanding) is not always appreciated in a society in which a widely known proverb claims that '*Alles verstehen heißt alles verzeihen*' (to understand all is to forgive all). Compassion is mostly out these days, and a sociology that dares explain why people do what they do by pointing out why they think it makes sense for them to do it, is easily considered advocacy in scientific guise, or bleeding-heart rhetoric, or *Gutmenschentum,* which is the enemy number one of the no-nonsense common-sense Sarrazin community.

This leads me to the question of the public to which a renewed public sociology could address itself. If anything, sociologists know that the public sphere is a social and institutional structure, not just a crowd. Is there, then, still an enlightened citizenry out there, a *Bildungsbürgertum* willing and able to shape a society-wide 'public opinion?' Are there political parties interested in seriously learning about the world, or trade unions looking for insights and arguments that could help their cause? Even without a lot of research, we are all reasonably certain that all of these are much less present today than they were a few decades ago, and clearly they are less interested than they used to be in sociology in particular. And what about the media through which sociology would have to make itself public? Print is declining while television and, recently, the internet are on the rise – less so perhaps than in the United States, but still. The 'pictorial turn' that is far from ended is not good for sociology, which deals mostly with subjects that cannot really be photographed; neurology and astronomy are incomparably better in delivering colourful images to newspaper editors and television stations. Moreover, the media seem to be becoming more specialized, making 'the public' more segmented than ever. If there was a *Strukturwandel der Öffentlichkeit* (structural transformation of the public) in the past three or four decades, it was one in the direction of modern niche markets. Today's consumers of commercialized information can pick what they expect to like, and avoid what they believe they will find boring, without ever having inspected it. Of course users of the newest, internet-based media are free to compose their news entirely by themselves, with no intervention whatsoever from anyone with authority to decide what a good citizen has to take notice of – which was what public broadcasting was able to do and did only a few years ago. Contemporary information consumers learn only what they want to learn, and nothing else. In a world of increasingly fragmented publics and communities, will public sociology be limited to speaking to those who, for whatever idiosyncratic reasons, happen to be interested in public sociology?

Sociology without Capitalism: A Problem of Supply?
That there are problems, and quite serious ones, on the *demand side* of a possible public sociology does not by itself mean that everything is in good shape on the *supply side* – that sociology as a social science actually does have insights to offer that are worth being assigned as required reading to citizens and their political representatives. I am afraid I am not and will never be an elder statesman of the discipline who can claim to overlook its full breadth and confidently point it into new directions. For this my substantive interests are too eclectic and my disciplinary identity is too tenuous – my only excuse being, perhaps, that sociology is as such too diverse to invite identification *tout court*. Also, like many others, I tend to be obsessed with whatever I happen to be currently working on, which easily makes me overestimate its importance. Still, with all due qualifications, I think a case can be made – and I will in the following make it – that the political-economic crisis that has for several years now held the world in its grip represents a historical turning point – one that, among many other things, offers a unique opportunity for making sociology once again a truly publicly relevant social science, provided it refocuses itself on what are shaping up to be the crucial issues of our time, *all of which have to do with a rapidly changing relationship between economy and society.*

In the time immediate aftermath of the crisis, economists were widely reproached for not having seen it coming, not least by sociologists. Three years later, public confidence in mainstream economics' ability to explain and help govern the economy is at a low – at a time when there is a widespread realiza-tion that, in the words of the German industrialist and liberal politician, Walther Rathenau, 'Die Wirtschaft ist unser Schicksal' (our fate depends on the economy). Remarkably, however, the crisis found sociologists by and large as unprepared as mainstream economists. While the latter apparently cannot but cling to their tautological models of self-stabilizing free markets, superfi-cial modifications notwithstanding, sociologists had for decades more or less eliminated the economy from their agenda, ceding it to the discipline of economics, under the historical peace treaty concluded in the 1950s by none other than Talcott Parsons himself. If the crisis of 2008 gave rise to a renewed sense of the centrality of the economy for modern society, modern sociology was in a bad position to respond since it has over the years essentially conceived its subject as *a society devoid of an economy*. In the process important discipli-nary traditions were marginalized or altogether externalized, like in particular political economy which fell into the hands of efficiency-theoretical econom-ics, whose dominance over the subject is today contested only by a handful of political scientists. Recent attempts to bring the economy back in, by establish-ing 'economic sociology' as a new subdiscipline, all too often limit themselves to suggesting alternative recipes for making economic transactions more effi-cient, for example by complementing markets with 'networks'.

I see the current crisis as a strong signal for our discipline that a theoreti-cal programme focused on a society cleansed of its economy is unsustainable, unless we are content with remaining as speechless on the leading social issues of our time as we were before, during and after the events of 2008. Many today feel that the current financial and fiscal crisis is not just an economic but fundamentally a social matter important enough to demand a revised inter-pretation of modern society – one that takes systematic notice of its being continuously revolutionized by expanding markets; of the fragility of social structures and political institutions that results from this; the growing uncer-tainty faced by governments and citizens as markets increasingly escape social controls; the inherent limits of the market as a site of social integration and a basis of social order, and the like. In principle, sociology with its history as a critical theory of modernity should be able to fill this need and offer to 'the public' insights that it could reject only at its peril. For this, however, sociology must restore the *economy* as a central subject of any theory of *society* worth its name – and not just as a neutral mechanism of wealth creation ruled by esoteric natural laws and governable by scientifically informed technicians. This will not be possible unless as a discipline we dispense with our interdisci-plinary peace agreement with economics and rediscover the political economy which sociology was when it was young, which it later abandoned in order to specialize on 'the society'. There cannot be a more auspicious moment for this than now, when the reputation of standard economics with the public has reached a well-deserved long-time low.

Why in the first place was it that sociology conceded the economy to the economists? How did we come to believe that a society without an economy could be a worthwhile subject of study, and that a macrosociology without a macroeconomics could be a viable approach to understanding modern society? Is there enough left for sociology if the social is separated from the economic – and often from the political as well? It may be interesting that in Germany, the exclusion of the economy from the domain of sociology apparently took place earlier than in the United States, and if I am not mistaken, not only or primarily for academic but to a large extent also for obvious political reasons. The story is more than just a little twisted. Max Weber, as we may remember, had a chair in economics (*Volkswirtschaftslehre*) and originally was a member of the professional association of economists, the Verein für Sozialpolitik. That he left it and founded the Deutsche Gesellschaft für Soziologie (DGS; German Sociological Association) was a political act as Weber strongly disapproved of contemporary economics' public advocacy of a reformist social policy. The DGS was to spare him from having to deal with the hated *Kathedersozialisten* (academic socialism), which was why it had to pledge itself to *Wertfreiheit* (value-free inquiry).[2] But this turned out to be unenforceable, and when the *soziale Frage* kept reappearing at DGS meetings Weber, having tried but failed to quell the subject, resigned from organized sociology as well. A few years later he died.

It is remarkable that German sociology after Weber never took up the grand themes of *Wirtschaft und Gesellschaft* (economy and society) that we today associate with him. They were essentially left to the institutional economists of the *Historische Schule* (Historical School), like Werner Sombart, who played no role in Weimar sociology at all. Their demise after the Nazi *Machtergreifung* (seizure of power) in 1933, not least their attempt at a *rapprochement* with German nationalism, cleared the ground for the post-war advance of 'theoretical' as opposed to historical economics. Sociologists, for their part, in their effort in the 1920s to establish themselves at the German

---

2   Weber's own social science was anything but *wertfrei*. His passionate rejection of the social policy advocacy of the economists of his time was that of a liberal nationalist for whom what he thought were the coming struggles for national survival and international supremacy, in particular with Britain, were of paramount importance. Social policy, just as democracy, was not for making people happy but had to help the newly formed German Reich to brace itself for an anarchic, conflict-ridden international world. That Weber could consider his position to be *wertfrei* was due to his conviction that *Realpolitik* was an objective fact and not something one was free to choose.

university, took great care not to be taken for socialists or, what was still almost the same then, Marxists. Indeed, Horkheimer and the Institut für Sozialforschung in Frankfurt never considered themselves sociologists, and never thought of joining the DGS. Theoretical sociology in Weimar seems to have basically pursued some kind of formalistic theory of social relations of which nothing is left (von Wiese's *Beziehungslehre* [Relationship Doctrine]). Empirical sociology busied itself mainly with demographic research, in particular settlement patterns in Germany and, increasingly, Central and Eastern Europe, under the label of *Siedlungsforschung* (settlement research). Unlike what the discipline's post-war mythology suggested, empirical sociology blossomed in the Third Reich and was respected by state and party, in particular in connection with urban and rural planning for the soon-to-be-annexed territories in the East. Capitalism, of course, never figured in what one might with some justification call a particular form of organic public sociology.[3]

In post-war Germany, sociology continued to stay away from the economy, regardless of the fact that economics was simultaneously becoming ever more *modellplatonistisch* (neoclassical), radically breaking with the tradition of the *Historische Schule* (Historical School). Institutional economics disappeared until it came back much later under 'modern', efficiency-theoretical auspices. Historical economics was marginalized, even in the form of historical econometrics, or 'cliometrics'. What was and what was not sociology was increasingly decided in the United States, from where the discipline was reimported as the Weimar and Nazi generations died off or retired. In the 1960s when post-war growth was at its height, the economy seemed no longer of sociological or, for that matter, political concern. Many believed, like Keynes had anticipated in one of his more optimistic moments, that economics had become like dentistry: a skilled trade to be called upon if there was a problem, with a toolkit of proven techniques painlessly to repair whatever there was to be repaired. At Frankfurt, where I was a student in the late 1960s, capitalism had been renamed *Tauschgesellschaft* (catallactic society) by Adorno, and nobody except for a few Soviet-Communist sectarians among the students

---

3   With a little bad luck, sociology as it had developed by the end of the Weimar Republic might have become a publicly recognized pillar of the regime. In 1934 the DGS met for the first time after the Nazi takeover. The issue on the agenda was whether to continue under new pro-Nazi leadership or dissolve in protest against it. A number of those present suggested electing as president one Reinhard Höhn, to succeed Ferdinand Tönnies. Höhn, a lawyer who worked as an assistant to the sociologist Franz Wilhelm Jerusalem in Jena, later became a professor of public law and a leading figure at the SS headquarters, where he headed a department at the Reichssicherheitshauptamt. While Höhn did not get enough votes, the members, in order not to antagonize the new government, decided to suspend the association for the time being rather than dissolving it. It was revived only after 1945. In the 1950s Höhn reemerged to set up and run, well into the 1970s, the leading management school of the Federal Republic.

expected 'the system' ever again to be vulnerable to *economic* crisis. (The crisis of the time, of course, being one of *legitimation*.) The view that the economy had become essentially a technical matter, and had finally and forever been tamed, was by no means limited to Frankfurt but was shared widely, by sociologists no less than by economists. One example among many is the 1968 book by Amitai Etzioni, *The Active Society*, which was easily the most ambitious attempt ever to spell out the conditions of modern democratic societies determining the direction of their development and governing their own fate.[4] On its 666 pages, it mentions the economy just once, and then only to remark that 'Western nations have gained confidence in their capacity to control societal processes with the wide use of Keynesian and other controls for preventing wild inflations and deep depressions and for spurring economic growth' (p. 10).

As indicated, it is my view that sociology's splendid isolation from the economic world is no longer tenable unless our discipline was prepared to render itself irrelevant for the big issues of our era. In view of the crisis, it would seem to be time to concede that sociology's bet on the non-economic in society has not paid off. The good news is that it may still be possible to reverse course. Since sociology is not (yet) as completely sold on rational choice as standard economics, we can more easily break away from an image of the world in which the rational pursuit of individual interests is capable of producing a stable order. Nor are we forever married to functionalist equilibrium models – which should in principle enable us to understand the inherent restlessness, the permanent imbalance and the continuing crisis-proneness of the modern society-cum-economy, aka contemporary capitalism. Most importantly, we still have access to older concepts of capitalism as a historical social formation, as a really existing, dynamically moving social structure, rather than an ideal type of economy, or a synonym for market economy, as in economics or in the economistic branch of the 'varieties of capitalism' literature. Just remember that as late as the 1970s, someone like Daniel Bell was acutely aware of and represented a tradition of sociological theories of capitalism that reached back to the likes of Marx, Weber, Sombart, Schumpeter and, why not, Keynes, even offering the occasional handshake across the ideological divide to a neo-Marxist like James O'Connor.

Public Sociology as a Return to Political Economy

What might a sociology aware of its political economy tradition have to say to a contemporary public that is more worried than it has been for a long time about where contemporary capitalism is going? At a minimum, we should be

---

4   Amitai Etzioni, *The Active Society*, New York: The Free Press, 1968.

able to impress on the public consciousness that the present crisis is not an accident – not the unfortunate result of accidental mismanagement of the American mortgage market – but arises from very basic tensions and contradictions inside the regime of democratic capitalism as we have known it in the Western world since the end of the Second World War. Inflation in the 1970s, rising public debt in the 1980s, the deregulation of private credit in the 1990s in compensation for a first wave of fiscal consolidation, and current attempts to restore 'sound money' under the pressure of a newly global *haute finance* are all expressions of a clash between a popular *moral economy* of social rights of citizenship and a capitalist *economic economy* insisting on allocation according to market justice and in line with the requirements of 'business confidence' (Kalecki). Over the decades the site of the battle changed, from collective bargaining and the labour market to electoral politics to markets for consumer credit to, as of now, international financial markets for the servicing and refinancing of public debt. While the issue was always the same – in David Lockwood's terms, how to deal with the conflicting requirements of system integration and social integration in a capitalist society – one cannot but note that the market-correcting capacity of popular democracy and its collective organizations, like trade unions and political parties, has continuously diminished from crisis to crisis. Today it is international financial diplomacy where the contradictions of democratic capitalism are being negotiated between states and investment banks – an arena almost entirely insulated from popular pressure whose logic is unintelligible to people apart, perhaps, from a few specialists in the employ of economic and political elites.

Sociologists are not expected to furnish advice as to how to restore sound money and make the economy grow again, and rightly so. But they can help the public understand that this is not the only issue at stake, and that restoring the social compact of democratic capitalism, on which the legitimacy of our social order depends, exceeds the powers of even the most expert economic management. Unlike most economists, sociologists understand that the job of politics is more complex than enforcing on a reluctant society the market justice of distribution by marginal productivity. Some sort of balance must be struck between the needs of people and the needs of capital. If providing for business confidence results in erosion of citizen confidence, nothing will in the end be gained for social stability. While political and economic elites may be tempted to use the crisis as an opportunity once and for all to insulate capitalism against democracy, sociologists are well-placed and well-advised to draw public attention to the risks such a strategy inevitably involves.

That we are in fact facing a severe crisis of democracy and not just of the economy should by now be obvious. In Europe, under the pressure of financial markets, national leaders are systematically transferring decision-making power to international organizations, taking authority away from national parliaments and, by extension, electorates. Debtor countries have no choice but to accept the dictates of their creditors, with national elections rendered meaningless for decades to come. Creditor countries, for their part, are driven by 'the markets' to respond rapidly and flexibly to the latter's fluctuating needs and capricious demands, which leaves little time for their parliaments to exercise their democratic prerogatives. Firmly institutionalized austerity policies radically narrow the range of political alternatives in all countries, rendering political participation increasingly inconsequential. Remarkably turnout in elections, at all levels, from local communities to Europe, has been steadily declining everywhere since the 1980s, and most steeply in areas with high rates of poverty, immigration, broken families and the like, where political mobilization would be most needed. As sociologists we know, and are competent to let others know, that where legitimate outlets of political expression are shut down, illegitimate ones may take their place, at potentially very high social and economic cost.

To add one more point, it has now become almost commonplace that the present crisis is to a large extent a crisis of trust – in the value of money, the willingness and ability of debtors to pay back their debt, the capacity of political leaders to resist the pressures of 'the market', and the capacity of markets to provide for an efficient, not to speak of fair, allocation of resources. Not only is there not much confidence that our governments and international organizations will be capable of preventing another crisis. There is also a rapid decline in trust among market actors themselves, in particular among banks dependent upon borrowing from one another. The result is that states and central banks may once again have to come in as trustees of last resort, which may force them to take over bad debt and extend guarantees of a dimension that may finally bring them to their knees. It is not so long ago that transaction-cost economics maintained that institutions are best built by market actors 'from below' looking after their own interests in efficient trading relations. Rational choice institutionalism in political science and sociology was eager to absorb the message and followed suit by replacing public government controlled by states with private governance constructed by market participants. The crisis has shown that private ordering can go only so far and is easily overburdened with the task of providing for social order. When it breaks down, public authority needs to be brought back for repair work. There is no reason not to draw public attention to what is the obvious bankruptcy of liberal theories of institutions and, incidentally, a resounding confirmation of the Durkheimian sociological legacy.

Drawing on the sociological tradition, we are able to see that what is at the bottom of our current predicament is the well-known tendency inherent in the capitalist social formation for markets to expand dynamically into other spheres of social life, typically disrupting them and often leaving them in disarray. That tendency today meets with a secular weakness of social counter-movements again marketization, of the protective-conservationist as well as the progressive-reconstructionist kind, in a historical period when global capital is about to superimpose itself on local, regional, national social structures and ways of life. Unlike contemporary economists, sociologists, informed not least by some of the great economists of the past, like Sombart and Schumpeter, possess in principle the conceptual tools to understand that the capitalist system is one that grows from within, in a way that tends continuously to turn social relations upside down. Rather than proceeding in harmony with the rest of society, capitalist development continuously causes frictions and contractions that demand and call forth ever new collective efforts at social stabilization, aimed at establishing some kind of – ever precarious – balance between economy and society.

Karl Polanyi, whose work a growing number of sociologists find inspiring, did not seek membership in the sociological profession of the 1950s and 1960s. He was content to be an economist, an economic historian, and a social anthropologist. It says something about our discipline, and something not very complimentary, that he was discovered by sociology only in the 1990s when neoliberalism was rampant and financialization was ushering in yet another revolutionary transformation of the capitalist economy. I believe there is no better summary account of our current predicaments than one drawing on the Polanyian notion of the three fictitious commodities, money, nature and labour, and the inherent limits to their commodification. Many believe that these limits may now be about to be reached, and with them the limits of further capitalist growth, at least of the sort that can still be made more or less compatible with existential human needs. The private-industrial manufacturing of *money* in the wake of the deregulation of the 'financial industry' has imposed unprecedented uncertainty on entire societies, exacerbating distributional conflict within and between them and raising as yet utterly unresolved problems of global re-regulation. As to *nature*, or *land*, we have slowly been learning that the fundamental characteristic of a fictitious commodity – that its supply is not and cannot be governed by the demand for it – applies to nature with full force. Indeed, indications are that unless we find ways to protect our global commons from further commodification, the very basis of life on earth as we know it may soon be consumed in the service of unbridled progress of capital accumulation. Finally, ever-increasing flexibility of *labour* markets and work organization has subjected individuals and families to relentless pressures to organize their lives in line with the unpredictable demands of increasingly competitive markets. Among other things, the result is growing polarization between an impoverished surplus population of losers; overworked middle-class families living an absurdly busy life and putting in ever more, and ever more intense, working hours in spite of unprecedented prosperity; and a small elite of winner-take-all super-rich whose greed knows no limits while their bonuses and dividends have long ceased to serve any useful function for society as a whole.

What, if not the political economy of contemporary capitalism, as anticipated in Polanyi's conception of critical limits to commodification, could be the subject of a renewed public sociology? A lot of work, of course, awaits doing. Sociologists have contributed little if anything on money and finance, *pace* Georg Simmel and apart from a few entertaining but politically irrelevant ethnographic accounts of life at Wall Street trading desks, written before disaster struck. On the natural environment sociologists have produced an endless number of studies on when and why people are willing to separate their garbage and make other low-cost sacrifices. But the question what it is that makes our societies so dependent on capitalist growth, even at the risk of destruction of their economic, natural and human foundations, we have left, strangely enough, to heterodox economists. The same applies to reflections on how a society compelled to grow might possibly be turned into one at peace with nature and itself. That economists turn to psychologists for advice on alternative, non-economic sources of human happiness cannot really be held against them, given that sociology has so carefully avoided the subject – although it could reasonably have insisted that the issue is a social and political rather than a psychological one. Relatively well, finally, are we doing on labour markets, family structures and the conflicts between participation in the intensifying rat race for income and advanced consumption on the one hand and social life, including the raising of children, on the other, as described by, well, public sociologists such as Arlie Hochschild and Richard Sennett.

The Demand Side Again

This brings me back to the old question: would anyone listen? Of course one should not be optimistic these days. But it seems that these are not normal times, or that normal times may well be coming to an end. Clearly a sense of crisis is building among elites as well as citizens, and not least in the academy, that goes far beyond what we have seen in decades. Perhaps we are approaching another *Sattelzeit* (Reinhard Koselleck): a period of accelerated change with uncertain event that will be of formative importance for a long time. An interesting symptom is how clueless standard economics presents itself when it comes to handling the post-2007 global economic disaster. Never were the world's leading economists as divided as today over what is to be done – something that even the trade press, like the *Economist* and the *Financial Times,* cannot but notice. Perhaps the explanation is simply that capitalist democracy has run out of technical fixes, as a result of which economic theory as we know it is losing its grip on the public discourse. Political leaders seem already to have lost faith, on both sides of the Atlantic. It is interesting that even inside economics itself doubts are emerging about, for example, the way we measure growth and prosperity, or the prospects for continued maximization of material prosperity in general.

Hauling the economy back into society, and indeed into sociology, may be a programme for which one could today find allies, in a world in which states are about to be turned into something like public corporations having to earn the confidence of capital givers; in which international organizations function as deposit insurance or debt collection agencies on behalf of private investors; and governments begin to resemble corporate managements pressed to extract 'creditor value' from citizens turned into workforces disciplined by capital markets. Perhaps there may also be demand for a renewed critical theory of political economy among the young who no longer join the political parties, avoid trade unions, and refuse to vote in elections. As with all 'basic research', that we cannot say who will use it and how, can be no reason for not doing it.

For sociology to become truly public sociology, I believe it must get ready for the moment in which the foundations of modern society will again have to be rethought, like they were in the New Deal and after the Second World War. That moment, I am convinced, is approaching, and when it will be here sociologists should have the intellectual tools at hand for society to understand what is at stake. Even if our only audience was, at first, in the academy, this would not necessarily render our efforts futile. In the final chapter of the *General Theory*, Keynes expounded on the power of 'ideas of economists and political philosophers, both when they are right and when they are wrong'. The world, he claimed, 'is ruled by little else', even though new ideas do not take hold immediately:

[F]or in the field of economic and political philosophy there are not many who are influenced by new theories after they are twenty-five or thirty years of age, so that the ideas which civil servants and politicians and even agitators apply to current events are not likely to be the newest. But, soon or late, it is ideas, not vested interests, which are dangerous for good or evil.[5]

There is no way of knowing, and perhaps good reason to doubt, if there will be enough time for trickle-down ideational change to come to our relief – the 'gradual encroachment of ideas', as Keynes calls it, which has worked so well for himself, at least for a time. Our need for a less suicidal political economy may be more urgent. But this can only mean that we cannot begin early enough to challenge the intellectual hegemony of contemporary economics over contemporary understandings of economy and society. The first public for public sociology, I suggest, is the academy, with its unprecedented numbers of students in economics and business administration, who are being taught, in essence, that society exists only as a grandiose opportunity for utility maximization by those capable of making the most rational choices. If we can't sow the seeds of doubt here, where then? The Parsonian peace treaty between sociology and economics has silenced the Kantian 'contest of faculties' (*Streit der Fakultäten*) where we would today most need it. Sociologists and political scientists, in alliance with heterodox economists of different stripes, have begun working on a new sort of political economy, a socio-economics that would again make the economic subservient to the social rather than *vice versa*, first as a theoretical and then, hopefully, as a political project. It is high time for the mainstream of the discipline to remember its roots and join the battle, even though we know that the capitalist reorganization of the university that is under way everywhere is not least designed precisely to eliminate critical reflection, for the all-powerful purpose of economic efficiency. But then, if public sociology cannot make itself heard in *this* public, how can it hope ever to be noticed in the world of YouTube, Facebook, Fox TV and the BILD-Zeitung?

5   John Maynard Keynes, *The General Theory of Employment, Interest and Money*, New York: Harcourt, Brace and Company 1967 [1936], chapter 24.

Index

If denotes figure

A

accumulated weaknesses, syndrome of, 13

The Accumulation of Capital (Luxenburg), 100

The Active Society (Etzioni), 245

Adidas, 101

Adorno, Theodor, 244

Andreotti, Giulio, 145

Argentina, borrowing practices of, 125

artificial intelligence, 9, 10

austerity, 19, 20, 69, 83, 84, 88, 90, 91, 92, 93, 126, 127, 128, 130, 132, 133, 134, 135, 136, 138, 141, 143, 148, 216, 219

at the level of government. *See* fiscal austerity

austerity regime, 134, 135, 136, 137–8, 139

austerity state, 69

authoritarian liberalism, 153, 154, 159, 161, 163

authoritarian state, 151, 152, 153, 155, 158, 161, 163

B

Babb, Sarah, 167

balanced budgets, 89, 117, 125, 126, 133, 135, 136–7, 141, 196

Banca d'Italia, 175

Bank for International Settlements (BIS), 50–1

bare Zahlung (naked cash), 102

Bell, Daniel, 45, 115, 245

Berlinguer, Enrico, 146

Berlusconi, Silvio, 104, 147

Bernanke, Ben, 51

Bindestrichsoziologie (hyphenated sociology), 223

Block, Fred, 227–35

border-crossing, 206

boutique production, 99

bracket creep, 82, 115–16

Bretton Woods model, 117, 181, 182

broken social contract (US, 1947–present), 64*f*

Bundesbank, 128, 175

Burawoy, Michael, 237

Bush, George W., 135, 237

Buying Time (Streeck), 181

C

Calhoun, Craig, 5, 6–7, 9, 13

Capital (Marx), 233

capital accumulation, 14, 24, 44, 45, 46, 47, 58, 61, 64, 67, 70, 91, 99, 115, 192, 205, 217, 229, 232, 248

capitalism

as always a fragile and improbable order, 13

compatibility of with democracy, 74–7, 185–99

contemporary capitalism. *See* contemporary capitalism

as culture, 204, 209–12

defined as modern society, 58–9

democracy as reconciling with, 52

democratic capitalism. *See* democratic capitalism

democratic welfare-state capitalism, 4

as denoting both economy and society, 201

development of as influenced by ideologies, wars and states, 7

dialectic of with democracy, 143

end of as a process rather than an event, 58

end of as death from a thousand cuts, 13

as endogenously dynamic and dynamically unstable social system, 203, 208

European capitalism, 55, 129, 156

financialization of, 67

as having outlived all predictions of its impending death, 4, 57

as history, 203, 204–9

how to study contemporary capitalism, 201–24

late capitalism, 5, 150

liberal capitalism, 4, 13, 155, 190

low-growth capitalism, 8

modern capitalism, 4, 16, 56, 119, 203

neoliberal capitalism, 13, 14, 16, 22, 36, 42

as not having any worthy opposition, 59, 60, 65

OECD capitalism, 15, 16, 21, 47, 50

as political economy in permanent disequilibrium, 222